AMERICAN HISTORY
Before 1877

About the Author

1. **Present Position**: Senior Research Associate, Henry E. Huntington Library. Formerly taught at Clark University, Smith College, and Northwestern University where he was William Smith Mason Professor of History. Has been president of Organization of American Historians, American Studies Association and Western History Association.

2. **Publications**: *The Protestant Crusade, 1830-1860* (Macmillan, 1938, Quadrangle, 1963); *Westward Expansion: A History of the American Frontier,* (Macmillan, 4th edn., 1974); *The Far Western Frontier, 1830-1860,* (Harper 1956); *The Westard Movement in the United States* (Van Nostrand, 1959); *The Historian's Contribution to Anglo-American Misunderstanding* (Hobbs, Dorman, 1966); *America's Frontier Heritage* (Holt, Rinehart & Winston, 1966); *The Genesis of the Frontier Thesis* (Huntington Library, 1971); *Frederick Jackson Turner: Historian, Scholar, Teacher* (Oxford, 1973). Co-author: *The United States: American Democracy in World Perspective* (Rinehart, 1947); *The Making of American Decocracy* (Rinehart, 1950); *America's Frontier Story* (Holt, Rinehart & Winston, 1970). Editor: numerous books, including *The Histories of the American Frontier Series* (Holt, Rinehart & Winston, 1963–). Has written articles and reviews for many journals.

About the Book

1. Material has been systematically arranged in outline form with important topics printed in bold type.

2. Basic facts, names, and dates have been <u>underlined</u> so .that all important information can be seen at a glance.

3. Interpretative sections in each chapter relate the past to present day America.

4. A list of eight or ten of the most useful books on special subjects are added to each chapter with brief comments.

5. Includes a complete section of questions and answers with helpful hints on how to prepare for examinations.

AMERICAN HISTORY
Before 1877

By
Ray Allen Billington
SENIOR RESEARCH ASSOCIATE,
HENRY E. HUNTINGTON LIBRARY

A HELIX BOOK

ROWMAN & ALLANHELD
Totowa, New Jersey

Reprinted in 1984 as A HELIX BOOK, published by
Rowman & Allanheld, Publishers (a division of
Littlefield, Adams & Company) 81 Adams Drive,
Totowa, New Jersey, 07512

Library of Congress Catalog Card Number — 51-12960

How to Use This Outline

Every student of history should have two objectives in mind: to *understand* man's past, and to *interpret* that past in the light of present-day experience. *Understanding* is possible only when the record of man's multitudinous activities is first freed of unimportant details, then arranged in an orderly pattern. When this has been done the student does not have to memorize a mass of unrelated facts; instead he can follow the course of history as he would a proposition in logic, reasoning from related event to related event. *Interpretation* is possible only when the student is sufficiently well versed in both past history and present-day problems to recognize the relationship between the two.

The purpose of this history in outline is to make easier the understanding and interpretation of America's past between the Civil War and the present. With this in view, several unique features have been introduced:

1. All factual details have been eliminated save those considered essential by most teachers. In addition, the most important information has been emphasized by underlining the basic facts, names, and dates.

2. Material has been systematically arranged in outline form, with headings and subheadings printed in **bold type.** By following the phrases in **bold type** through a section or a chapter, the student can construct a brief and easily memorized outline of any subject.

3. Each chapter concludes with a section interpreting the material, and showing the connection between events discussed there and modern America.

The careful student who wishes to benefit most from these features should follow a standard procedure in studying for any examination. First, he should read thoroughly and carefully the text and collateral material assigned in the

course he is taking, making notes on the outside reading. Then he should study this outline, noting that certain facts and interpretations are in both the text and the outline, while others are in the text alone. These latter are less essential than the former, but should be remembered if possible.

Next, the student should prepare an outline of this outline by copying out the topics in bold type in the chapter or chapters he is studying. This is recommended because most of us have visual memories; by writing something down we store that information in our minds. Moreover, that skeleton outline, which will fill less than a sheet of paper, will be easy to remember. Having learned that outline thoroughly, the usual student in an examination will be able to recall the more detailed treatment of the subject in this fuller outline, and from that most of the subject matter in the text. He should also pay attention to the names and events underlined, remembering that those are of such importance that they appear commonly on examinations.

Finally, having learned the factual story, the student should study the interpretative sections carefully, seeking to supplement them from his own knowledge of the past and present. By thinking about the material in this way he will not only achieve better understanding, but will be equipped to apply his knowledge in his own life.

Two other features of this history in outline are designed to help the student. At the end of each chapter is a section entitled "Additional Reading" which lists eight or ten of the most useful books on the subjects considered, together with brief comments indicating their nature and point of view. These bibliographies should help the student select, from the longer lists given in most texts, the few books that are essential if he wishes to do further reading. Finally, the volume ends with a section in which various types of examination questions are discussed and a number of sample questions given. The student should study carefully those questions pertaining to the section of the subject on which he is to be examined, and if possible should write out answers to several of them. By comparing his answers with the corresponding sections of this outline, he will be able to realize and correct his own defects before taking an actual examination.

R. A. B.

Contents

CONTENTS

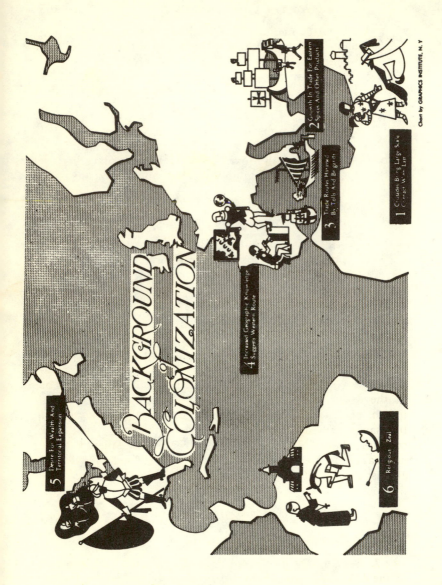

BACKGROUND of COLONIZATION

1 Crusades Bring Large Scale Contact With East

2 Growth In Trade For Eastern Spices And Other Products

3 Trade Routes Hampered By Tolls And Brigands

4 Increased Geographic Knowledge Suggests Western Route

5 Desire For Wealth And Territorial Expansion

6 Religious Zeal

Chart by GRAPHICS INSTITUTE, N. Y.

CHAPTER I

The Colonization of North America
1492-1600

ℂ THE EXPANSION OF EUROPE

The colonization of North America was only one phase of a mammoth movement of peoples known to historians as the "expansion of Europe." This began in the twelfth century when Christian crusaders attempted to wrest the holy city of Jerusalem from infidel hands, and ended only when all livable portions of the world were occupied. During its height — in the sixteenth, seventeenth, and eighteenth centuries — hundreds of thousands of Europeans left their homelands to plant new colonies in Asia, Pacific Oceania, Africa, and America. The occupation of the American continent can be understood only against this broader background of expansion.

I. THE AGE OF DISCOVERY, 1100 - 1492

A. The European Background

1. Beginnings of Commercial Expansion. At the end of the eleventh century eastern Europe stagnated under Byzantine rule, while western Europe had succumbed completely to

1

feudalism. Trade and learning had virtually disappeared as the minor lords who governed each isolated community warred on each other or wrung new concessions from their serfs.

a. INFLUENCE OF THE CRUSADES. Between 1095 and 1291 warlike Christian crusaders periodically marched against Jerusalem. They failed to capture the Holy City, but they brought back luxuries unknown to frugal Europe: silks, gems, tapestries, and especially the spices that were so highly prized in that prerefrigeration era. Soon these items were demanded as necessities by Europeans. Merchants in such Italian city states as Genoa, Venice, Pisa, and Florence undertook to supply this demand. Their long row galleys regularly visited the Levantine coast, returning with luxuries that were distributed over Europe by pack trains that trudged northward across the Alps.

b. EUROPE'S ADVERSE TRADE BALANCE. As Europe's bulky agricultural produce could not be marketed in the Near East, gold was constantly drained eastward to pay for these luxuries. By the year 1300 an acute money shortage had plunged the continent into a prolonged depression. As the people were by this time dependent on these luxuries, the only solution was to find a cheaper source of supply.

2. The Demand for Oriental Trade

a. ADVANTAGES OF TRADE WITH THE ORIENT. Europeans believed that a more direct route to the Orient was the only solution, for such travelers as *Marco Polo* (1298) told them that this was the source of the goods they had obtained in the Near East. This would eliminate two sets of middlemen: 1) Levantine traders who brought goods from China or Japan to the eastern end of the Mediterranean; and 2) Italian merchants who distributed them over Europe.

b. PREPARATIONS FOR ORIENTAL TRADE.

I. *Rise of National States.* During the fourteenth century such nations as Portugal, Spain, France, and England gradually emerged, as strong kings welded feudal estates into kingdoms. Only these united nations had the resources necessary to finance voyages to the Orient.

II. *The Commercial Revolution.* As control of commerce shifted from feudal lords to national monarchs, modern business methods were introduced. These included most of the features of *capitalism* : the taking of interest, emphasis on competition, and individual initiative. They provided merchants with the economic means necessary for long voyages of exploration.

B. The Search for a Route to the Orient

1. Portugal and the Eastern Route. Portugal, under the able leadership of *Prince Henry the Navigator* (1394-1460), took the initiative in seeking a direct route to the Far East. His navigators pushed farther and farther down the African coast until *Bartholomew Diaz* rounded the Cape of Good Hope in *1487*. A short time later *Vasco da Gama* reached India (1498) by following this African route, opening a Far Eastern trade that brought prosperity to Portugal.

2. Spain and the Western Route

a. VOYAGE OF CHRISTOPHER COLUMBUS. With Portugal monopolizing the eastern route, Spain was forced to reach the East by sailing west, a project deemed feasible, as all intelligent Europeans knew the world was round. The voyage was delayed until *1492* by wars against Moorish invaders from Africa, but in that year the Spanish monarchs, *Ferdinand and Isabella,* sent *Christopher Columbus* westward with three small ships. Columbus returned after making his landfall in the Bahamas on *October 12, 1492,* convinced that he had hit upon an outlying portion of Asia.

b. DIVISION OF THE NEW WORLD. When Portugal protested, the Pope awarded that country all heathen lands east of a *Demarcation Line* (May 4, 1493) drawn 100 leagues west of the Cape Verde Islands. A year later the *Treaty of Tordesillas* between the two powers shifted the line to a point 370 leagues west of the Cape Verde Islands, giving Brazil to Portugal, and the rest of America to Spain.

c. LATER SPANISH VOYAGES. Among later explorers who demonstrated that Columbus had found a new world were: 1) Americus Vespucius, who gave America its name; 2) Balboa, who crossed the Isthmus of Panama (1513) ; and 3) *Ferdinand Magellan,* who circumnavigated the globe (1519-1522).

II. BEGINNINGS OF EUROPEAN COLONIZATION
1493 - 1600

A.   Origins of the Spanish Empire in America

1. Occupation of the West Indies

a. THE FIRST SPANISH COLONIES. On his second voyage (1493) Columbus carried 1500 Spaniards to Hispaniola (Haiti). Enslaved natives, put to work in primitive mines, were by 1513 producing $1,000,000 worth of gold yearly. In the meantime other islands were gradually overrun; Puerto Rico was 'pacified' in 1508, Jamaica in 1509-1510, and Cuba in 1511-1515.

b. THE SPANISH COLONIAL SYSTEM. The conquest was carried on by minor noblemen, or _conquistadores,_ who were authorized by the king to "pacify" specific regions. Areas thus subdued were known as _encomiendas,_ and each was under the absolute control of the nobleman. As the empire expanded, larger administrative units, _viceroyalties,_ were created, each under a viceroy, who governed with the aid of an _audiencia_ of appointed officials which served as both supreme court and legislature.

2. Expansion Into North America

a. EXPLORATION OF THE SOUTHEAST. The conquest of Mexico's Aztec Indians by _Hernan Cortés_ (1519-1521) rewarded Spain with a fortune in gold and silver. Other _conquistadores,_ seeking to duplicate this rich find, swarmed out over all America in the next years. One group turned toward the northern mainland, which had been discovered by _Juan Ponce de Léon_ (1513). _Panfilo de Narvaez_ led one party (1528) which explored north of Florida, then tried to reach Mexico by boat. All were wrecked save _Cabeza de Vaca_ and three companions; after six years of wandering they finally emerged in Mexico with tales of a barren countryside. Undiscouraged by this, _Hernando de Soto_ undertook a more thorough exploration of the interior (1539-1543) which ended with his death on the banks of the principal river that he had discovered, the Mississippi. His sacrifice convinced Spain that the Southeast held neither surface wealth nor advanced natives who would welcome salvation.

b. EXPLORATION OF THE SOUTHWEST. A similar expedition from Mexico under _Francisco Coronado_ (1540-1542) advanced as far as present-day Kansas without finding gold or silver. The Coronado and de Soto expeditions turned Spanish interest from North America to South America, where wealth did exist.

c. THE FIRST SPANISH SETTLEMENTS.

I. _The Occupation of Florida_. When French adventurers occupied the Florida east coast as a base to attack Spanish treasure ships (1564), interest in North America revived. _Pedro Menéndez_, a soldier, was sent to drive out the intruders, then build the town of _St. Augustine_ (1565) to hold the region. The Florida colony was on the brink of failure until the 1590's when Franciscans and Jesuits established _mission stations_ there to convert and civilize the Indians. By 1606 missionaries had won control of the coast as far north as the Carolinas.

II. _The Occupation of New Mexico_. In a similar attempt to protect Mexico from invaders, _Juan de Onate_ was sent northward to occupy New Mexico (1598). The important town of Santa Fe (1609) soon became the center of this outpost.

B. Origins of the French Empire in America

1. Early French Exploration. The first official French explorer to visit America was Giovanni Verazzano (1524), who searched the coast from Cape Fear to Maine, seeking the fabled _Northwest Passage_. More important were the three voyages of _Jacques Cartier_ (1533-1541) which gave France a claim to the St. Lawrence Valley.

2. Founding of Quebec. French fur traders became active in the St. Lawrence Valley during the late sixteenth century. Their activities led to the founding of Quebec (1608) by _Samuel de Champlain_, the greatest French explorer. Traders and missionaries soon advanced far into the interior, taking advantage of the easy water routes that led to the Great Lakes.

C. Beginnings of English Expansion

1. Reasons for Delay in Expansion. Despite a claim to North America established by the voyage of _John Cabot_ (1497), England was late in entering the race for colonies. This was because: 1) internal conflicts accompanying the consolidation of the kingdom under the _Tudor_ monarchs depleted its resources; 2) dependence on Italian merchants prevented it from developing commercial enterprises of its own until after 1550; and 3) under the early Tudors England and Spain were so closely united by religious and diplomatic ties that the former did not dare challenge the latter's New World monopoly.

2. The War with Spain

a. ORIGINS OF ANGLO-SPANISH CONFLICT. Under _Queen Elizabeth_ the alliance between England and Spain was severed. Responsible for this important break were: 1) the refusal of Elizabeth to marry King Philip of Spain, who sought in this way to extend his influence over England; 2) the steady growth of Spanish strength which endangered the balance of power in Europe; and 3) the _Protestant Reformation_ under Elizabeth's father, Henry VIII, which converted Britain into Europe's leading defender of Protestantism against Catholic Spain.

b. ATTACKS ON SPANISH SHIPPING.

I. _Raids on the Spanish Main_. Although England and Spain remained technically at peace during the early years of Elizabeth's reign, bold _"sea dogs"_ began raiding Spanish shipping with the queen's secret support. Their leader was John Hawkins, who in the 1560's made numerous raids on Caribbean ports.

II. _Exploits of Francis Drake_. After repeated attacks on Spanish towns and ships, Francis Drake sailed into the Pacific, where he raided at leisure before completing the circumnavigation of the globe (1578-1580). On his return to England he was knighted by Elizabeth, in open defiance of Spain.

c. OUTBREAK OF OPEN WARFARE. Drake's raid precipitated open warfare that was climaxed by the _defeat of a Spanish armada_ (1588) on its way to attack England. This established Britain as mistress of the seas, and started Spain's decline as a world power.

3. First Attempts at Colony Planting

a. EFFORTS OF SIR WALTER RALEIGH. As antipathy toward Spain mounted, many noblemen sought to check that nation's expansion in America by planting English colonies there. Most active was _Sir Walter Raleigh,_ a wealthy court favorite, who in 1583 inherited a patent authorizing him to establish a colony from his half-brother, Sir Humphrey Gilbert. Raleigh made three attempts to found a settlement on _Roanoke Island,_ North Carolina (1585-1587). The first two failed; the colonists sent out on the third expedition (1587) disappeared before a supply ship could reach them. The fate of the _"lost colony of Roanoke"_ remains one of the mysteries of history.

b. REASONS FOR RALEIGH'S FAILURE. As a result of Raleigh's failure, Englishmen learned that: 1) colonies must create their own wealth through agriculture rather than depending on exploitation of the country or its primitive natives; and 2) the wealth of no one man was sufficient to nurture a colony to the point that it would return profits. In the future colony planting was entrusted to _joint stock companies,_ which sold stock to many "adventurers" (investors). This shifted control of overseas expansion from the individualistic noble class to the rising middle class.

4. _Motives for English Colonization_. England was ready to apply these lessons, for by 1600 conditions were ripe for expansion.

a. RELIGIOUS MOTIVES. The Protestant Reformation: 1) made Englishmen anxious to convert American natives before they were won to Catholicism by Spain; and 2) created numerous dissenting sects whose members were eager to move to colonies where they could worship as they pleased.

b. SOCIAL MOTIVES.

I. _Overcrowding at Home_. The enclosure of farm fields for sheep growing and the influx of American gold increased food prices fourfold between 1500 and 1600. Wages, however, remained stable, as former farm laborers competed for jobs. Englishmen believed that prosperity would never return until the excess population was drained away into colonies.

II. _Desire for Adventure_. A strong spirit of wanderlust was shown by the popularity of the narratives of voyages published by _Richard Hakluyt,_ the greatest propagandist for overseas expansion.

c. ECONOMIC MOTIVES.

I. _Need for Outlets for Capital_. England's commercial and industrial enterprises had created surplus capital for which there was no market at home.

II. *Need for Raw Materials.* Under the prevailing system of *mercantilism* (which measured national wealth in terms of gold) every nation sought to export more than it imported. England was forced to import sugar, tobacco, and other semi-tropical produce, as well as lumber and naval stores (masts, pitch, and tar). Colonies would supply her with these items, allowing her to keep her wealth at home.

III. *Need for Markets.* England's woolen manufacturers were unable to sell cloth in Europe, as most nations forbade imports in an effort to preserve their gold supplies. Colonies would provide a profitable market.

III. FOUNDING OF THE SOUTHERN COLONIES
1600 - 1660

A.   Occupation of Virginia, 1606 - 1612

1. End of the Spanish War. The death of Elizabeth (1603) elevated to the throne *James I,* the first of the *Stuart monarchs,* who lacked his predecessor's fanatical hatred of Catholicism. When he ended the war with Spain, Englishmen could no longer prey on Spanish wealth, but must found their own colonies to enjoy the benefits of the New World.

2. The Virginia Company

a. THE CHARTER OF 1606. Two groups of merchants in London and Plymouth applied for charters authorizing them to plant colonies. They were united as the *Virginia Company* (1606), with the London group authorized to occupy southern North America (34° to 41°) and the Plymouth group northern America (38° to 45°). Each colony was to be governed by a local council, appointed by a royal council in England whose members were named by the king. The Plymouth group lapsed into inactivity after an unsuccessful attempt to occupy the Maine coast (1607).

b. THE JAMESTOWN COLONY, 1607-1612. Three ships with 105 colonists sent by the London group established a colony on a peninsula jutting into the James River (*May, 1607*).

I. *The "Starving Time."* During the first years disease and starvation took a terrible toll; only a constant supply of new colonists sent by the company kept the colony alive. In 1609 Captain *John Smith,* a member of the governing council, provided some of the leadership necessary, but his return to England that fall again reduced the colonists to extreme want.

II. *Reasons for Near Failure.* Responsible for the "starving time" were: 1) the inadequacies of the colonists, who were either decayed "gentlemen" or unambitious paupers; 2) lack of knowledge of a "frontier technique" which would have allowed the colonists to pick a healthier site for Jamestown and utilize the riches of nature; 3) inefficient management by the bickering council members; 4) Indian hostility; and 5) a labor system that forced the settlers to work entirely for the company rather than themselves, thus reducing incentive.

B. Virginia Under Company Rule, 1612 - 1624
1. Success of Virginia Colony

a. PRODUCTION OF A STAPLE. The need for an export crop was satisfied in 1612 when John Rolfe began raising *tobacco.* As the European market was limitless, high profits brought prosperity to the colony.

b. CHANGES IN THE ECONOMY.

I. *Transition to Private Ownership.* Settlers refused to work for the company and its absentee stockholders, even under threat of harsh punishments decreed by Governor *Thomas Dale* (1611-1616). Hence between 1616 and 1619 land was divided among private owners. With a new incentive, production mounted until the colony was self-supporting and prosperous.

II. *Growth of Labor Supply.* Most labor was performed by *indentured servants* (men who sold their services for from four to seven years to the farmer who paid their way to America). To encourage their importation, the company granted a *"head right"* of fifty acres of land to anyone paying the passage of a servant. This transferred more land to private hands, further stimulating production.

c. GOVERNMENTAL CHANGES.

I. *Charter of 1609.* This remedied the mistakes of the old charter by: 1) revising the boundaries to include 400 miles along the coast with the interior area running "west and northwest" to the Pacific; 2) providing that the governing council in England be elected by the stockholders; and 3) replacing the squabbling local council with a governor.

II. *The First Legislature.* To encourage migration, the company in *1619* authorized a legislature composed of two elected representatives of each plantation to meet with the governor and council in framing laws.

2. Dissolution of the Virginia Company, 1624

a. REASONS FOR DISSATISFACTION WITH COMPANY.

I. *Internal Conflicts.* The election of the liberal *Sir Edwin Sandys* to head the company (1619) angered the tyrannical James I, who was already annoyed by a conflict over the collection of customs duties on tobacco. Sandys proved a vigorous leader, sending out 4000 colonists in the next four years.

II. *Bad Times in Virginia.* The influx of "unseasoned" immigrants multiplied the death rate in Virginia, as well as weakening the colony's defenses against Indians. An Indian massacre in 1622 cost 357 lives. This allowed Sandys' enemies within the company to accuse him of incompetence.

b. END OF THE COMPANY. James I seized on these conflicts to charge mismanagement of the company. A legal suit that he instituted forced it to surrender its charter in 1624.

C. Virginia as a Royal Colony, 1624 - 1660

1. Form of Government. Virginia became a *royal colony*, ruled by a governor and council named by the king, and an elected assembly chosen by the people. Although the king could veto acts of the assembly, the people enjoyed a large degree of self-government, especially after 1624, when the governor was forbidden to levy taxes without the consent of the House of Burgesses. During the Puritan Revolution in England (1642-1660) the colony virtually ruled itself.

2. Economic Progress

a. NATURE OF THE ECONOMY. Virginia remained a land of small farms, operated by owners and indentured servants. All grew foodstuffs for their own use, plus tobacco for export to England.

b. EXPANSION OF SETTLEMENT. Settled areas expanded rapidly due to: 1) soil exhaustion as successive tobacco planting wore out the land and drove farmers westward; 2) a steady influx of indentured servants and other colonists, particularly after the Puritan Revolution drove royalists abroad; and 3) the ease with which land could be obtained under the "head right" system. By 1660 the river bottoms of the James, York, and Rappahannock rivers were occupied by some 30,000 settlers.

D.   The Founding of Maryland, 1632 - 1660

1. The Maryland Charter

a. AMBITIONS OF LORD BALTIMORE. In 1632 the region between the Potomac River and the 40th parallel was granted to *George Calvert*, the first *Lord Baltimore*, a prominent English Catholic who was anxious to found a haven for persecuted members of his faith.

b. NATURE OF PROPRIETARY COLONIES. The charter established a pattern for *proprietary colonies*. The proprietor was authorized to dispose of the land as he wished, and to make all laws subject only to the advice and assent of the people.

2. Beginnings of the Maryland Colony

a. THE FIRST SETTLERS. A shipload of colonists reached America early in 1634. There they laid out the town of *St. Mary's* on a healthy site. Profiting by Virginia's mistakes, the colonists prospered from the beginning as they turned to growing corn, tobacco, and livestock.

b. GOVERNMENTAL BEGINNINGS. Although the Calvert family attempted autocratic rule for a time, a legislature was soon called and self-government introduced. The governor and council were appointed by the proprietor, while the assembly was elected by the people.

c. RELIGIOUS CONFLICTS. As Protestants outnumbered Catholics from the beginning and steadily increased their majority, Lord Baltimore realized that the religious freedom of his Catholic followers must be protected. The *Toleration Act of 1649* which he sponsored was a landmark in the history of liberty. It granted freedom of worship to all who accepted the divinity of Christ.

IV. FOUNDING THE NEW ENGLAND COLONIES
1620 - 1660

A.   English Background of New England Migrations. The New England colonies were founded for both economic and religious purposes. Responsible for the latter was the establishment under Queen Elizabeth of the Anglican Church as the official Church of England. This displeased numerous dissenting groups, including the *Puritans* who wished to "purify" Anglicanism of its "popish" practices, and the *Separatists* who wanted to separate from the Church of England altogether. Members of both of these groups became interested in founding American colonies where they could worship as they pleased

B.   The Plymouth Colony

1. The Migration of the Pilgrims

a. THE VOYAGE TO PLYMOUTH. A group of *Separatists* from the town of Scrooby, after living for a time in Holland, determined to move to Virginia. Obtaining a grant of land from the Virginia Company and the financial backing of a number of London merchants who banded together as a joint stock company for the purpose, they sailed on the *Mayflower* late in *1620*. Storms drove the vessel from its course, landing the Pilgrims on the Massachusetts coast, where they decided to remain. On December 21, 1620, they began building homes on the shore of Plymouth Harbor.

b. THE MAYFLOWER COMPACT. The Pilgrims realized that they were occupying land to which they had no title. To protect themselves from eviction, and to provide a system of government, they signed a compact that bound each to obey the majority will. This was the first of a series of *"squatters' agreements"* entered into by frontiersmen who found themselves temporarily beyond the pale of the law. In 1621 they secured a patent to the land from the *Council for New England,* which had succeeded the Virginia Company as owner of the region.

2. Expansion of the Plymouth Colony

a. ACHIEVING SELF-SUFFICIENCY. To pay off their London backers, the Pilgrims: 1) developed an extensive fur trade in Maine; and 2) divided all land among the people (1623). By 1627 the colony was out of debt and self-supporting. This impressed contemporaries more than the religious freedom secured by the colonists.

b. GOVERNMENT OF PLYMOUTH COLONY. At first an elected governor (*William Bradford* for thirty years) and assistants met with all the people to draft laws. As the population increased this became impossible; after 1639 the towns sent representatives to a General Court, or legislature.

c. EXPANSION OF PLYMOUTH. The colony slowly expanded as new towns were established along the coast and on lower Cape Cod. Cereals and livestock were its principal products. Its backers never succeeded in securing a royal charter, however, and in 1691 Plymouth Colony was absorbed by Massachusetts.

C. The Massachusetts Bay Colony

1. The Massachusetts Bay Company

a. FOUNDING OF THE COMPANY. A group of Puritan businessmen secured from the Council for New England a grant to the area between the Charles and Merrimac rivers (1628), and immediately established a trading post at Salem. A year later a royal charter incorporated the group as the Massachusetts Bay Company. Several Puritan leaders, noting that this charter did not force the company to hold its meetings in England, recognized an opportunity to found a colony that would be virtually self-governing. Led by *John Winthrop*, they signed the *Cambridge Agreement* (August, 1629), binding themselves to migrate to America if the government and charter were transferred as well.

b. MIGRATION TO MASSACHUSETTS. In 1630 John Winthrop, who was chosen governor, reached Massachusetts with 1000 followers. Settlement expanded rapidly as towns sprang up about Boston, the center of the colony. Between 1630 and 1640 the *"Great Migration"* brought 25,000 Puritans to Massachusetts, for during that period Charles I ruled England without Parliament and vigorously persecuted all dissenters. Cereals and livestock were produced in large quantities, while fishing also helped the colony enjoy prosperity.

2. Evolution of a Governmental System

a. PURITAN POLITICAL THEORY. The Puritan leaders disliked democracy, believing instead in a *theocracy* that would allow the state to force all people to live and worship in an orthodox way. This theory, which was based on the teachings of

John Calvin, a Reformation leader, underlay their plans for a governmental system.

b. PERIOD OF ABSOLUTE CONTROL. The charter vested control in the "freemen" (stockholders), who were authorized to elect eighteen "assistants" (a board of directors), and a governor (president). In the first migration only twelve "freemen" reached Massachusetts, all of them officers of the company. Their plans to rule the colony were upset in the fall of 1630 when 109 settlers asked to be made "freemen." The twelve did not dare to refuse, but before acceding ruled that the sole function of "freemen" would be to elect assistants for life. The assistants would then elect a governor, and with him would rule Massachusetts.

c. DEMOCRATIC BEGINNINGS. Sensing something wrong, the people in 1634 appointed a committee to examine the charter. When they discovered that they, rather than the assistants, were authorized to enact laws, a legislature was demanded. This was composed of two "deputies" from each town, who thereafter met with the assistants to levy taxes and make all laws. After 1644 the "deputies" and assistants met separately in a two-house legislature. The government was far from democratic, however, as only selected church members were admitted to the ranks of "freemen."

D. Establishment of Other New England Colonies

1. Founding of Rhode Island

a. EFFECT OF PURITAN INTOLERANCE. The undemocratic government of Massachusetts bred a whole series of rebels who founded other New England colonies. Most famous among them were *Roger Williams,* who was banished in 1635 for stating that the government had no authority over the personal habits and opinions of individuals, and *Anne Hutchinson,* who was expelled in 1637 for criticizing certain Boston clergymen. The followers of these two rebels founded Rhode Island.

b. THE FIRST SETTLEMENTS. In the spring of 1636 Roger Williams and his followers laid out the town of *Providence.* Complete religious and civil freedom was promised all settlers. A short time later supporters of Anne Hutchinson established Portsmouth. When they quarreled over religious matters, a faction broke away to occupy Newport. Warwick was settled by *Samuel Gorton,* a religious eccentric from Massachusetts Bay.

c. THE RHODE ISLAND CHARTER. A preliminary charter authorizing the settlement of Rhode Island (1644) was followed by another (1663) which established a permanent government based on that of Massachusetts but not requiring church membership of voters. The complete political and religious freedom allowed attracted dissenters from all over America and Europe.

2. Founding of Connecticut

a. THE RIVER TOWNS. Followers of the Reverend *Thomas Hooker,* a liberal clergyman from Cambridge, Massachusetts, who had quarreled with the Boston ministers, migrated westward in 1636 to found *Hartford.* Before the year was out other immigrants from Massachusetts established Wethersfield, Windsor, and Springfield. In 1639 representatives of the Connecticut towns drew up the *Fundamental Orders,* a written constitution that established a government similar to that of Massachusetts but with the governor's powers restricted.

b. THE NEW HAVEN COLONY. Another Puritan colony was established at New Haven in 1637 by the Reverend *John Davenport,* an English clergyman, and Theophilus Eaton, a merchant. In their rigid Bible commonwealth church members alone had a voice in the government.

c. CHARTER OF 1662. The New Haven Colony and the River Towns were united as the colony of Connecticut under a charter issued by the king in 1662. The liberal frame of government allowed almost complete self-rule.

3. Maine and New Hampshire.

The region north of Massachusetts was granted to *Sir Ferdinando Gorges* and Captain John Mason (1623). Six years later they divided the area between them, Gorges taking Maine and Mason taking New Hampshire. Neither established settlements; instead most pioneers came from Massachusetts, including the Reverend *John Wheelright,* a follower of Anne Hutchinson, who founded Exeter, New Hampshire (1638). This allowed Massachusetts to assert its authority over both New Hampshire and Maine. New Hampshire was made a royal colony in 1679, but Maine remained part of Massachusetts until 1820.

E.   Development of the New England Colonies

1. Expansion of Settlement. Settlement advanced slowly over the coastal areas and in the lower Connecticut River valley, checked only by the *Pequot War* (1637) which ended in the extermination of that Indian tribe. For the next half century the New England frontier enjoyed peace.

2. The New England Confederation. The intrusion of Dutch traders from New York and French traders from Canada at a time when England was so absorbed in the Puritan Revolution that it could afford no protection led the New England colonies to form the *New England Confederation* (1643). This provided for yearly meetings of commissioners from each colony, who were authorized to wage war and to appropriate men and money. As the commissioners had no power to enforce their decisions, they served in only an advisory capacity. The Confederation, however, endured until 1684.

V. SIGNIFICANCE OF EARLY COLONIZATION

A.   Motives for Colonization

1. The Religious Motive. Despite arguments to the contrary, most historians today agree that religion was an important force inspiring migration, especially to New England. Doubtless many Puritans and Separatists were also motivated by a desire for gain, but far fewer would have risked immigration had dissent been accepted in England. This did not mean that the colonists favored freedom of conscience; they simply wanted a place where they could worship as they pleased.

2. The Economic Motive. Even the most zealous dissenters could not have reached America had the profit motive been nonexistent; the Puritans relied on wealthy church members to finance their migrations, just as the Separatists were dependent on rich London merchants. Moreover all comers hoped to find greater economic opportunity than in overcrowded England. Thus the economic motive for colonization was always present; the religious motive was influential at certain times and places.

B.   Results of Colonization

1. Freedom of Worship. In most colonies before 1660 religious freedom was as restricted as it was in England, but in Maryland and Rhode Island liberty of conscience was allowed most men. This was an important contribution in a world where toleration was almost unknown.

2. Freedom of Political Thought. None of the colonies was completely democratic; voting was restricted to persons of proper religious views or economic status. Yet Americans by 1660 enjoyed greater political freedom than Englishmen. These democratic beginnings were traceable to: 1) the vision of such liberals as Sir Edwin Sandys and Roger Williams; and 2) the frontier demand for self-rule to deal with problems so unique that they could not be solved by a distant parliament.

3. Freedom of Economic Opportunity. The presence of vast quantities of cheap land in America opened opportunities for economic advancement unknown in overcrowded Europe, where nearly all land was engrossed by the gentry. For the first time in modern history men could capitalize on their own abilities, rather than on the accident of birth. The resulting impulse toward economic democracy was destined to change the whole nature of western civilization.

ADDITIONAL READING

C. P. Nettles, *Roots of American Civilization* (1947) is a competent factual survey, but more recent interpretations are in Clarence Ver Steeg, *The Formative Years*, 1607-1763 (1964). J. B. Brebner, *The Explorers of North America* (1933), is brief but adequate; the most important explorer receives fitting tribute in S. E. Morison, *Admiral of the Ocean Sea* (1942). Excellent on the background of English colonization is Wallace Notestein, *The English People on the Eve of Colonization* (1954). The best study of the early southern colonies is F. W. Craven, *The Southern Colonies in the Seventeenth Century* (1949), but newer points of view on two colonizers are in W. M. Wallace, *Sir Walter Raleigh* (1959) and P. L. Barbour, *The Three Worlds of Captain John Smith* (1964). Good on early New England is T. J. Wertenbaker, *The Puritan Oligarchy* (1947), although his anti-Puritan bias should be balanced with S. E. Morison, *Builders of the Bay Colony* (1930), and Alan Simpson, *Puritanism in Old and New England* (1935). E. S. Morgan, *The Puritan Dilemma* (1958) is a fine biography of Governor John Winthrop, and Bernard Bailyn, *The New England Merchants in the Seventeenth Century* (1955), a penetrating analysis of economic growth. Perry Miller, *Roger Williams* (1953) provides sound information on early Rhode Island.

CHAPTER II

The Maturing
of Colonial America
1660-1763

⊄ THE EXPANSION OF EMPIRE

Haphazard colony planting by individuals or groups came to an
end with the restoration of the Stuarts in 1660. For the next
half century a serious effort was made to weld the growing
empire into a compact unit and to plan its extension with care.
Eventually distance and royal indifference again slackened England's interest in its overseas possessions; through most of the
eighteenth century the colonies went their own ways, unhampered by royal restraint. This period of "salutary neglect" so
weakened imperial ties that England received little colonial aid
in the decisive wars against France and Spain, fought to determine the ownership of the North American continent.

I.   DEVELOPMENT OF BRITISH COLONIAL
POLICY — 1660 - 1754

A.   Planned Colony Planting. After his restoration to
the throne in 1660, Charles II was anxious to reward both cava-
liers and merchants who had aided him. To the former he
granted new colonies; to the latter a system of economic controls designed to aid England's commercial classes.

1. Founding of the Carolinas

a. THE CAROLINA CHARTER. The region between Virginia and Florida was granted (1663) to eight proprietors, who were authorized to make any provision for government that they chose. They engaged the philosopher, *John Locke,* to draft the *Fundamental Constitutions,* a document that provided for an archaic system of rule based on feudal practices. The Constitutions were soon abandoned as unsuited to conditions in America.

b. SETTLEMENT OF CAROLINA. Pioneers from Virginia were already in the region about *Albemarle Sound,* where they resisted all attempts of the proprietors to establish a government or collect taxes. More attention was paid the settlement established at Charles Town (later *Charleston*) in 1670. Tobacco did not thrive there, but a trade in deerskins soon brought the colonists prosperity. After 1693 rice culture spread rapidly, while an influx of Scots and French Huguenots also stimulated the growth of the colony. Negro slaves were imported after 1700 to work in the rice fields.

c. SEPARATION OF THE CAROLINAS. By 1700 South Carolina was becoming a land of large plantations and slavery, North Carolina a region of small farms and free labor. When the proprietors sold out their interests to the crown (1729) this difference was recognized by the creation of the royal colonies of North and South Carolina.

2. Founding of New York and New Jersey

a. FOUNDING OF NEW NETHERLAND. Basing their claims on the voyage of *Henry Hudson* (1609), the Dutch in 1624 occupied New York and New Jersey. The *Dutch West India Company,* which was granted the region, first tried to attract settlers with the *patroon system;* large estates were granted wealthy men who promised to bring out a number of tenant farmers. When this failed amidst the plentiful land of America (only one patroonship was settled), the company turned to the *fur trade. Fort Orange* (Albany) was soon the center of a profitable commerce with the *Iroquois Indians* of the Mohawk Valley, while Ft. Nassau (opposite Philadelphia) attracted furs from the Delaware Valley. By 1660 New Netherland boasted 10,000 inhabitants, including a number of *Swedish colonists* who had been absorbed (1655) after trying to found their own settlement (1638) near the mouth of the Delaware River.

b. BRITISH CONQUEST OF NEW NETHERLAND. Irritated by the presence of the Dutch in North America and by their conflicts with New England fur traders, Charles II granted the area between the Connecticut and Delaware rivers to his brother, the Duke of York (1664). The latter, seizing on an impending war between England and Holland as an excuse, captured New Netherland in August, 1664. The colony, renamed New York, was ruled with an iron hand by its proprietor, who did not even allow an assembly until 1683.

c. SEPARATION OF NEW JERSEY. The southern portions of New York were given to two friends of the Duke of York, one of whom soon sold his interests to a group of Quakers (1674). This led to its division into two colonies, East New Jersey (adjacent to New York) and West New Jersey (adjacent to Pennsylvania). The former was settled largely by New Englanders, who developed an economy based on agriculture and commerce; the latter was peopled by a miscellaneous group who patterned their economy on that of Virginia. In 1702 the two were united as the royal colony of New Jersey.

3. Founding of Pennsylvania

a. GRANT TO WILLIAM PENN. Penn, a wealthy English Quaker, was granted proprietory rights to the region along the Delaware River (1681) to satisfy an old family claim against Charles II. The charter bound him to obtain the settlers' consent when making laws.

b. SETTLEMENT OF PENNSYLVANIA.

I. *The "Holy Experiment."* As a leading humanitarian, Penn was interested in a government guaranteeing both religious and political freedom. In a *Frame of Government* (1682) and a *Charter of Privileges* (1701) he decreed complete freedom of worship and a democratic government in which most power was vested in a one-house elected legislature. In no other colony did the people enjoy such freedom.

II. *Nature of Population.* Penn's tolerance attracted settlers from all over Europe to Philadelphia; others were lured by his advertising in Germany and elsewhere. By 1689 Pennsylvania's population of 12,000 was the most cosmopolitan in America. The colony prospered from the first.

c. SEPARATION OF DELAWARE. In 1682 Penn purchased Delaware from the Duke of York to protect the water route to Pennsylvania. Delaware was given an assembly of its own in 1702, but remained under the Pennsylvania governor until the Revolution.

4. Founding of Georgia

a. MOTIVES FOR SETTLEMENT. Although founded after the Restoration period, the same motives influenced England: 1) a desire to erect a buffer state between the Carolinas and Spanish Florida; 2) expansion of the empire at the expense of other colonizing powers; and 3) the erection of a haven for debtors who clogged England's jails and for persecuted European Protestants.

b. SETTLEMENT OF GEORGIA. A group of proprietors under *James Oglethorpe,* a prominent humanitarian, in 1732 were granted the region between the Savannah and Altamaha rivers. The charter provided that the proprietors should own no land and secure no profits from the colony, authorized them to appoint a governor but no assembly, and decreed that the colony should revert to the king in twenty-one years. Under this grant, Oglethorpe led the first settlers to Savannah in January, 1733.

c. DEVELOPMENT OF GEORGIA. The colony grew slowly because: 1) English debtors did not migrate in the numbers expected; 2) land holdings were restricted to 500 acres as a defense measure; 3) Negro slaves were forbidden for the same reason, preventing the growth of a plantation economy; and 4) constant conflicts with Spanish Florida deterred timid settlers. These restrictions were modified after *1751* when Georgia became a *royal colony,* but its population was only 9000 in 1760.

5. Founding of Minor Colonies.

Other outposts occupied included: 1) *Bermuda,* which was settled as a tobacco colony by the Somers Island Company in 1612 and became a royal colony in 1679; 2) several *West Indian islands* including Barbados (1625) and Jamaica (1655) as centers for sugar production; and 3) the area about Hudson Bay, which was granted to the *Hudson's Bay Company* (1670).

B. Economic Reorganization of the Empire

1. Economic Theory Underlying Reorganization. Under the prevailing theory of mercantilism each nation constantly worked to : 1) strengthen itself at the expense of its rivals ; and 2) sell more than it purchased, thus securing a favorable trade balance that could be met by imports of gold or silver. To fit properly into this scheme, colonies must : 1) supply the mother country with goods that could not be produced at home ; 2) purchase the mother country's goods with gold or silver from colonial mines ; and 3) allow themselves to be exploited in any other way for the benefit of the home country. In practice within the British empire this meant : 1) the regulation of colonial trade to prevent goods from leaving the empire ; and 2) the stamping out of colonial manufactures that would compete with England's own industries.

2. Application of the Theory of Mercantilism

a. REGULATION OF COLONIAL COMMERCE.

I. *Navigation Act of 1660.* This was the first of a series of Acts of Trade and Navigation (except for a temporary law passed in 1651). It provided that : 1) all goods entering England must be carried in British ships or the ships of the producing country ; 2) trade with British colonies was confined to English ships with three-quarters of the crews English ; and 3) certain *enumerated articles* (tobacco, sugar, cotton, indigo, ginger, dyewoods) produced in the colonies could be sold only in England. To compensate the continental colonies for the loss of their European tobacco market, the law forbade further production of the crop in England or its importation from abroad. The "enumerated list" was gradually expanded during the next years, with the addition of rice, naval stores, furs, iron, and lumber.

II. *Navigation Act of 1663.* This stated that all European goods on the way to the colonies must pass through England, paying the usual customs duties. On leaving England for the colonies, however, a *drawback* (a large portion of the customs duty) was returned to the shipper. This allowed colonists to buy goods through England about as cheaply as directly from the continent.

III. *Navigation Act of 1673.* Shippers had violated the provision in the 1660 act concerning "enumerated articles" by carrying these items from one colony to another, then (considering the law fulfilled) taking them to a European country. The act of 1673 required merchants to post a bond as guarantee that goods would be taken only to England.

IV. *Navigation Act of 1696.* This law was designed to allow the earlier acts to be enforced. It provided that: 1) all colonial governors must take an oath to obey trade regulations; and 2) the laws were to be enforced by a *Board of Trade and Plantations* appointed by the king.

V. *Molasses Act of 1733.* This placed prohibitive duties on all non-English sugar, molasses, and rum imported into North America. It was passed at the insistence of the British West Indian sugar planters, but was never enforced.

b. REGULATION OF MANUFACTURING. Laws designed to stamp out colonial industries threatening to compete with those of the mother country included: 1) the *Woolens Act* (1699) forbidding the production of woolen cloth for export; 2) the *Hat Act* (1732) prohibiting the manufacture of hats; and 3) the *Iron Act* (1750) preventing the production of certain types of iron implements. The first two did not interfere seriously with the colonial economy, while the third was not enforced.

3. Effect of Economic Regulation on the Colonies

a. EFFECT ON THE TOBACCO COLONIES. Some historians maintain that the "enumeration" of tobacco so restricted the market that resulting low prices brought depression to Virginia and Maryland after 1660. Others argue that overproduction caused the depression, and that the Navigation Acts aided tobacco sales by: 1) giving the colonies a monopoly in England; 2) allowing the royal navy to protect tobacco fleets; and 3) giving shippers the benefit of the *drawback* on tobacco re-exported to the continent.

b. EFFECT ON THE NORTHERN COLONIES.

I. *Growth of Shipbuilding.* As the acts required the use of English (including colonial) ships, a thriving shipbuilding industry developed in New England. By 1776 one-third of the British carrying trade was in American-built vessels.

II. *The Triangular Trade.* If enforced, the Molasses Act would have ended a thriving trade in food, slaves, and sugar carried on between the northern colonies, Africa, and the French and Spanish West Indies. The act, however, was not enforced.

II. POLITICAL REORGANIZATION OF THE EMPIRE — 1660 - 1754

A. The Extension of Royal Control, 1660-1688

1. Political Theory of the Stuarts. During the Restoration period, the absolutist Stuart monarchs sought to bring colonial administration under their control by: 1) converting all older colonies into royal colonies; and 2) merging the colonies into larger administrative units.

2. Effect on the Tobacco Colonies. A tyrannical governor, *Sir William Berkeley,* completely suppressed popular rule in Virginia. His absolutism, combined with an economic depression and Indian attacks, finally goaded the colonists into *Bacon's Rebellion* (1676). The sudden death of Nathaniel Bacon, its leader, ended the uprising before reforms were secured; Berkeley continued his absolutist rule through the Restoration period. A similar uprising in Maryland was suppressed without bloodshed.

3. Effect on the New England Colonies

a. KING PHILIP'S WAR. Massachusetts especially resisted royal control after 1660, as its Puritan leaders had no sympathy with the Anglican Stuarts. This defiant attitude secured for the colony a brief period of virtual self-rule, during which expansion was rapid. Advancing settlement so alarmed the Indians that they struck back in *King Philip's War* (1675-1676). For two years the back country was ravaged before native resistance was crushed.

b. REASSERTION OF ROYAL AUTHORITY, 1674-1684. In 1674 Charles II ordered Massachusetts to obey the Navigation Acts and repeal laws conflicting with those of England. When the colonists refused to obey, Massachusetts: 1) lost New Hampshire, which was made into a royal colony (1679); and 2) was deprived of its charter (1684). Two years later all the New England colonies were welded into the *Dominion of New England,* to which New York and New Jersey were added.

A royal governor, *Sir Edmund Andros*, and an appointed council, were placed in control, with the people having no voice in their government. Andros enforced the Navigation Acts, levied taxes without legislative approval, secured religious liberty for Anglicans, and in other ways aroused a storm of opposition.

B. Political Organization After the Glorious Revolution, 1688-1763

1. Effect of the Glorious Revolution. A bloodless revolution against the unpopular James II (1688) placed William III and Mary on the throne, but established the supremacy of Parliament over the king. An immediate result in the colonies was the collapse of the Dominion of New England. Massachusetts, with Plymouth and Maine added to it, was made a royal colony (1691), as was New Hampshire. Rhode Island and Connecticut were allowed to retain their corporate charters. In New York a revolution against Andros, led by *Jacob Leisler*, ended with New York a royal colony, while a similar status was awarded New Jersey (1702) and the Carolinas (1729). Pennsylvania and Maryland were eventually restored to their proprietors. By 1754 all were royal colonies except: 1) Maryland and Pennsylvania (including Delaware) which were proprietary; and 2) Connecticut and Rhode Island which were *chartered*.

2. Organization of the Empire. The governmental system developed at this time was employed for the rest of the colonial period.

a. ENGLAND'S ADMINISTRATIVE MACHINERY. Control over the colonies was vested in: 1) the king and his Privy Council; 2) Parliament; and 3) the royally appointed courts. Actual administration was handled by the Privy Council through a subordinate committee, the *Board of Trade* (1696-1776). Judicial functions were performed by: 1) the Privy Council, which could disallow unconstitutional colonial laws or hear appeals from colonial courts; and 2) the English courts, including the *admiralty courts* which heard cases involving the Navigation Acts. After 1696 vice-admiralty courts in the colonies handled such cases without juries.

b. Colonial Administrative Machinery.

i. _Governor and Council._ Governors were appointed by the king in royal colonies, by the proprietors in proprietary colonies, and were elected in chartered colonies. In addition to the usual administrative powers, they enjoyed the right to veto acts of the colonial legislatures, and were entrusted with enforcing the Navigation Acts (after 1696). An appointed council of from ten to twenty-eight members not only advised each governor, but sat as the upper house of the legislature and as the court of highest appeal. Council members were normally conservative aristocrats.

ii. _The Assembly._ Colonists who could fulfill the property qualifications for voting chose an assembly. This body could initiate tax bills, and make other laws subject to veto by the governor or Privy Council. The assembly's viewpoint was represented in England by _colonial agents,_ who lobbied for measures desired by the colonists.

iii. _The Courts._ Each colony had local courts, county courts presided over by justices of the peace, and a superior court. As judges were appointed by the governors or king, they represented the royal viewpoint rather than that of the assemblies.

c. Assemblies _vs._ Governors. A constant conflict between popularly elected assemblies and royally appointed governors symbolized the struggle for self-rule that went on through the eighteenth century. In this the assemblies gradually increased their power at the expense of the governors, largely bcause their control of the purse strings allowed them to deny appropriations to executives who defied the popular will. England's _"salutary neglect"_ of her colonies during the eighteenth century also allowed the legislatures to expand their activities. Should the mother country ever decide to resist a further extension of popular rule, however, a serious conflict was inevitable. England was forced to take this stand as a result of the eighteenth-century wars with Spain and France.

III. THE IMPERIAL WARS FOR
NORTH AMERICA — 1689 - 1763

A . Expansion of New France in the Seventeenth Century, 1608-1689

1. Expansion in the Great Lakes Country, 1608-1663

a. LACK OF AGRICULTURAL EXPANSION. The colony of New France grew slowly in the first fifty years after the founding of Quebec (1608). This was because: 1) the cold climate discouraged farming; 2) France refused to allow non-Catholics to migrate; and 3) the feudal land system was poorly suited to a new country. Large estates were granted to *seigneurs*, who parceled out the land in strips to *habitants* in return for an annual rental and services.

b. BEGINNINGS OF THE FUR TRADE. Hence New France turned to the fur trade for prosperity. Using the easy water routes along the St. Lawrence and Ottawa rivers, traders and *coureurs de bois* (unlicensed traders), pushed far into the interior, seeking unsophisticated Indians who would barter a maximum quantity of furs for a minimum quantity of trading goods. Before the death of Samuel de Champlain (1635), Frenchmen reached Wisconsin. Between 1642 and 1653 they were driven back by the Iroquois, who had received arms from the Dutch at Albany. Expansion began again in 1656 as traders returned to Wisconsin and, under the leadership of Pierre Radisson and Sieur de Grosilliers, penetrated into Lake Superior.

2. Expansion Into the Mississippi Valley, 1663-1689

a. NEW FRANCE AS A ROYAL COLONY. In 1663 New France was made a royal colony, with administration vested in a governor, intendant (who headed the judicial system and supervised expenditures), and bishop. The resulting efficiency led to a new burst of expansion under the first intendant, *Jean Talon*. In impressive ceremonies at Sault Ste. Marie an expedition took formal possession of the whole Great Lakes country (1671), while both traders and missionaries overran Wisconsin. To extend the trading area, Talon sent Father *Jacques Marquette* and *Louis Joliet* to explore the Mississippi River (1673). After descending as far as the Arkansas River, they returned with news of an all-water route to the Gulf of Mexico.

b. EXPANSION UNDER COUNT FRONTENAC. Frontenac, who became governor in 1672, sent his associate *Sieur de La Salle*, down the Mississippi again, with instructions to establish a series of posts that would dominate all the interior waterways. Although La Salle built forts on Lake Ontario and in Illinois, he failed in an attempt to occupy the mouth of the Mississippi (1684), losing his life in the venture. These efforts greatly alarmed England, which feared encirclement of its own colonies if New France continued to expand over the interior.

B. The First Two Imperial Wars, 1689-1713

1. King William s War, 1689-1697

a. ORIGINS OF THE WAR. Responsible for the war were: 1) the efforts of William III of England to prevent Louis XIV of France from overrunning William's native Holland; and 2) a clash of trading empires at two points in America. In *New York* an ambitious governor, Thomas Dongan, goaded the Iroquois into striking at the pro-French tribes of the Great Lakes, then when the French struck back with an expedition through the Iroquois country, to stage the *La Chine Massacre* (1689) in which they killed some 200 villagers near Montreal. In *northern Canada* the Hudson's Bay Company had been intruding on a French trading domain since its founding in 1670.

b. INDECISIVE NATURE OF THE WAR. The French, under Governor Frontenac, took the initiative with a series of raids in upper New York and New England, the most important being the massacre at Schenectady (1690). A New England naval force captured Port Royal, a strong French base on Acadia (Nova Scotia), but failed to take Quebec. Fighting in the Hudson Bay country ended with the English in possession of three posts there and the French in possession of one. The *Treaty of Ryswick* (1697) provided for a mutual restoration of all conquered territory.

2. Preparations for Renewal of Hostilities, 1697-1701

a. FRENCH EXPANSION IN THE INTERIOR. Fearful lest illegal French traders, who opened a trade with the Carolinas along the Tennessee River, lead Englishmen into the Ohio Valley, France built forts at Mackinac and Detroit, at the same time sending missionaries to found the villages of Kaskaskia and Cahokia in the Illinois country. To secure the lower Missis-

European Claims AD 1664-178?

Spanish
English
French
Independent

1664

1713

1763

1783

sippi Valley, Pierre d'Iberville was dispatched to build a post in _Louisiana_ at the mouth of that river (1699). Thus New France gained a precarious hold over all the interior.

b. THE EUROPEAN BACKGROUND. On the death of the Spanish monarch (1700), Louis XIV of France attempted to place his grandson on the throne. England, Holland, and Austria, uniting to prevent this step that would upset the balance of power, began the _War of the Spanish Succession,_ or Queen Anne's War as it was known in America.

3. Queen Anne's War, 1701-1713. Fighting in the south between French from Louisiana, Spaniards from Florida, and Englishmen from the Carolinas proved indecisive. In the north a New England expedition captured Port Royal, Acadia (1710), renaming it Annapolis. Again an attack on Quebec failed. England's successes on the European continent were reflected in the _Treaty of Utrecht_ (1713), which forced France to surrender the Hudson Bay country, Newfoundland, and Acadia (renamed Nova Scotia). Britain also received the fortress of Gibraltar.

C. Expulsion of the French from North America, 1713-1763

1. Clash of Trading Frontiers, 1713-1754

a. THE PERIOD OF PEACE, 1713-1744. During this long truce England strengthened its position by: 1) winning the friendship of most of the southern tribes; and 2) founding the colony of Georgia (see p. 21). France retaliated by: 1) weakening the Iroquois-English alliance; 2) building new posts in the interior; 3) inspiring Indian raids on the New England back country; and 4) erecting the powerful fortress of Louisbourg on Cape Breton Island.

b. KING GEORGE'S WAR, 1744-1748 Neither nation was ready for war when Frederick the Great of Prussia joined with France to seize portions of the Austrian empire. England met the challenge by starting the _War of the Austrian Succession,_ or King George's War (1744). The only decisive American engagement was a successful New England attack on Louisbourg. The _Treaty of Aix-la-Chapelle_ (1748) forced each nation to return its conquests.

c. The Struggle for the Ohio Valley, 1748-1754.

I. *English Expansion Into the Valley.* Two English advances into the valley threatened the French hold on the interior. 1) A group of Virginians, organized as the *Ohio Company of Virginia,* secured a 200,000-acre grant from the crown (1749) on the upper Ohio River and began active preparations for trade and settlement there. 2) Traders from Pennsylvania began invading the Ohio Valley during King George's War when the French were unable to import trading goods. Their leader, *George Croghan,* built a fortified post at *Pickawillany* on the Miami River in 1748. France realized that the superior British goods could soon allow the Pennsylvanians to win the Indians of the whole interior.

II. *French Retaliation.* A military force under *Charles la Langlade* (1752) drove the English from the West and destroyed Pickawillany. To hold the area, an expedition was sent to build a chain of forts across the back country of Pennsylvania from Lake Erie to the Forks of the Ohio, thus closing the interior to British traders or speculators. Forts Presque'Isle, Le Boeuf, and Venango were built in 1753, but construction of the principal *Ft. Duquesne* at the Forks of the Ohio was delayed until the next year.

III. *Protests of Virginia.* Virginia, which claimed the Forks of the Ohio under its Charter of 1609, sent *George Washington* to warn the French away, then ordered a work force to the spot to build a fort. When the small army under Washington that was sent to guard the workers reached the Forks, Ft. Duquesne was already under construction. A skirmish between the two parties at Great Meadows touched off the last of the imperial wars.

2. The Seven Years' War, 1754-1763

a. Preparations for War. Commissioners from seven colonies met at the *Albany Congress* (1754) to: 1) discuss means of bringing the Iroquois into the war; and 2) perfect a machinery for intercolonial cooperation in Indian and military affairs. The first objective failed when the Iroquois decided to remain neutral. The *Albany Plan* of union, drafted by *Benjamin Franklin,* proposed that defense problems be handled by a royally appointed president general and a federal council of delegates chosen by the colonies. The plan was accepted by the congress but rejected by the individual colonies, which were too provincial to cooperate.

b. THE YEARS OF DEFEAT, 1754-1757. General _Edward Braddock,_ the English commander, divided his inadequate force into four armies, three of which suffered defeats during 1755. His own force was routed by a smaller army of French and Indians as it approached Ft. Duquesne, while assaults on French forts at Niagara and Crown Point (Lake Champlain) also failed. Only Ft. Beauséjour on Nova Scotia was captured (June, 1755). The 5000 French Acadians there were then cruelly moved to Maryland or Virginia lest they prove disloyal. These defeats forced England into defensive tactics, which allowed the brilliant French commander, _Marquis de Montcalm,_ to Capture Ft. Oswego (1756) and Ft. William Henry (1757), controlling water routes to the St. Lawrence Valley. British assaults on Louisbourg and Ft. Ticonderoga also failed.

c. THE YEARS OF VICTORY, 1758-1760. In 1756 war began in Europe, with Frederick the Great of Prussia on the side of England, thus weakening the French position on the continent. The tide did not turn in England's favor, however, until _William Pitt_ became prime minister (1758). In July, 1758, one of his able young generals, Jeffery Amherst, captured Louisbourg, opening the eastern gateway to the St. Lawrence. Fort Frontenac on Lake Ontario fell a month later, cutting New France in two, while Ft. Duquesne was captured by General _John Forbes,_ to be rebuilt as Ft. Pitt. In 1759 a large army under General _James Wolfe_ defeated the French defenders of _Quebec_ on the _Plains of Abraham_ at the gates of that key city. Montreal, the last stronghold of New France, capitulated in 1760.

d. THE TREATY OF PARIS, 1763. England continued to win victories over France and Spain after fighting stopped in America. These were reflected in the _Treaty of Paris_ (February, 1763) in which Britain received Canada from France and the Floridas from Spain. French Louisiana was given to Spain in compensation. Guadeloupe and other French and Spanish West Indian islands were returned to their former owners, largely because English sugar planters of the Caribbean did not welcome competition.

IV. THE PROBLEM OF EMPIRE — 1763

A. The New Empire

1. Changed Nature of Empire. The addition of Canada and the Floridas complicated England's governmental problems because: 1) these two provinces contained alien peoples with different traditions, language, and religion; and 2) the removal of France from America allowed Americans to adopt a more truculent attitude toward the mother country without fear of attack from a northern neighbor.

2. Changed Purpose of Empire. Until 1763 the empire was considered valuable only to the extent that it enriched the commercial classes at home. After 1763 the vastly enlarged empire was viewed as a source of both men and revenue to maintain Britain's world supremacy. In this capacity it must be carefully guarded and rigidly administered. As defense and administration would cost heavily, Englishmen wanted the colonists to assume a fair share of the empire's expenses.

3. Changed Methods of Empire Administration. The failure of the laissez-faire policy of colonial administration employed during the period of "salutary neglect" was shown when the colonies failed to support the mother country during the Seven Years' War.

a. REFUSAL OF FINANCIAL SUPPORT. To avoid taxing the colonists, England employed the *requisition system*: sums needed for each year's campaigns were requisitioned among the colonies. Most refused to meet these requests; only Massachusetts, Connecticut, and New York supplied the men and money demanded of them.

b. TRADE WITH THE ENEMY. New England and Middle Colony merchants continued the triangular trade with French and Spanish West Indian islands, thus preventing the British navy from starving them into submission. This illegal trade was carried on through neutral West Indian ports, or under flags of truce that were sold openly by some colonial governors. With such a flag, a merchant could visit a French island with a few prisoners to exchange and a cargo of foodstuffs to sell. Much produce was also shipped to Canada to feed the French armies.

B.   England's Problem.   This disloyalty convinced England that the colonies had drifted too far from the empire for their own or the mother country's good. To restore them to a proper position, however, would necessitate interference with popular liberties. How far could she extend authority without inciting rebellion? Britain's failure to solve that problem launched the American Revolution.

ADDITIONAL READING

The best discussions of trade regulation are in L. A. Harper, *English Navigation Laws* (1939), and O. M. Dickerson, *The Navigation Acts and the American Revolution* (1951). L. W. Labaree, *Royal Government in America* (1930) traces the growth of royal power, while the same author's *Conservatism in Early American History* (1948) shows the growing influence of upper classes in politics. J. P. Greene, *The Quest for Power: The Lower Houses of Assembly in the Southern Royal Colonies* (1963) explores a counter-influence in a book of wider importance than its title indicates. The delightful volumes by Francis Parkman, *LaSalle and the Discovery of the Great West* (1898), and *Frontenac and New France* (1898) remain unsurpassed for readability, but newer interpretations are to be found in W. J. Eccles, *Canada under Louis XIV* (1963). A brief account of the intercolonial wars is in R. A. Billington, *Westward Expansion* (2nd edn., 1960), and a fuller story in H. H. Peckham, *The Colonial Wars, 1789-1762* (1964).

CHAPTER III

Life and Thought
in Colonial America

❡ INTELLECTUAL PREPARATION FOR INDEPENDENCE

By the close of the Seven Years' War the American people were prepared — economically, socially, and intellectually — to sever the bonds that held them to England. Their way of life, they believed, differed so radically from that of the mother country that Parliament was incapable of governing them wisely. This spirit of independence stemmed from: 1) the unique nature of the population that resulted from a mingling of peoples; 2) the distinctive economic enterprises of the New World; and 3) the unusual environment offered by a frontier of cheap land. These three forces gradually Americanized the transplanted Europeans who occupied the thirteen colonies, making easier the break that came after 1763. The Revolution is understandable only in the light of the social, economic, and intellectual developments that endowed the American people with their unique characteristics.

I. THE PEOPLE OF COLONIAL AMERICA

A. The Colonial Population

1. The Population in the Seventeenth Century. Most of the 250,000 people who lived in America in 1700 were of

English ancestry, although a sprinkling of Dutch, Germans, Swedes, and French Huguenots gave the Middle Colonies a cosmopolitan atmosphere. The lower middle class contributed a majority of the English settlers, with a higher portion of the lower classes in the tobacco colonies as a result of the influx of indentured servants there.

2. Population Changes in the Eighteenth Century

a. Coming of Non-English Colonists. During the eighteenth century colonial society was strengthened by the addition of three alien groups: 1) *Palatine Germans*, some 250,000 of whom were driven from their homeland by wars or religious persecution to settle in the back country of Pennsylvania and Virginia. There their descendants are known today as the "Pennsylvania Dutch." 2) *Scotch-Irish* pioneers began arriving in 1718 in the wake of economic depression and religious persecution in their native Ulster. Like the Germans, they sought cheap lands in the interior. By 1776 some 200,000 were scattered along the frontier from Pennsylvania to the Carolinas. 3) *Negro slaves* were first introduced in 1619, but few reached America until after 1697, when the monopoly of the Royal African Company was broken. During the eighteenth century 500,000 were imported, largely to the southern colonies. Slavery existed in all the colonies, however; the smaller numbers owned in the North indicated that the institution was less profitable there rather than moral opposition. Treatment of the slaves varied with their masters, but nearly all worked hard amidst unpleasant conditions. Almost half of those imported died during the voyage or in the "seasoning" process that followed.

b. Influence of the Non-English Groups. By 1776 one-third of the people were of non-English stock. Their coming: 1) made possible a more rapid utilization of the natural resources; and 2) stimulated the growth of unique American characteristics as each alien group contributed to the social order.

B. Nature of Colonial Society

1. The Structure of Society. Despite the greater economic opportunity available in America, tradition was so strong that class lines existed, although less rigidly than in Europe.

a. The Aristocracy. A small group of governors, judges, clergymen, and wealthy merchants with English backgrounds held themselves aloof from the lower castes, modeling their lives on those of Britain's aristocracy.

b. The Native Aristocracy. More numerous were the native aristocrats — southern planters, northern merchants, and wealthy landholders of the Middle Colonies. Known as "gentlemen," they dressed in knee breeches and frock coats, controlled the colonial legislatures, and dominated economic affairs.

c. The Lower Classes. The farmers and artisans who made up the bulk of the population dressed in homespun garments resembling those of today, were seated in special sections of churches, and enjoyed few political privileges. The presence of cheap land in America, however, allowed members of this group to "rise above their station" as they could not in Europe.

2. Life in Colonial America

a. Manner of Living. Life was provincial, for roads were nonexistent until the eighteenth century, and then connected only the most important cities. Travel was by horseback or stagecoach, with frequent stops at taverns where much social life centered. The ordinary homes were usually unattractive, with one or two rooms heated by a fireplace and lighted by candles. Water, hauled from wells that were frequently contaminated, accounted for the high percentage of sickness. Food was plentiful, with bread, hominy, and pork serving as staples. Rum, cider, and later whisky were consumed on all social occasions; coffee and tea did not become common until the eighteenth century.

b. Sports and Amusements. Quilting parties, corn-husking bees, and weddings offset the monotony of life. Dancing was also popular except in Puritan New England. Among the upper classes the common sports were cockfighting, horse racing, and hunting. Gambling was not frowned upon; lotteries to raise money for public enterprises were accepted everywhere. Nor could clerical opposition prevent the young people from "bundling."

c. Life on the Frontier. Life on the western edge of the colonies was dedicated to the conquest of the wilderness. Pioneers, skilled in frontier techniques, learned to "girdle" trees by cutting a notch around the trunk, to plant their crops amidst the still standing timber, to build log cabins, and to protect themselves against Indians and wild animals. Their unique skills gave them a sense of distinction; most believed that eastern legislatures were incapable of understanding or solving their problems. This _provincialism_ stimulated a belief in _democracy_ as the best means of government, as well as an emphasis on _individualism_ natural in a region where limitless opportunity made men less dependent on the social group. These were basic frontier characteristics.

II. THE ECONOMY OF COLONIAL AMERICA

A. Agriculture as the Basic Industry

1. Farming in New England

a. DISTINCTIVE FEATURES OF NEW ENGLAND AGRICULTURE. The unique features of New England's agricultural economy resulted from: 1) the hilly country and short season that discouraged the growing of staple crops for export (tobacco, rice, cotton, etc.) and encouraged _diversified farming_ for home consumption (cereals, livestock, etc.) ; and 2) the intensity of Puritan religious belief which led men to settle in groups about churches and schools.

b. THE NEW ENGLAND LAND SYSTEM. The legislatures, which were interested in spreading religion rather than making profits, granted six-mile tracts to groups of _proprietors_ who laid out a "town," with the understanding that they allot the land free to newcomers of proper orthodoxy. Newcomers and proprietors had an equal voice in the _town meeting_ that settled political questions, but only the proprietors owned the undivided land. Conflicts between proprietors and nonproprietors over further divisions drove many persons westward. During the eighteenth century the system broke down as a desire for profits increased.

c. AGRICULTURAL METHODS. Farmers lived in town, walking out each day to care for their fields. Corn, barley, oats, and sometimes wheat were the usual crops, while livestock was pastured in a community-owned field. Implements were primitive: a plow made from a crooked stick and pulled by oxen, a scythe for reaping, and a flail for threshing. Emphasis on the group persisted as New Englanders moved westward; among no other Americans were the desires of individuals so subordinated to the needs of society.

2. Farming in the Middle Colonies

a. LAND SYSTEM OF THE MIDDLE COLONIES. Land, which belonged to the proprietor or king, was granted individuals in return for a small *quitrent.* As the rentals could not be collected, *ownership in fee simple* soon became common. At first no provision was made for the sale of land, forcing the colonists to use the *head right* system for this purpose. This allowed anyone paying the passage of an indentured servant to receive fifty acres of land. Head rights became the common means of land sale in the seventeenth century; in the eighteenth outright sales were substituted.

b. FARMING METHODS. As the climate was less severe than in New England, farms were larger, with farmers living on their own land rather than in villages. Wheat was the principal crop; New York and Pennsylvania were known as the "bread colonies." Fruit and livestock were also produced.

3. Farming in the Southern Colonies

a. LAND SYSTEM IN THE SOUTHERN COLONIES. The land system was like that of the Middle Colonies. During the seventeenth century small farms were common, with few over 500 acres. In the eighteenth century, however, slave labor allowed a few favored individuals to expand their holdings into *plantations* of 1000 or more acres. Few plantations existed in proportion to small farms, but their owners dominated southern life.

b. AGRICULTURAL METHODS. The level lands and long growing season of the south were ideal for the production of the *staples* of colonial agriculture: *tobacco* in Maryland, Virginia, and North Carolina; *rice* and *indigo* in South Carolina and Georgia. The routine tasks involved in producing staples allowed slave labor to be employed.

B. Colonial Industries. The abundance of natural resources, and the high prices charged for transporting manufactured goods across the Atlantic, encouraged colonial industry, despite the fact that the cheap lands of the frontier kept wages up by draining the excess labor supply westward.

1. Home Industries. Most farmers produced their own food, furniture, and agricultural implements, while their wives spun wool or flax into thread which was woven into cloth on home looms. This allowed them to attain virtual self-sufficiency.

2. Forest Industries. Shipbuilding was a prominent industry in New England and the Middle Colonies, where hundreds of wooden vessels ranging from 30 to 500 tons burden were constructed at small yards. After 1750 ships were also built in the South from live oak. *Naval stores* (timbers, masts, pitch, tar, and turpentine) were also produced in large quantities for export.

3. Metal Industries

a. IRON MINING. Bog iron was mined in New England and Virginia, but after 1750 production shifted to Pennsylvania where ore was abundant and the wood used in smelting plentiful. By 1776 iron was produced in every colony save Georgia. Colonial production was greater than that of England.

b. PRODUCTION OF HARDWARE. Many small establishments manufactured guns, ironware, locks, clocks, and other metal implements that could not be made by farmers. Most were managed by independent *artisans,* aided by *apprentices* whose hours of labor and working conditions were regulated by law.

4. Extractive Industries

a. THE FUR TRADE. Although the trade was common throughout the back country, the most important centers were at : 1) *Albany,* where the Iroquois Indians served as middlemen between traders and the Great Lakes tribes; 2) *Charleston,* where as many as 160,000 deerskins were exported annually. After 1763 Montreal became the headquarters for a trade that extended over Canada.

b. FISHING. Fish were plentiful on the *Newfoundland Banks,* a submerged tableland in the North Atlantic that was visited by hundreds of New England fishermen yearly. Fish not consumed at home was salted for export to the West Indian sugar plantations or the Catholic countries of Europe. By 1776 the 350 vessels engaged in fishing earned profits of $2,000,000 yearly. *Whaling,* which was centered in New Bedford, Nantucket, and other New England towns, was another important industry.

c. DISTILLING. Molasses obtained in the West Indies in return for fish was distilled into rum at distilleries in Massachusetts and Connecticut. Whisky production increased in the eighteenth century, but rum remained the principal colonial drink.

d. GRISTMILLING. Water-powered mills to turn corn or wheat into flour sprang up everywhere, but especially in New York and Pennsylvania. Large quantities of flour were exported from those two colonies.

C.   Colonial Commerce

1. Trade of the Southern Colonies. The tobacco, rice, and indigo produced in the southern colonies were sent to England, where they were traded for manufactured goods. About one-half of all colonial commerce was with England.

2. Trade of the Middle and New England Colonies As the fish and grain available for export from the northern colonies were also produced in England, merchants were forced to seek other markets. Better grades of fish and cereals were sent to *southern Europe,* where they were exchanged for wine, spices, and gold. Lumber, meat, grain, horses, and poorer grades of fish were shipped to the *West Indies,* to be traded for sugar, molasses, and gold. The molasses, after being transformed into rum, was re-exported to *Africa,* together with provisions, iron implements, and trading goods. There Negro slaves, spices, and gold were obtained in return. The slaves were taken to the West Indies and traded for more sugar, molasses, and gold. This *Triangular Trade* allowed the northern colonies to secure the gold they needed to purchase manufactured goods from England.

3. Results of Commercial Activity

a. THE CURRENCY PROBLEM. Farmers could transact necessary business by barter, but merchants trading in the West Indies or Europe required currency. This was scarce in the colonies as in all new countries; the only coins available were those brought out by settlers or secured through trade. Spanish dollars, or pieces of eight, minted in Mexico, were commonly used in commercial transactions. To meet the demand for additional currency, the colonial legislatures in 1690 began issuing paper money. In Massachusetts this was done through "land banks" which secured the currency with the colony's land holdings. When business confusion resulted from the depreciation of this money, Parliament forbade the New England colonies to issue money (1751). The restriction was applied to all colonies in 1764.

b. RISE OF THE SEABOARD TOWNS. Commercial activity created such cities as Philadelphia, New York, Boston, and Charleston. Although small by modern standards, Philadelphia with 30,000 inhabitants (1775) was the second largest city in the empire, surpassed only by London. The cultural activities of the colonists were centered in these cities, especially in the eighteenth century.

III. INTELLECTUAL DEVELOPMENT OF COLONIAL AMERICA

A. The Seventeenth Century Mind

1. The Religious Basis for Colonial Culture

a. NEW ENGLAND PURITANISM. Intellectual progress was directly related to religious enthusiasm, which was highest in New England. There the Puritans based their belief on the teachings of _John Calvin_, who held that Christ's sacrifice had moved God to select certain of the "elect" for salvation, while all others were predestined to damnation. This doctrine of _predestination_ led Puritans into intensive soul searching in an effort to discover whether they were of the elect. Moreover all sought to live exemplary lives that they might be ready to appear before the heavenly throne, and to see to it that others behaved similarly. All Puritan colonies passed _"blue laws"_ requiring church attendance, protecting the holiness of the Sabbath, and regulating individual conduct.

b. SOUTHERN ANGLICANISM. The Episcopal Church was established in all southern colonies, where attendance was required by law and the church was supported by taxation. The emphasis on secular affairs, however, made religion a less important force than in New England.

c. MIDDLE COLONY RELIGIONS. Many small sects existed in the Middle Colonies: Presbyterians, Quakers, Lutherans, and

Huguenots in Pennsylvania; Dutch Reformed and German Reformed in New York; Baptists in Rhode Island; and Catholics in Maryland. As no one church was dominant, _toleration_ was necessary. The Middle Colonies contributed more to the theory and practice of religious freedom than all others. Also developed there was the system of _voluntarism_ through which churches were supported by voluntary contributions rather than taxes.

2. Intolerance in Seventeenth Century America

a. UNDEMOCRATIC ASPECTS OF COLONIAL THOUGHT. Intolerance varied with the intensity of religious belief; Puritans were more intolerant than Presbyterians; Presbyterians more intolerant than Anglicans. Puritans especially believed that all dissenters must be converted, banished, or executed as the only means of protecting God's chosen people from contamination. Democracy was also disliked as the rule of those who did not know God's will. In Massachusetts nonchurch members were at first banned from voting; after 1662 the "Half-Way Covenant" opened church membership and political privileges to those unable to give proof of a spiritual experience, but denied them the right to participate in the Lord's Supper or to vote in church elections.

b. PERSECUTION OF RELIGIOUS DISSENTERS. Massachusetts and Connecticut not only banished Baptists but whipped those who persisted in returning. Quakers were also imprisoned, beaten, and banished. Four who insisted on preaching were executed in 1659-1660.

c. PERSECUTION OF WITCHES. All men believed in witches (persons who sold their souls to the devil in return for wealth or supernatural powers), but only in New England were victims executed. That section's most important epidemic occurred at _Salem_ (1692) when young girls who had listened to the voodoo lore of a West Indian slave accused several old women of bewitching them. Before the mania subsided nineteen persons were hanged, while one was pressed to death for refusing to plead to the indictment.

3. Intellectual Progress in the Seventeenth Century

a. PURITANISM AND LITERATURE. Religious enthusiasm fostered intellectual outpourings as well as intolerance. Hence progress was greatest in New England. There an important sermon literature was produced by *Cotton Mather,* Increase Mather, John Cotton, and others. More enduring were the many histories written to glorify the sacrifices made for religion : *William Bradford's History of Plymouth Plantation* (1646) ; John Winthrop's *History of New England* (1649), and Edward Johnson's *Wonder-Working Providence of Zion's Savior* (1654). Puritanism also inspired countless poets in various ways : *Michael Wigglesworth (The Day of Doom,* 1662) issued a grim warning of the fate awaiting sinners at the Last Judgment, *Anne Bradstreet* found evidence of the glory of God in nature, and *Edward Taylor* wrote passionate eulogies to his Savior. Two outstanding works written beyond New England were William Byrd's *History of the Dividing Line Betwixt Virginia and North Carolina,* an excellent history by a Virginia gentleman, and the *Journal* of John Woolman, a Quaker businessman from Pennsylvania.

b. Origins of Colonial Education. A desire to train ministers and educate congregations inspired the first New England schools. Massachusetts pioneered with a law (1642) requiring parents or masters of apprentices to teach their charges to read. A more important law (*1647*) forced towns of fifty or more families to maintain a primary school, and those of one hundred families or more a secondary school. In the Middle Colonies church-supported schools provided some education, while in the South "field schools" or private tutors cared for children of the wealthy. Secondary schools were virtually nonexistent outside of New England, where Latin grammar schools prepared youths for college. In the mid-eighteenth century private "academies" began to appear, but they did not become prominent until after the Revolution.

c. Colonial Colleges. The first college was *Harvard* (1636) in Massachusetts, followed by William and Mary (1693) and Yale (1701). The remaining colonial colleges were not established until the middle of the eighteenth century. Of the nine founded in the colonial period, four were in New England. All were church schools, stressing training in the classical languages and theology essential in the training of ministers.

d. BEGINNINGS OF A NEWSPAPER PRESS. New England also pioneered in newspaper publishing. The first paper, *Publick Occurrences* (1690), was founded in Boston by Benjamin Harris, but succumbed to censorship after one issue. The *Boston News-Letter* (1704) was the first to be published regularly. The *Boston Gazette* and the *American Weekly Mercury* (Philadelphia) followed in 1719. All were weekly journals which stressed foreign rather than local news. By the mid-eighteenth century newspapers were published in nearly all colonies. No magazines appeared until 1741 when Andrew Bradford, a Philadelphia printer, launched the *American Magazine*.

B. The Eighteenth Century Mind

1. Impact of the Enlightenment on Colonial Thought

a. EUROPEAN ORIGINS OF THE ENLIGHTENMENT.

I. *The Medieval Mind in America.* Until the eighteenth century most Americans lived in the medieval world intellectually. They believed, as had the philosophers of the Middle Ages, that: 1) all men must unquestionably obey their spiritual and secular rulers; 2) society and thought were static, with progress not to be expected; 3) life on earth was an unpleasant interlude to be borne without complaint in the hope of eternal salvation; and 4) man was at the complete mercy of an arbitrary God who personally decreed each event of nature for the benefit of His creatures.

II. *Beginnings of the New Science.* These concepts were first challenged by *Nikolaus Copernicus,* a Polish scholar, whose *On the Revolutions of the Heavenly Bodies* (1543) proved that the earth was not the center of the universe, but a minor planet revolving about the sun. Subsequent observations by other scientists·demonstrated the correctness of this theory. This was important because: 1) scientists now pictured a universe governed by natural laws rather than special decree; and 2) as one basic medieval belief had been proved wrong, all could be questioned.

III. *Social Implications of the New Science.* Scholars in the eighteenth century applied these findings to human behavior, thus broadening the New Science into the Enlightenment.

If natural laws governed the universe, they reasoned, similar laws of nature should govern society. *John Locke,* an English philosopher, in his *Essay Concerning Human Understanding* (1690), argued that man's character was the product of his environment rather than of divine decree. Jean Jacques Rousseau's *Social Contract* (1762) refuted the divine right of kings by showing that man, as the creator of the social order, could demand from his rulers protection for his natural rights to life, liberty, and property. Adam Smith, an English economist, held in his *Wealth of Nations* (1776) that natural laws (such as the law of supply and demand) should govern the economy rather than tariffs, monopolies, or royal decrees. By the mid-eighteenth century enlightened thinkers believed in: 1) a universe governed by natural laws; 2) a social order in which every man was entitled to natural rights; 3) unlimited progress for all persons; and 4) an unhampered economy.

b. THE ENLIGHTENMENT IN THE COLONIES.

I. *Progress in Colonial Science.* Several colonial scientists not only showed a remarkable ability to accept the New Science, but made important contributions. *John Bartram,* a Pennsylvania botanist, made observations that were later used by Linnaeus. John Winthrop, a Harvard professor, explained in 1755 that earthquakes were of natural origin rather than divine warnings to man. The greatest scientist was *Benjamin Franklin.* He studied the movement of hot and cold air, invented the Franklin stove and street lamps, plotted the course of the Gulf Stream, made important contributions in the study of electricity, demonstrated that lightning resulted from natural conditions rather than God's wrath, and performed countless other experiments. He also organized the American Philosophical Society (1743) to stimulate scientific progress.

II. *Social Effects of the Enlightenment.* The colonists readily accepted two basic teachings of the Enlightenment: the inevitability of progress, and the right of all to freedom of opportunity, which fitted well in a frontier environment. Their relations with England also inclined them to embrace the doctrine that natural rights protected all men from political tyranny. The right of revolution against tyrants was upheld by clergymen for decades before 1776. Editors were similarly ready to protest any interference with freedom of expression. Outstanding was *John Peter Zenger,* a New York editor, who was arrested for a written attack on the governor (1735). His acquittal after a moving plea for freedom of the press was a landmark in the evolution of liberty. These incidents showed that the colonists were ready to challenge the king whenever they became convinced that he had violated their fundamental rights.

2. Religious Conflicts in the Eighteenth Century

a. GROWTH OF RELIGIOUS APATHY. The failure of theologians to accept the concept of a benevolent Deity who ruled through natural laws drove many people from the churches in the early eighteenth century. Also responsible for the decline in religious zeal were: 1) the excesses of the Salem witchcraft epidemic; 2) the growth of secular interests as economic activities broadened; and 3) the passing of the older generation.

b. THE GREAT AWAKENING.

I. *Origins of the Great Awakening.* Alarm at the mounting apathy inspired ministers to greater efforts. Results began to show in the 1720's when a revival spread through New Jersey and Pennsylvania. During the next decade the movement swept into New England, where its leader was *Jonathan Edwards.* The coming of an evangelical preacher from England, *George Whitefield,* also helped fan the flames of enthusiasm. From 1734 to 1744 the colonists were in a state of evangelical excitement unparalleled in their history. After 1745 the revival spirit died rapidly, burned out of its own excesses.

II. *Results of the Great Awakening.* The revival: 1) divided churchmen into *Old Lights* whose condemnation of the revival's emotionalism drove them toward a more rationalistic theology, and *New Lights* who supported evangelism; 2) strengthened such sects as the Baptists who gained many members; 3) inspired the founding of colleges (Princeton, Brown, Rutgers, and Dartmouth) as New Lights and Old Lights vied in establishing training grounds for their own clergymen; and 4) gave the common people more control over the churches.

3. The Fine Arts in Colonial America

a. EVOLUTION OF COLONIAL ARCHITECTURE. The growing secular interests that inspired the Great Awakening stimulated cultural growth; as men acquired wealth and leisure they could afford to patronize the arts. This was shown at the end of the seventeenth century, when better homes began replacing the crude frame dwellings of the earliest colonists. In the North, where cold winters made compact houses essential, they were usually oblong, with a central chimney from which fireplaces opened into several rooms, a steep roof to shed snow, and small porches. In the South homes were built with wide halls that opened at both ends for ventilation, detached kitchens, flat roofs, and spacious porches. The predominant style was _Georgian,_ which was based on the Renaissance architecture popular in England.

b. COLONIAL PAINTING. In the seventeenth century a few "primitives" such as John Smibert eked out an existence by painting portraits of wealthier citizens. Two artists of importance emerged in the eighteenth century. _Benjamin West_ of Pennsylvania, after study in Europe, settled in England where he spent most of his life. His London studio became the training school for American painters through the late colonial and Revolutionary periods. _John Singleton Copley_ of Boston, after studying with West, painted portraits of many prominent colonists before settling permanently in England in 1776.

c. COLONIAL MUSIC. Organized musical entertainment did not begin until 1733 when the first song recital was given at Charleston. An opera was performed in the same city two years later. The first singing societies were the Orpheus Club of Philadelphia (1759) and the Saint Cecilia Society of Charleston (1762). The only composer of note was _Francis Hopkinson,_ whose hymns are still sung today.

d. BEGINNINGS OF THE THEATER. Stage shows were frowned upon as immoral influences and time wasters. Not until 1716 was the first theater built at Williamsburg, Virginia; others followed in New York and Charleston in the 1730's but few existed before the Revolution. Troups of English actors began touring the colonies in the 1750's, marking the real beginning of the American theater. In 1767 the first native play, Thomas Godfrey's _Prince of Parthia,_ was performed in Philadelphia.

IV. THE AMERICAN PEOPLE ON THE EVE OF THE REVOLUTION

By the close of the Seven Years' War the American people had achieved partial social, economic, and intellectual independence from England; political independence was sure to follow.

A. Social Independence

1. Nature of Population   One-third of the people were of non-English stock who felt no loyalty to the mother country. Moreover the mingling of peoples had created a new society, strengthened by the contributions of each alien group, that little resembled England's social order.

2. Influence of the Frontier. Americans who lived near the western edge of settlement had developed frontier characteristics — provincialism, belief in democracy, individualism — that stamped them as different from Englishmen. Moreover they firmly believed that no distant Parliament could solve their unique problems; self-rule was the only answer.

B. Economic Independence.

In theory the colonists accepted the principle that natural laws rather than royal decrees should govern the economy. In practice only the southern colonies were bound to England by the tobacco trade. The New England and Middle Colonies, unable to find markets in Britain, found prosperity by trading outside the empire. Any attempt to stop this trade would lead to rebellion.

C. Intellectual Independence.

The Enlightenment had taught the colonists that society, like nature, was governed by natural laws. A ruler who interfered with their freedom of progress or their political freedom would become, in their eyes, a tyrant guilty of violating the laws of nature. For generations ministers and writers had taught the duty of resisting such a tyrant. The American Revolution began when the colonists became convinced that George III was denying them their God-given rights.

ADDITIONAL READING

Stimulating interpretations are in D. J. Boorstin, *The Americans: The Colonial Experience* (1958), and H. M. Jones,

O Strange New World. American Culture: The Formative Years (1964). V. L. Parrington, *The Colonial Mind* (1927), may still be read with profit. Broader in scope are L. B. Wright, *The Cultural Life of the American Colonies* (1957), and Max Savelle, *Seeds of Liberty* (1948), which describe all cultural achievements. A similar role for the New England colonies is played by S. E. Morison, *The Intellectual Life of Colonial New England* (1956). The urban impact on colonial culture is the theme of two books by Carl Bridenbaugh, *Cities in the Wilderness, 1625-1742* (1938), and *Cities in Revolt, 1743-1776* (1955). The survey treatment in W. W. Sweet, *Religion in Colonial America* (1942), should be supplemented with the excellent account of the most important religious event in E. S. Gaustad, *The Great Awakening in New England* (1957). Perry Miller, *Jonathan Edwards* (1949) brilliantly illuminates that clergyman's thought. The witchcraft illusion is pleasantly described in M. L. Starkey, *The Devil in Massachusetts* (1948), while the scientific capabilities of the colonists are appraised in the biography of a leading scientist, Brook Hindle, *David Rittenhouse* (1964).

Chapter IV

The American Revolution
1763-1783

❡ **AUTHORITY *vs.* NATURAL RIGHTS**
Since the drafting of Magna Carta by feudal barons, the English people had sought to protect their liberties by imposing restraints on rulers. At first this effort was directed toward creating a strong Parliament to act as a check on the king; within fifty years after the Glorious Revolution, however, liberals realized that an arbitrary legislature from which representatives of the people were excluded could be as tyrannical as an absolute monarch. Hence, borrowing a doctrine from the Enlightenment, they began insisting that Parliament's authority was limited by an unwritten constitution which guaranteed to every man his natural rights to life, liberty, and property. This theory was universally accepted in the colonies by 1763. From this time on Americans had only to be convinced that an arbitrary ruler — whether Parliament or king — was violating their inherent rights, to feel that rebellion was justified. This conviction was bred in them by the series of events that occurred between 1763 and 1776.

I. INAUGURATING THE NEW IMPERIAL POLICY — 1763 - 1770

A. Reasons for Inauguration of the Policy

1. Rebellious Attitude of the Colonists. During the Seven Years' War England was not only alarmed by the colonists' insistence on trading with the enemy (see p. 33), but an-

51

noyed by two minor disputes: 1) In 1761 Boston merchants hired *James Otis* to protest the legality of *writs of assistance* (general search warrants) used to hunt out smuggled goods. The courts upheld the crown, but Otis' denial of Parliament's authority to issue such writs was significant. 2) When a Virginia law setting the salaries of Anglican clergymen in cash rather than tobacco was disallowed by the Privy Council, several ministers brought suit to recover the back sums due them. Although the law was on their side, the colony's attorney, *Patrick Henry*, argued so vehemently against the Privy Council's right to disallow colonial laws that the jury awarded the ministers only one penny. This case of the *Parsons' Cause* also alarmed England.

2. The Western Problem

a. THE PROCLAMATION OF 1763. Colonists who viewed the Seven Years' War as a struggle to open the Mississippi Valley for settlement began migrating westward before peace was signed. When the alarmed Indians struck back with *Pontiac's Rebellion* (May, 1763) royal officials decided that migration must be stopped until the red men could be pacified. The *Proc-*

Causes of the American Revolution

ECONOMIC SUBORDINATION OF COLONIES TO ENGLAND.

CHANNELIZING OF ALL TRADE THROUGH ENGLAND.

STRUGGLE FOR MORE HOME RULE.

LIMITING OF COLONISTS TO RAW MATERIALS PRODUCTION.

APPEARANCE OF MANY SKILLED COLONIAL LEADERS.

war for freedom

Chart by GRAPHICS INSTITUTE, N.Y.

lamation of 1763 (October 7, 1763): 1) forbade settlement west of a *Proclamation Line* drawn down the crest of the Appalachians; 2) placed the West under military rule; and 3) opened the colonies of East Florida, West Florida, and Quebec to pioneers. The Proclamation was resented by Americans, who demanded the right to settle anywhere in the West.

b. READJUSTMENT OF THE PROCLAMATION LINE. Colonial pressure forced royal officials to shift the demarcation line westward in two treaties negotiated with the Indians in 1768: the Treaty of Ft. Stanwix and the Treaty of Hard Labor. Together these opened much of West Virginia and western Pennsylvania. An attempt by a group of speculators organized as the *Grand Ohio Company* to establish the proprietary colony of *Vandalia* in the newly opened area almost succeeded, but languished as the Revolution approached.

c. EARLY SETTLEMENT OF THE WEST.

I. *Course of Settlement.* Undeterred by England's law, pioneers occupied three frontier areas after 1763: 1) the region around Pittsburgh; 2) the Watauga Valley in eastern Tennessee, where they formed the *Watauga Association* (1772) as a squatters' agreement to protect themselves from eviction; and 3) the Kentucky country, which was illegally purchased from the Indians by the *Transylvania Company* (1775), a speculating concern headed by Judge Richard Henderson of North Carolina. *Daniel Boone* led the first settlers to Boonesborough that year, to be followed by other adventurers who laid out several small towns, or "stations."

II. *Need for Defense of the Frontier.* Officials realized that unrestrained migration would arouse the Indians to attack; *Lord Dunmore's War* (1774) which followed the early occupation of Kentucky only proved their point. Hence the frontiers must be defended. The ministry in 1763 decided to station 10,000 men in America at an annual cost of £350,000. The colonists, Englishmen believed, should be forced to pay at least one-third of this amount. Efforts to raise this money by taxation launched the revolutionary movement.

B. Early Tax Measures, 1763-1766
1. The Grenville Ministry
a. NATURE OF THE MINISTRY. George Grenville, a business-minded politician, headed one of the many small factions

remaining after the breakup of the English Whig party. Like leaders of the other factions, he was more interested in political power than in principles of empire. Eventually _George III_, who ascended the throne in 1760, was to take advantage of this divided opposition to place his own "king's friends" in control of Parliament. Grenville, although intelligent, had neither the knowledge nor principles necessary to inaugurate a taxation program that would be acceptable to the colonists.

b. THE GRENVILLE TAXATION PROGRAM.

I. _Reform of the Customs Service_. Grenville: 1) ordered all customs collectors to their posts; 2) instructed the navy to run down smugglers; and 3) enlarged the jurisdiction of vice-admiralty courts, which operated without juries.

II. _The Sugar Act_ (1764). This measure: 1) lowered the duty on molasses imported from French or Spanish West Indian islands from 6 pence to 3 pence a gallon; 2) levied new taxes on sugar; 3) forbade the importation of rum. Although milder than the earlier Molasses Act (see p. 23), its enforcement threatened the triangular trade.

III. _Currency Reform_ (1764). Parliament forbade all colonies to issue paper money, thus reducing the supply of currency just as the Sugar Act and improved customs collections were draining specie from the colonies.

IV. _The Stamp Act_ (1765). Grenville planned to raise one-third of the money for American defense with this law. It provided that revenue stamps must be affixed to legal and commercial papers, newspapers, pamphlets, and other printed matter.

2. Colonial Opposition to the Taxation Program

a. REASONS FOR OPPOSITION. Although Grenville expected that his program would be accepted, the colonists objected because: 1) the Stamp Act required payments just after customs reform and the Sugar Act checked the flow of currency into the northern colonies; 2) the Americans were in the grip of a postwar depression that they could blame on the tax laws; and 3) the Stamp Act not only affected all people but fell most heavily on vocal groups: lawyers, merchants, and editors.

b. Forms of Opposition.

I. *Legal Protests.* The Virginia assembly adopted the *Virginia Resolves* denying the right of Parliament to tax the colonies without their consent, an example imitated by other legislatures. A *Stamp Act Congress* (October, 1765) passed a similar resolution. This was the first united action of the colonists.

II. *Extralegal Protests.* The lower classes, organized as the *Sons of Liberty*, used mob violence so effectively that within a few months all stamp agents resigned.

III. *Nonimportation Agreements.* More effective were agreements among merchants to import no more English goods until the Stamp Act was repealed. The trade stagnation that resulted was partly due to the depression.

c. The Constitutional Issue. Two important constitutional questions were raised in this controversy: 1) Were the colonies represented in Parliament? They were under England's system of "virtual representation" in which each member represented the entire empire; they were not under America's system of "actual representation" in which each represented his own district. 2) Did Parliament have the legal right to tax the colonists? Americans admitted Britain's right to regulate their trade, even through taxation, but distinguished between "*external taxes*" (for trade regulation) and "*internal taxes*" (for revenue) such as the Stamp Act.

d. Repeal of the Stamp Act. British merchants whose business was hurt by the Nonimportation Agreements soon joined with liberals to demand repeal of the Stamp Act. Parliament responded (March, 1766), but at the same time passed: 1) the *Declaratory Act* asserting its right to legislate for the colonies "in all cases whatsoever"; and 2) a revenue act reducing the tax on molasses from three pence to one penny a gallon. The colonists were too busy celebrating to object to the dangerous principles involved in these measures.

C. The Townshend Acts, 1767-1770
1. Passage of the Townshend Acts
a. Need for Additional Revenue. Charles Townshend, a weakling serving as chancellor of the exchequer in a new

ministry that took office in 1766, consented to a reduction in the English land tax, planning to offset this by raising revenue in the colonies.

b. TIGHTENING IMPERIAL REGULATIONS. At the same time Townshend showed his hostility to the colonies by: 1) suspending the New York legislature when it refused to grant adequate supplies to British troops; and 2) creating a _Board of Commissioners of the Customs,_ with authority to use writs of assistance, to enforce the Navigation Acts. Revenue used in this way was used to pay the salaries of royal governors, thus lessening their dependence on colonial legislatures.

c. THE TOWNSHEND DUTIES. In 1767 he pushed through Parliament new customs duties on glass, paper, painters' supplies, and tea. These, he held, were "external taxes" such as the colonists had declared legal.

2. Opposition to the Townshend Acts

a. CONSTITUTIONAL PROTESTS. Townshend's constitutional argument was answered by _John Dickinson,_ whose _Letters From a Farmer_ held that "external taxes" were illegal unless their primary purpose was to regulate trade rather than to raise revenue. This implied that Americans could judge for themselves whether or not to abide by any law. At the same time _Nonimportation Agreements_ spread among coastal merchants, although they were less effective than before because of the passing of the postwar depression.

b. PROTESTS OF THE LOWER CLASSES. Led by _Samuel Adams,_ radicals in the Massachusetts legislature drafted a _"Circular Letter"_ to all colonies urging strict enforcement of the Nonimportation Agreements. The result was a period of disorder as customs agents were mobbed, tarred, and feathered. These activities were climaxed when soldiers sent to protect agents in Boston were attacked by a mob. Four persons were killed in this _Boston Massacre_ (March 5, 1770), which aroused resentment all over America.

3. Repeal of the Townshend Duties. A new ministry of "king's friends" under _Lord North_ in 1770 recommended repeal of all duties save that on tea. This was done because: 1) English business had suffered under the Nonimportation

Agreements; and 2) the North ministry realized that taxes on goods exported from England were unwise. Americans believed that they had won a second victory.

II. THE DRIFT TOWARD INDEPENDENCE
1770 - 1776

A. Underlying Factors Responsible

1. The Constitutional Factor. Until 1770 the colonists held that Parliament could regulate their trade, but not tax them. The Townshend Acts showed that commercial legislation could be used for taxation purposes. Hence Americans retreated to a position where they maintained their right to examine the *purpose* of each law passed, refusing to obey those designed to raise revenue. Parliament, which had repeatedly asserted its right to legislate on all matters, would never accept such a proposition.

2. Influence of Social Conflicts

a. LOWER-CLASS DISCONTENT. The lower classes had long been dissatisfied, objecting to: 1) property qualifications for the franchise that barred them from voting; 2) established churches; 3) aristocratic inheritance laws; and 4) outworn guild systems of labor that interfered with free employment. That they were on the verge of rebellion at this time was shown by: 1) an uprising in western Pennsylvania (1763) in which a group of *"Paxton Boys"* marched on the legislature to demand protection from Indian attack; and 2) the organization of a Regulators' Association among frontiersmen of North Carolina to protest high taxes and corrupt courts. The *Regulators* met an eastern army in the *Battle of the Alamance* (1771) before they were finally dispersed.

b. EFFECT ON THE REVOLUTIONARY STRUGGLE. When the conflict with England began, the upper classes were delighted to use lower-class support, but they soon became alarmed at the growing strength of the masses. Yet the lower classes, having tasted power, continued their protests against England, hoping that they would be rewarded with political and social equality. Thus Britain was faced with two groups, each trying to out-protest the other.

B.   The Period of Calm, 1770-1773. During this period of peace, colonial radicals such as *Sam Adams* labored in vain to arouse discontent. At the same time they prepared for the future by forming *"Committees of Correspondence"* (1772) in each town and colony to spread immediate word of any new English aggression. This propaganda network was to show its worth when Parliament again blundered with the Tea Act.

C.   The Tea Act, 1773

1. Passage of the Tea Act. To aid the East India Company, which was in financial difficulties, Parliament in 1773 decided to: 1) remit the entire English duty on tea destined for the colonies, thus subjecting it only to the three pence duty required by the Townshend Act; and 2) allow the company to sell tea through its own agents, rather than through American retailers.

2. Colonial Resistance. Merchants, outraged by the East India Company's monopoly on tea, joined the radicals in protest once more. Thus strengthened, mobs turned back tea ships at Philadelphia and New York. In Boston, where the colonial governor would not allow the vessels to depart, a band of radicals staged the *Boston Tea Party* (December, 1773), dumping the tea into Boston harbor.

3. The Coercive Acts, 1774. Parliament retaliated with four measures known to the colonists as *"Intolerable Acts"*: 1) the *Boston Port Act* which closed the port until the tea was paid for; 2) the *Massachusetts Governing Act* suppressing town meetings and making the upper house of the legislature appointive; 3) the Administration of Justice Act transferring important trials involving royal officials outside of New England; and 4) the Quartering Act allowing governors to requisition buildings to house troops. Americans linked with these the *Quebec Act* which: 1) allowed freedom of worship to Canadian Catholics; 2) restored French civil law to the colony; and 3) extended Quebec's boundaries to the Ohio and Mississippi rivers. These measures convinced all colonists that their liberties were so endangered that they must decide between servile submission and active resistance.

D. The Decision to Rebel, 1774-1776

1. The First Continental Congress

a. RADICAL vs. MODERATES. On a call from Virginia, all colonies save Georgia sent delegates to a Continental Congress which met at Philadelphia in September, 1774. The fifty-five delegates were narrowly divided between radicals who favored resistance, and moderates who advocated conciliation, but with the radicals in a slight majority. This was shown when Congress: 1) adopted the *Suffolk Resolves* pledging members not to obey the coercive acts; and 2) rejected by one vote the *Galloway Plan* for a colonial union under a royally appointed president general and a popularly elected grand council, which could pass laws subject to the approval of the president general and Parliament.

b. ACTION OF THE CONGRESS. With radical control established, the members: 1) adopted a *Declaration of Rights and Grievances* which promised obedience to the king but denied Parliament's right to tax the colonies; and 2) set up the *Continental Association* to prohibit the importation of English goods after December, 1774, and the export of goods to England after September, 1775. Congress then adjourned to meet again in May, 1775, if its grievances were not redressed.

2. The First Bloodshed

a. OPERATION OF THE CONTINENTAL ASSOCIATION. Local committees enforced nonimportation so effectively that trade virtually ceased. Radicals were encouraged by this to adopt an increasingly nonconciliatory attitude toward England. This was shown when they rejected Lord North's *Resolution on Conciliation* (February, 1775) which promised any colony that would provide for its own government and defense virtual immunity from taxation.

b. BATTLES OF LEXINGTON AND CONCORD. When General *Thomas Gage,* the British commander at Boston, decided to send troops to Concord to capture rebel supplies, militiamen gathered to resist. They met the redcoats on the village green at Lexington at daybreak on *April 19, 1775,* losing eight men in the skirmish that followed. The soldiers then marched on to Concord, only to find that most of the supplies had been removed. They were pursued into Boston by a growing force of patriots, leaving the countryside inflamed with wrath.

3. The Final Break with England

a. THE SECOND CONTINENTAL CONGRESS. Congress met on May 10, 1775, amidst the excitement created by the first bloodshed. Moderates such as John Dickinson of Pennsylvania prevented an immediate declaration of independence; instead radicals contented themselves by giving _George Washington_ of Virginia command of the army that was being formed to besiege the British in Boston.

b. THE INEVITABILITY OF INDEPENDENCE.

I. _Military Necessity._ Between May, 1775, and June, 1776, continued military activity showed the colonists that fighting would continue until they won their independence. This centered in: 1) _Boston,_ where the patriots first suffered defeat at the _Battle of Bunker Hill_ (June 17, 1775), then won a complete victory when Washington's army forced the British to evacuate the city (April 1776); 2) Lake Champlain, where Forts _Ticonderoga_ and _Crown Point_ were captured by an American force under Ethan Allen and Benedict Arnold; 3) _Canada,_ which was invaded by a patriot army that captured Montreal (November, 1775) but failed to subdue Quebec (December, 1775); and 4) _Charleston,_ where an attack by a British fleet was beaten off (June, 1776).

II. _Uncompromising Attitude of England._ The open hostility of George III was evidenced by: 1) the rejection of an _Olive Branch Petition_ drafted by John Dickinson (July, 1775); 2) the royal denunciation of the colonists as rebels (August, 1775); 3) the hiring of German mercenaries, or _Hessians,_ to fight against the Americans; and 4) a Parliamentary decree closing all American ports to trade until the colonists capitulated (December, 1775). With the latter step, independence became increasingly necessary to open trade with other countries.

III. _Shifting American Opinion._ The people were won to the necessity of independence by: 1) the publication of _Thomas Paine's Common Sense,_ a simply worded pamphlet that argued for separation; and 2) the realization that this was necessary to improve the lot of the lower classes. In Pennsylvania the common people seized control of the government, while else-where they greatly increased their strength in the assemblies. These were the colonies that began instructing their delegates in Congress to declare independence.

c. The Declaration of Independence. On June 7, 1776, Richard Henry Lee of Virginia introduced a resolution calling for independence. Four days later a committee headed by *Thomas Jefferson* was named to draft a declaration. Lee's motion was approved on July 2, and Jefferson's Declaration of Independence on *July 4*. This immortal document contained: 1) a preamble justifying rebellion on the basis of natural rights; and 2) a list of grievances demonstrating that the natural rights of Americans had been violated by the tyrannical George III. This section was aimed at the king rather than Parliament, as Americans held that Parliament had no authority over them.

III. THE WAR FOR INDEPENDENCE
1776 - 1783

A. The Opposing Forces

1. Loyalists vs. Patriots. About one-third of the colonists remained loyal to England. Most of the Tories were from the upper class, including officials, Anglican clergymen, and the wealthier merchants whose dislike of the "rabble" inclined them toward monarchy. The loyalists were so mistreated by patriot mobs that thousands fled to the West Indies, Canada, or England.

2. Differences in Military Strength

a. The Patriot Army. Americans were so provincial or so indifferent to the war that troops could be obtained only by offering large land bounties for enlistment and cutting the term of service to three months. Even with these inducements, the patriot army never numbered more than 18,000 men. Most of these were poorly trained, and such believers in democracy that discipline was impossible to maintain. To make matters worse, the lack of manufacturing establishments meant they would have to fight without adequate guns, ammunition, clothing, or food. Only the unflinching courage of General *George*

Washington, who could instill others with his faith in ultimate victory, allowed the patriots to win.

b. THE BRITISH ARMY. The seasoned troops sent to fight in America could always be supplemented with hired "Hessians," loyalists, and Indians. Hence they regularly outnumbered their opponents. England failed to subdue the colonies only because: 1) the problem of supplying a force fighting 3000 miles from its base could not be solved; 2) the task of subduing a rebellious people who were thinly scattered over a vast area soon exhausted its resources; and 3) the colonists received the aid of much of Europe in their struggle for freedom.

3. Problems of the Home Front

a. PROBLEM OF GOVERNMENT. The patriots were further weakened by the lack of any central authority. The Continental Congress, having no legal basis, could only ask the states to contribute men or money to Washington's army. When they refused, as they usually did, Congress could do nothing.

b. PROBLEM OF FINANCE. Having no power to levy taxes, Congress issued *bills of credit* (notes in the form of currency) against funds that it hoped would eventually be supplied by the states. The states also issued paper money without backing. The rapid depreciation of this currency caused acute distress among the people. After 1781 when *Robert Morris* became Superintendent of Finance, conditions improved, but only because he was able to borrow money from friendly European nations.

B. Military Operations, 1776-1777

1. British Campaigns of 1776

a. THE BATTLE FOR NEW YORK. A British army of 34,000 men under *Sir William Howe* landed near New York in July, 1776. Washington with 18,000 troops contested their advance on the city, but was badly defeated at the *Battle of Long Island* (August, 1776). The patriots then withdrew to New York, but recognized the impossibility of holding back the superior English force, and retreated into New Jersey.

b. THE NEW JERSEY CAMPAIGNS. With the British in pursuit, the American army retreated across New Jersey, crossing the Delaware River into Pennsylvania at Trenton (December 8, 1776). Howe waited for the river to freeze, stationing his troops at Trenton. Knowing that discipline would be relaxed at Christmas, Washington led 2500 soldiers back across the river to defeat Howe at the *Battle of Trenton* (December 25-26, 1776). A British detachment sent to inflict revenge was overpowered at the *Battle of Princeton* (January 3, 1777). That ended fighting until spring.

2. British Campaigns of 1777

a. PLAN OF CAMPAIGN. General Howe planned to move against Philadelphia, where he would await an army under General John Burgoyne that was marching southward from Montreal along Lake Champlain. With the New England colonies isolated, the combined force would then advance southward to subdue the southern colonies.

b. FAILURE OF BRITISH CAMPAIGN. Howe did not start for Philadelphia until August, 1777, when he moved his troops by water to a point fifty miles from the city. Washington's attempt to check their advance at the *Battle of Brandywine* (September, 1777) failed. In the meantime Burgoyne's army, advancing southward along Lake Champlain, met surprising resistance from a gathering army of patriots and frontiersmen. This so slowed his march that his supplies ran out. Surrounded by patriots, he had no choice but surrender at the *Battle of Saratoga* (October, 1777). Howe then settled down for the winter of 1777-1778 in Philadelphia, while Washington's dwindling force waited nearby at Valley Forge.

C. The French Alliance

1. French Sympathy with the American Cause. The Battle of Saratoga brought France into the war, but before this the French had exhibited open sympathy for the colonists. This was because: 1) the French desired revenge against England for the defeat they had suffered in the Seven Years' War, and wanted to restore the European balance of power by lessening Britain's strength; 2) as disciples of the Enlightenment, they hailed the Revolution as a struggle for "natural rights" against tyranny; and 3) an independent America would benefit French trade, which had been restricted since France lost its own colonies in 1763.

2. Early French Aid to the Colonies. As early as March, 1776, Congress sent Silas Deane to Paris to solicit the help of France. Although fearful of antagonizing England by open aid, the foreign minister, the *Comte de Vergennes,* authorized: 1) the sending of supplies through the fictitious firm of *Roderique Hortalez et Cie;* and 2) the fitting out of American privateers in French ports.

3. Winning a Military Alliance

a. MISSION OF BENJAMIN FRANKLIN. With independence, Benjamin Franklin was sent to press for a military alliance. Although sympathetic, Vergennes refused to act until reasonably assured that England could be defeated. He was convinced by: 1) the victory at the Battle of Saratoga; and 2) a British offer of peace on any terms short of independence. On *February 6, 1778,* he signed two treaties: 1) a treaty of amity and commerce which assured American shippers commercial privileges in France; and 2) a *treaty of alliance* which bound both nations to continue fighting until American independence was won and each was ready for peace.

b. RESULTS OF THE FRENCH ALLIANCE. As a result of the alliance: 1) England declared war on France (June, 1778), forcing a dispersal of its forces to defend the empire; and 2) unlimited French aid in the form of supplies, officers, money, and naval support was made available to the Americans. Without this they could never have won their independence.

4. Aid from Other European Nations

a. SPAIN ENTERS THE WAR. With the French alliance, Spain became interested in the struggle as the two nations were united in a "family compact." The Spanish hesitated to enter the war, however, lest American success encourage rebellions in Latin America. France finally overcame this reluctance by offering to continue fighting until Gibraltar was wrested from England. The Franco-Spanish agreement (April, 1779), brought Spain into the war, further weakening England.

b. THE DUTCH ALLIANCE. Holland capitalized on the war by seizing much of England's carrying trade, and by supplying Americans with arms through Dutch West Indian islands such as St. Eustatius. To stop this, the British declared war in December, 1780. The patriots were strengthened by loans from .Holland, and by aid from the Dutch navy.

c. The League of Armed Neutrality. The Baltic countries, enraged by England's interference with their shipping, formed the League of Armed Neutrality (1780), which constantly threatened to take up arms against England.

D. Military Operations, 1778-1781

1. The War in the North, 1778-1781. Sir Henry Clinton, who replaced Howe as British commander, moved his force from Philadelphia to New York, narrowly escaping defeat at the hands of the pursuing Washington in the *Battle of Monmouth* (June, 1778). Washington hoped to attack New York, but a French fleet sent to aid him made an unsuccessful assault on Newport, Rhode Island, instead. This ended fighting in the North.

2. The War in the West, 1778-1781. A series of American defeats in the West were climaxed by the massacres at Wyoming Valley (1778) and Cherry Valley (1778). The tide turned that summer, however, when a force under *George Rogers Clark* captured Kaskaskia, Illinois, and Vincennes, Indiana. British and Indians from Detroit retook Vincennes, but Clark led 175 men in a heroic march through flooded lands to win the fort again (February, 1779). This aggressive policy proved so successful that an army was sent to punish the Iroquois for the Wyoming and Cherry Valley massacres.

3. The War in the South, 1778-1781

a. Campaigns in the Carolinas, 1780. In May, 1780, Clinton and *Lord Cornwallis* landed a large army at Charleston, planning to move northward to subdue the southern colonies. An American army under General Horatio Gates was defeated at the *Battle of Camden* (August, 1780), but a smaller British force under Major Patrick Ferguson was cut to pieces by patriot frontiersmen at the *Battle of King's Mountain* (October, 1780). The resulting delay allowed Americans to regroup and defeat the British at the *Battle of Cowpens* (January, 1781), although Cornwallis' main army won a costly victory at the *Battle of Guilford Court House* (March, 1781).

b. Impending American Defeat: Winter, 1780-1781. This was the low point of the war for Washington. Cornwallis seemed certain to resume his northward march in the spring, while the patriot force was too depleted and exhausted to offer serious resistance. Moreover, a trusted officer, *Benedict Arnold,* turned traitor. His plot to surrender West Point to the British was detected in time, but Arnold's treason was a sad blow to Washington.

c. THE YORKTOWN CAMPAIGN. In the spring of 1781, Cornwallis advanced northward to Yorktown, on the tip of the peninsula between the York and James rivers. Seizing his chance, Washington marched overland to this point, while a French fleet moved into Chesapeake Bay from the sea. By September, 1781, the British escape route by sea was blocked, while 16,000 Americans faced them on land. Cornwallis held out until *October 19, 1781,* when he surrendered his entire command. The victory at Yorktown ended fighting.

IV. THE PEACE NEGOTIATIONS — 1782 - 1783

A. Preliminary Peace Negotiations

1. The Peace Commissions. *Lord Shelburne,* who became prime minister after the fall of the North ministry, sent as his agent *Richard Oswald,* with instructions to treat with "the Thirteen United States," thus conceding independence from the outset. At Paris, where negotiations were conducted, he met the American commissioners: *John Adams, John Jay,* and *Benjamin Franklin.* Only Franklin was in Paris when negotiations began (April, 1782), the others arriving later.

2. Conflicts Among the Allies

a. BASIS OF THE CONFLICTS. Negotiations were complicated by the wartime alliances. The United States was pledged to continue fighting until France stopped; France was bound to stay in the war until Spain received Gibraltar. As this fortress was still in England's hands, the Americans were technically still involved, even though their independence was won.

b. THE FRENCH SOLUTION. The *Comte de Vergennes,* who was anxious for peace, sought to resolve the difficulty by offering Spain other territorial concessions as a bribe to end the war. To this end, he proposed dividing the region west of the Appalachian mountains into three parts, the northernmost going to England, the central to the United States, and the southern to Spain. This proposal was made to Spain secretly, but news of it soon reached the American commissioners.

c. SEPARATE PEACE NEGOTIATIONS. The American commissioners took the stand that Vergennes' proposal was so hostile to their interests that they were justified in making a separate treaty with England, despite their instructions to work always with France. Hence negotiations with Oswald were begun in September, 1782, and a preliminary treaty signed on November 30, 1782. The final treaty was not signed until *September 3, 1783.*

B. The Treaty of Paris. The final treaty provided: 1) for American independence; 2) boundaries extending north to the 45th parallel and the Great Lakes, westward to the Mississippi, and southward to the 31st parallel — with a secret provision that if England rather than Spain eventually secured the Floridas the southern boundary should be the line of 32°28′; 3) "liberty" for Americans to fish in Canadian waters; 4) freedom for nationals of both nations to navigate the Mississippi River; 5) that "no lawful impediment" be placed in the way of British merchants seeking to collect debts due them in America; and 6) that Congress "earnestly recommend" that the states restore confiscated loyalist property. The generosity of these terms was due to: 1) the war weariness of the English people; and 2) the far-sighted policy of Lord Shelburne.

V. SIGNIFICANCE OF THE REVOLU-TIONARY WAR

A. Political Significance. The Revolution was the first of a series of conflicts inspired by men seeking to achieve the ideals promised them by the philosophers of the Enlightenment: life, liberty, and happiness. The American struggle was watched eagerly by liberals everywhere, while the Declaration of Independence became the inspiration of millions who found solace in Jefferson's noble words. The success of the colonists in their war against tyranny gave heart to those later generations who struck for freedom through the French Revolution, the Latin-American rebellions, and a host of other struggles for liberty.

B. Social Significance. Washington's ragged soldiers endured the trials of battle because they fought not only for liberty, but for democracy. The new nation created by their sacrifices, they knew, would sweep away those relics of aristocracy that had persisted in colonial times: rule by the few, an established church, inheritance laws shaped to perpetuate great estates, antiquated guild systems of employment, and other measures that discriminated against the masses. Nor were their sacrifices in vain. Although generations were to pass before true democracy blossomed in the United States, the Revolution was a landmark in the world-wide struggle for equality among men.

Additional Reading

Excellent interpretative accounts are in E. S. Morgan, *The Birth of the Republic, 1763-1789* (1956), and Edmond Wright, *Fabric of Freedom, 1763-1800* (1963). The causes of conflict are best appraised in J. C. Miller, *Origins of the American Revolution* (1943), and L. H. Gipson, *The Coming of the Revolution, 1763-1775* (1954), although C. M. Andrews, *The Colonial Background of the American Revolution* (1924) is still challenging. Specific causes are discussed in: A. M. Schlesinger, *Colonial Merchants and the American Revolution* (1918), P. G. Davidson, *Propaganda and the American Revolution* (1941), and A. M. Schlesinger, *Prelude to Independence: The Newspaper War on Britain, 1764-1776* (1958). L. W. Labaree, *The Boston Tea Party* (1964) re-interprets that important event. Essential biographical studies include: J. C. Miller, *Sam Adams, Pioneer in Propaganda* (1936), C. D. Bowen, *John Adams and the American Revolution* (1949), R. D. Meade, *Patrick Henry* (1957), and Lewis Namier and John Brooks, *Charles Townshend* (1965). The events of the war are compactly described in W. M. Wallace, *Appeal to Arms* (1951) which is largely military history, Howard Peckham, *The War of Independence* (1958) a brief account, John Alden, *The American Revolution* (1954), and Piers Mackesy, *The War for America, 1775-1783* (1964). Diplomatic aspects are treated in S. F. Bemis, *Diplomacy of the American Revolution* (1935), and Richard Van Alstyne, *Empire and Independence: The International History of the American Revolution* (1965).

CHAPTER V

Confederation and Constitution
1783-1789

～～～～～～～～～～～～～～～～～～～～～～～～～～

ℭ LIBERTY vs. AUTHORITY

With the close of the American Revolution, the people found themselves facing the same problem that had precipitated that struggle: how could central authority be reconciled with personal liberty? England's failure to find an answer had aroused the colonists to rebellion; they feared that their fundamental rights were threatened by the overemphasis on authority. Now they must seek their own solution. For the next half dozen years they experimented with various forms of government, always seeking one strong enough to be workable, but so restrained that their sacred liberties would not be imperiled. Not until they drafted the federal Constitution in 1787 and added a Bill of Rights in 1791 did they find a partial answer.

I. FROM COLONIES TO COMMONWEALTHS

A. Drafting the State Constitutions

1. Writing the Constitutions. Between May, 1776, when the Continental Congress recommended that state governments be set up, and 1780, all former colonies drafted state constitutions save Rhode Island and Connecticut, which retained their former charters.

2. Method of Adoption. The legislatures of three states drafted and adopted constitutions, but in others the people were given a larger voice. Only in _Massachusetts_ was a modern method employed; there popularly elected delegates drafted a constitution, which was then submitted to the voters for ratification.

B. Nature of the State Constitutions

1. Theoretical Basis for Constitutions. Written constitutions were adopted, as the people were accustomed to colonial charters. All were based on the "social compact" popularized during the Enlightenment, with the government resting on an agreement among the people.

2. Content of State Constitutions

a. BILLS OF RIGHTS. As the people were anxious to preserve liberties that had been threatened by England's pre-Revolutionary laws, each contained a section guaranteeing freedom of speech and press, liberty of conscience, protection from arbitrary arrest, jury trial, and the like.

b. SEPARATION OF POWERS. All provided for three governmental branches that would serve as checks upon each other: 1) governors who were elected for only one year (usually by the legislatures) and given no veto power; 2) legislatures with frequently changing membership in which most power was vested; and 3) courts whose judges were named for life by the legislature or governor. Although not granted the power of _judicial review_ (the right to declare acts of the legislature unconstitutional), state courts exercised this function in three cases before 1787, the most famous being that of _Trevett v. Weeden_ (1786) in Rhode Island.

c. LIMITATIONS ON THE FRANCHISE. Property qualifications for voting and officeholding restricted control of the government to the upper classes in all states. In addition many constitutions contained religious tests that barred Jews, Catholics, and atheists from voting. Probably three-fourths of the adult males were kept from the polls by these restrictions.

II. THE FIRST NATIONAL CONSTITUTION

A. Origins of the Articles of Confederation

1. Need for a National Government. The need for a central government was recognized early in the Revolutionary War. Hence Congress in 1776 appointed a committee under *John Dickinson* to draft a written constitution. The committee acted on the principle that this should codify existing practices rather than introduce innovations. After prolonged debate, the *Articles of Confederation* were adopted by Congress (November, 1777) and submitted to the states for ratification.

2. Nature of the Articles of Confederation

a. THEORY UNDERLYING THE ARTICLES. Each state retained its complete sovereignty and independence; the central government acted for the states as an administrative agency. Hence the United States was, in effect, a league of nations banded together to solve common problems.

b. FORM OF GOVERNMENT.

I. *Powers of Congress.* Executive, legislative, and judicial functions were vested in a single-house legislature composed of delegates from each state who voted as a unit. The votes of two-thirds of the states were required to pass any measure. All powers not delegated to Congress were reserved by the states; those that were delegated included: 1) making war and peace; 2) drafting treaties and alliances; 3) controlling Indian affairs; 4) establishing standards of coinage, weights, and measures; and 5) maintaining a postal service.

II. *Powers of the States.* Among the powers reserved by the states were: 1) the *power to tax*, which forced Congress to exist by borrowing or requisitioning federal expense among the states; and 2) the *power to regulate commerce*, which deprived the nation of a uniform commercial policy.

3. Merits and Defects of the Articles

a. MERITS OF THE ARTICLES. A *national citizenship* was created; citizens were assured the same privileges in all states that they enjoyed in their own. This laid the basis for the more workable union soon to emerge.

b. DEFECTS OF THE ARTICLES. These included: 1) lack of an executive to provide leadership; 2) lack of a judicial system; and 3) *lack of any national compulsive power* over states or individuals. This left the central government helpless.

B. Ratification of the Articles of Confederation

1. The Ratification Process. The Articles, by their own provisions, were to become operative only when ratified by all the states. This process started in 1777 and proceeded slowly until only Maryland had failed to ratify.

2. Maryland's Refusal to Ratify

a. WESTERN LAND CLAIMS. Maryland's refusal was connected with the western land problem. Seven of the states claimed territory west of the Appalachians on the basis of their colonial charters. The largest claimant was Virginia, Maryland's neighbor, which began selling its western holdings during the Revolution. Maryland feared that the resulting income would allow Virginia to lower taxes, thus creating dissatisfaction among Marylanders. Hence it refused to ratify the Articles until the land-owning states surrendered their claims to Congress. Especially insistent on this was a group of Pennsylvania and Maryland speculators, organized as the *Indiana Company* and the *Illinois-Wabash Land Company,* who had purchased from the Indians large tracts lying within Virginia's western claims. They realized that Virginia would never allow them to occupy their plots, but hoped that Congress would. Their influence in the Maryland legislature was a primary factor in that state's refusal to ratify.

b. RATIFICATION BY MARYLAND. As most people knew nothing of the speculative intrigue involved, popular pressure demanded that Virginia cede its lands, especially after February, 1780, when New York turned over its claims to Congress. Virginia responded by offering its lands, but only on condition that previous Indian cessions there be invalid. Although the speculators persuaded Congress to refuse this gift until 1784, Maryland could no longer delay. It ratified the Articles in *March, 1781.*

III. PROBLEMS OF THE CONFEDERATION

A. The Western Problem

1. Land Cessions by the States. Several thousand pioneers lived in the West by 1783, most of them concentrated in:

1) western Pennsylvania; 2) Kentucky; 3) eastern Tennessee; and 4) the Nashville region, which had been occupied in 1780 by a group under James Robertson. All were demanding that government be extended over them, but Congress could not act until the states ceded their claims to the West.

a. THE CESSION PATTERN. Virginia's cession not only forced all other states to cede but established an important precedent: the retention of large western reserves. The Old Dominion retained title to the *Virginia Military Reserve* in central Ohio to use in satisfying military bounties. When *Massachusetts* ceded (1784) it kept title to western New York, later dividing ownership of the region with New York. *Connecticut* (1786) retained a triangle in northeast Ohio known as the *Western Reserve.*

b. SOUTHERN LAND CESSIONS. When *North Carolina* ceded its western lands (1784) frontiersmen there organized the *State of Franklin* with John Sevier as governor. This was resented by North Carolina, which regained control in 1788 after a period of controversy. By 1789, when the final cession was made, all the western lands had been sold. *South Carolina* relinquished a narrow strip running westward along the Tennessee border in 1787. *Georgia,* hoping to profit from its holdings, twice sold them to speculating concerns. Each time the sale was revoked, but the state did not finally surrender its lands until 1802.

2. Evolution of a Western Policy

a. ESTABLISHING A LAND SYSTEM. The *Ordinance of 1785* provided that: 1) the public domain be surveyed into "townships" six miles square, with each being subdivided into thirty-six "sections" one mile square; 2) the "sections" be sold at auction at a minimum price of $1 an acre. The "rectangular" surveying system introduced ended confusion in land sales, but frontiersmen objected to the Ordinance because: 1) buyers must take bad land with the good rather than selecting the plot they wanted; and 2) no farmer needed or could afford a 640-acre "section," thus forcing speculators to serve as intermediaries in parceling out land in small lots and on credit to actual users.

b. PROVIDING PROTECTION FROM INDIANS. Five Indian commissioners were named to draft Indian treaties that would open parts of the Northwest for settlement. In the Treaties of Ft. Stanwix (1784) and Ft. McIntosh (1785) several tribes ceded much of southern Ohio. As a number of the most important tribes were not included, the treaties meant nothing. They were soon repudiated by the Indians, whose hostility to the Americans was only increased.

c. PROVIDING GOVERNMENT FOR THE WEST.

I. *Evolution of a Theory of Government.* Congress from the beginning accepted the principle that the western territories would eventually be admitted into the Union on terms of full equality with the older states. This theory was applied when *Thomas Jefferson* drew up the *Ordinance of 1784* which stated that: 1) the first settlers in a western territory should adopt the constitution of an older state as their form of government; 2) when the population reached 20,000 they could draft their own constitution; and 3) when the population equalled that of the smallest state they could enter the Union on equal terms with the other states. Although this Ordinance was adopted by Congress, it was displaced before it became operative.

II. *Influence of the Ohio Company.* The stimulus that led Congress to adopt a governmental system came from the Ohio Company, a speculative concern formed to occupy the Muskingum Valley of Ohio (1786). The agent that it sent to Congress to make the purchase, the *Reverend Manasseh Cutler,* was unable to interest Congress until he took into partnership a group of politicians organized as the *Scioto Company.* Together these two concerns agreed to buy 5,000,000 acres of Ohio land. Cutler, however, refused to agree to the sale until a government was provided for the region. Congress finally acted as a result.

III. *The Ordinance of 1787.* This important measure was in three sections: 1) The area north of the Ohio was to be divided into not less than three nor more than five territories. 2) Each should go through three stages of government. In the first it would be ruled by a governor appointed by Congress; in the second (when the male population was 5000) a popularly elected legislature was added and a delegate sent to Congress; in the third (when the total population was

60,000) the territory could enter the Union as a state. 3) A *bill of rights* protected freedom of speech, liberty of worship, and other basic liberties, as well as prohibiting slavery.

3. *The Settlement of Ohio*. Congressional policy led to the founding of three settlements in the *Northwest Territory* which was created under the Ordinance of 1787, with General *Arthur St. Clair* as governor: 1) *Marietta* (1788), the Ohio Company colony at the mouth of the Muskingum; 2) Gallipolis (1790) founded by a group of Frenchmen who had been duped into buying land from the Scioto Company; and 3) *Cincinnati* (1788), laid out on a tract purchased by a private speculator, *John Cleaves Symmes.*

B. Foreign Problems of the Confederation Period

   1. *Anglo-American Controversy Over the Northwest Posts*

   a. ENGLAND'S RETENTION OF THE POSTS. At the close of the Revolution England held Oswego, Niagara, Detroit, and other posts south of the Canadian border. These she refused to relinquish, taking advantage of a loosely worded phrase in the Treaty of 1783 which provided that they be evacuated "with all convenient speed." By retaining the posts, Britain hoped to: 1) keep control of the fur trade; 2) prevent an Indian war which would almost certainly follow if the natives were abandoned to the Americans; and 3) force the United States to live up to its promises to pay British creditors and loyalists.

   b. DIPLOMATIC EFFORTS AT SOLUTION. *John Adams,* who was sent to London to demand that the posts be abandoned (1785), failed because: 1) the United States was too weak to enforce its demands; and 2) Congress could not force the states to repay British creditors or return loyalist property, giving Britain an excuse to retain the posts.

   2. *Disputes Between Spain and the United States*

   a. POINTS IN DISPUTE. Several issues were in dispute. 1) Both Spain and the United States claimed the *Yazoo Strip* between the 31st parallel and the line of 32°28', basing their claims on their treaties with England in 1783 (see p. 67). 2) Spain controlled the mouth of the Mississippi and was able to close that stream to American commerce. This threatened the economy of the Ohio Valley, which could export its bulky crops only via New Orleans. 3) The Indian tribes of the South-west were friendly to Spain, especially the Creeks under their chief, _Alexander McGillivray._ The frontiers would suffer should Spaniards in Florida or Louisiana incite the natives to attack. 4) Americans hoped to obtain a commercial treaty that would open the Spanish West Indies to their ships.

   b. THE JAY-GARDOQUI NEGOTIATIONS.

   i. _Course of the Negotiations._ Spain closed the Missis-sippi to Americans in 1784, then sent _Diego de Gardoqui_ to negotiate. He proposed to _John Jay,_ the American foreign sec-retary, that Spain would grant a commercial treaty in return for closing the Mississippi for twenty-five years. When Jay asked Congress to change his instructions so that he could negotiate along those lines, Congress agreed by a vote of seven to five. As the nine votes needed to ratify any treaty could clearly not be obtained, the Jay-Gardoqui conversations ended.

   ii. _The Spanish Conspiracy._ Western anger was high when the Ohio Valley learned that seven northern states were willing to strangle their economy in return for a commercial treaty. This discontent was capitalized upon by _James Wil-kinson_ of Kentucky, who conspired with Spain to separate Ken-tucky from the Union in return for financial rewards for him-self. His conspiracy finally collapsed in 1788 when Spain reopened the Mississippi, although charging heavy duties on American goods. Ill feeling remained high for another decade.

   3. The Barbary Pirates. Mediterranean pirates had long preyed on the commerce of any nation that could not afford the tribute they demanded. The United States persuaded one of the Barbary states, _Morocco,_ to respect American ships (1787), but the remaining states continued their attacks.

IV. FAILURE OF THE ARTICLES OF CONFEDERATION

A. Collapse of American Commerce

   1. Commercial Relations with Other Powers. As Con-gress had no power to regulate customs duties, it could not make the guarantees to foreign nations needed to secure commercial treaties. _England_ not only refused to consider such a treaty, but in 1783 banned American vessels from the West Indies, ruled that American goods could be carried there only in British ships, and barred all trade in salt meat and fish. John Adams spent three years in London seeking a treaty, but finally returned home in disgust (1788). _Spain_ also refused to grant a treaty. Treaties with Sweden (1783) and Prussia (1785) benefited commerce only slightly. The decline in American shipping that resulted created dissatisfaction with the Confederation government.

2. Decline of Domestic Commerce. The states began using their power to levy tariffs just after the war when England dumped such quantities of cheap goods in America that domestic producers were threatened with ruin. As the tariffs were not uniform, commerce gravitated toward such low-tariff states as Rhode Island. Other states, jealous of this trade, began levying retaliatory tariffs against the goods of those favored states. These barriers slowed domestic trade to a standstill, creating further dissatisfaction with the government.

B. Collapse of the Monetary System
1. Financial Problems of the National Government
a. FAILURE OF THE REQUISITION SYSTEM. Congress needed money for current expenses and to pay interest on the national debt of $40,000,000. To obtain this it relied on 1) borrowing from abroad, which was almost impossible; 2) sale of public lands, which yielded only a slight return; and 3) the _requisition system,_ by which each state was asked to pay its share of the expenses. Most refused.

b. FAILURE TO GRANT POWER TO CONGRESS. On two occasions Congress requested amendments to the Articles which would allow it: 1) to levy 5 per cent import duties (1781); and 2) to levy import duties for twenty-five years (1783). In each case the states refused to grant it this power. Congress was so impotent that even members lost interest in attending its sessions.

2. Financial Problems of the States
a. ISSUE OF PAPER MONEY. States where debtors gained control of the legislatures issued large quantities of paper money

which depreciated in value rapidly. In *Rhode Island* the small farmers in the assembly then adopted a *Force Act* requiring creditors to accept the money at par. Although this was eventually declared unconstitutional by the state supreme court in *Trevett v. Weeden* (1786), it brought business to a temporary standstill as merchants closed their shops rather than accept payment in depreciated money. Elsewhere the resulting inflation caused suffering. Creditors were also discriminated against by *mortgage stay laws* which prevented mortgage foreclosures for indefinite periods.

b. Mob Action by Debtors. In the six states where the creditor classes retained control of the legislatures, high taxes and ruthless mortgage foreclosures drove debtors to mob action. In Massachusetts interior farmers under Daniel Shays marched on Boston to take control of the state by force. *Shays' Rebellion* was ended when troops were called out, but showed the temper of the people. Everywhere the lower classes talked of an equal division of property or the abolition of all debts.

C. Movement for a Stronger Government

1. The Alexandria Conference. Alarmed men of property realized that their rights could be protected only by creating a national government that would be strong enough to curb the states. They first expressed themselves when delegates from Virginia and Maryland met at Alexandria (1785) to consider means of improving the navigability of the Potomac River. Instead of acting, the commissioners asked Virginia to invite all states to send delegates to a convention at Annapolis where the broad problem of commerce could be considered.

2. The Annapolis Conference. Although only five states were represented, the Annapolis Conference (1786) adopted a report prepared by *Alexander Hamilton* urging all states to send delegates to a convention at Philadelphia where the problem of amending the Articles of Confederation could be discussed. Congress gave its approval in February, 1787, and in May, 1787, the convention that was to draft the Constitution of the United States began its sessions.

V. THE CONSTITUTIONAL CONVENTION

A. Preliminary Steps

1. Membership of the Convention

a. CHARACTERISTICS OF THE FRAMERS. Most of the fifty-five framers were young (their average age was forty-two), while over half were lawyers. Outstanding among them were: *James Madison* of Virginia, *Benjamin Franklin,* who proved adept at calming ruffled feelings in periods of crisis, and *George Washington* as presiding officer. *Alexander Hamilton,* while brilliant, was too conservative to influence the delegates.

b. ECONOMIC INTERESTS OF THE FRAMERS. All the framers represented the propertied upper classes. Moreover most were personally interested, through their own investments, in creating a strong central government. Yet instead of acting selfishly, their primary concern was to create a workable government that would preserve the Union. Disliking aristocracy, and made distrustful of democracy by events of the Confederation Period, their ambition was a government that would avoid the extremes of both despotism and popular rule.

2. Preliminary Plans

a. THE VIRGINIA PLAN. Two previously prepared plans which were laid before the Convention showed the basic *conflict between large and small states.* The Virginia, or *large-state plan,* proposed: 1) a two-house legislature with membership in both houses proportional to population; 2) voting in the legislature by individuals; and 3) a president and courts chosen by the legislature.

b. THE NEW JERSEY PLAN. Presented by *William Patterson* of New Jersey and representing the *small-state view,* this suggested: 1) a Congress similar to that under the Articles with each state having one vote; 2) separate executive and judicial branches; and 3) an enlargement of the powers of Congress to include the right to levy tariffs, regulate commerce, and force states to pay requisitions.

B. Drafting the Constitution

1. The Problem of Representation

a. LARGE STATES *vs.* SMALL STATES. As the large states were in a majority (because Rhode Island sent no delegates and those of New Hampshire arrived late) the New Jersey Plan was defeated. Small-state delegates continued to work against the Virginia Plan, however. The result was the *Great Compromise* which provided that: 1) membership in the lower house should be proportionate to population; 2) each state should have two representatives in the upper house; and 3) money bills should originate in the lower house. This settled the basic differences between large and small states.

b. COMPROMISES WITH THE SOUTH AND WEST. Southerners wanted to count slaves in determining state representation in the lower house, but Northerners were opposed. After long debate, the framers agreed to count *three-fifths of the slaves*

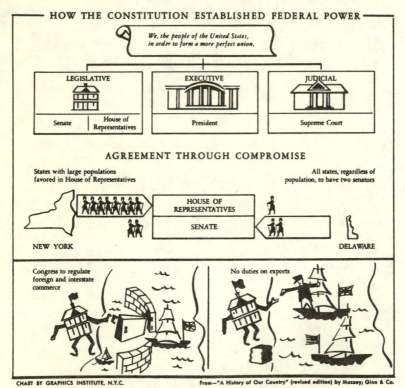

HOW THE CONSTITUTION ESTABLISHED FEDERAL POWER

We, the people of the United States, in order to form a more perfect union,

LEGISLATIVE	EXECUTIVE	JUDICIAL
Senate / House of Representatives	President	Supreme Court

AGREEMENT THROUGH COMPROMISE

States with large populations favored in House of Representatives

All states, regardless of population, to have two senators

HOUSE OF REPRESENTATIVES

SENATE

NEW YORK   DELAWARE

Congress to regulate foreign and interstate commerce

No duties on exports

CHART BY GRAPHICS INSTITUTE, N.Y.C.   From—"A History of Our Country" (revised edition) by Muzzey; Ginn & Co.

in apportioning both representation and taxes. Easterners also wished to restrict representation from the West, fearing control of Congress by agricultural interests. In the end the Convention voted Congress *power to admit new states into the Union.*

c. NATURE OF REPRESENTATION. The framers left to the states the right to determine who should vote for members of the legislature. In effect this excluded many from voting, as property qualifications restricted the electorate in most states.

2. The Powers of Congress

a. POWERS DELEGATED TO CONGRESS. Congress was specifically delegated the power to: 1) collect taxes, duties, and excises; 2) regulate foreign and interstate commerce (except that, to please the South, it was forbidden to levy export duties or to stop the importation of slaves before 1808); 3) coin or borrow money; 4) declare war; 5) maintain an army; 6) establish post roads; and 7) make all rules necessary to carry out its delegated powers.

b. POWERS WITHDRAWN FROM THE STATES. The states were forbidden to: 1) coin money or make anything but gold and silver legal tender; 2) levy customs duties; and 3) pass ex post facto laws or laws impairing the obligation of contracts. These were powers that had been abused by the states during the Confederation period.

3. The Executive Branch

a. METHOD OF ELECTING THE PRESIDENT. To avoid election by Congress or the people, the framers set up an *electoral college,* composed of delegates from each state equal in number to its total representation in Congress. Each elector would then vote for two persons; the one receiving the highest number would become President, the second highest Vice-President. If no candidate had a majority, the election would be decided in the House of Representatives, with each state having one vote. The framers, not foreseeing the rise of the two-party system, believed the electoral college (dominated by the small states) would nominate, while the House (dominated by the large states) would elect a President.

b. POWERS OF THE PRESIDENT. The framers, believing in a *separation of powers* that would allow the executive and judicial branches to check the legislative, granted the President the right to: 1) make treaties with the "advice and consent" of two-thirds of the Senate; 2) serve as commander of the army and navy; 3) name diplomatic agents with the consent of the Senate; 4) execute the laws passed by Congress; and 5) veto acts of Congress, with the qualification that vetos could be overridden by a two-thirds vote.

4. The Judicial Branch

a. THE FEDERAL COURT SYSTEM. Congress was authorized to create a Supreme Court and such inferior courts as were deemed necessary, with judges named for life by the President. The federal courts were granted jurisdiction over: 1) cases arising under the Constitution, laws, and treaties; 2) cases affecting relations with other powers; 3) cases in which the United States was a party; and 4) controversies between two or more states or between citizens of two or more states.

b. DOCTRINE OF JUDICIAL REVIEW. The Supreme Court was not given specific power to declare void acts of Congress or the state legislatures that conflicted with the Constitution. That the framers intended the court to have this power was indicated by: 1) the fact that all were familiar with the doctrine through practices of state courts; and 2) the inclusion of the *supreme law of the land clause* which made the Constitution, federal laws, and federal treaties supreme over state laws in case of conflict.

5. Amending the Constitution.

Congress was given power to propose amendments, or they could be drafted by a convention called on the demand of two-thirds of the states. Amendments were to become effective when ratified by three-fourths of the states acting through their legislatures or special conventions.

C. The Division of Sovereignty

1. Necessity for Division.

The framers realized that the national government could never enforce its laws unless given some sovereignty, but were aware that the states would object to surrendering any of their sovereign powers. They solved this problem by dividing sovereignty between the two, using three devices for this.

2. Method of Division

a. PRINCIPLE OF DELEGATED POWERS. Certain powers were specifically delegated to the national government; all others were reserved for the states. Thus *the national government can do only those things the Constitution allows it to do; the states can do all things not forbidden them in the Constitution.*

b. THE SUPREME LAW OF THE LAND CLAUSE. In cases of conflict between national and state governments, the framers ruled that the national Constitution, laws, and treaties were to be the "supreme law of the land," taking precedence over state laws. *The judges in each state* were to determine when such a conflict existed, and to declare the state laws void.

c. PRINCIPLE OF DUAL CITIZENSHIP. To give the national government a workable *compulsive power,* all people were made citizens of both the state in which they lived and the United States. This allowed the national government to compel each to pay taxes, obey its laws, and the like. This was the most important principle used to create an effective federal government.

D. Ratification of the Constitution

1. The Opposing Factions

a. THE ANTI-FEDERALISTS. When the framers finished their labors (September 17, 1787) and submitted the Constitution to the states for ratification, a division in opinion immediately developed. Opposing ratification were: 1) small farmers and other debtors who disliked restrictions on the states' power to issue paper money; 2) Westerners who feared the new government would barter away their right to navigate the Mississippi; and 3) liberals who had learned from history that strong governments tended toward tyranny. Leaders of this group included *Patrick Henry, Sam Adams,* and other pre-Revolutionary radicals.

b. THE FEDERALISTS. Favoring the Constitution were planters, merchants, and others of the upper classes who were concentrated along the seaboard where they could make their weight felt. They were ably led by *George Washington, Alexander Hamilton,* and *James Madison.* The latter two men, with John Jay, produced *The Federalist,* a book of eighty-five essays that argued effectively for ratification.

2. Ratification by the States

a. THE FIRST CONTESTS. The small states were so pleased with the "Great Compromise" that they ratified almost at once. The first important contest occurred in *Massachusetts* (February, 1788) where the Federalists triumphed only after winning over the lower-class leader, John Hancock, by promising him political rewards, and agreeing to add a Bill of Rights to the Constitution. New Hampshire (June, 1788) was the ninth state to ratify, putting the new frame of government into effect.

b. THE FINAL CONTESTS. In *Virginia* ratification was secured after a long debate (June, 1788), only when Federalists agreed to add a Bill of Rights. Opponents of the Constitution in *New York* included not only small farmers but large landholders under George Clinton, who feared import duties. The Federalists under Alexander Hamilton did not carry the day until news of Virginia's ratification reached the convention. North Carolina delayed action until the Bill of Rights was actually added, while Rhode Island refused to ratify until threatened with an economic boycott.

VI. THE CONSTITUTION: 1787 AND TODAY

A. The Democratic Trend in American History

1. An Undemocratic Constitution in 1787. Although a liberal document for the eighteenth century, the Constitution as adopted contained few of its democratic features of today.

a. SYSTEM OF CHECKS AND BALANCES. The courts could check the legislature and President; the President could use his veto power to negate the popular will expressed in Congress; Congress could frustrate the President by refusing to ratify treaties or appointments. Although designed partially to prevent any branch of the government from developing tyrannical powers, the system also frustrated the popular will.

b. DENIAL OF POPULAR RULE. Despite the fact that property qualifications kept many from voting, the framers allowed the people to choose only the House of Representatives. The Senate was removed two steps from the people; they chose members of a state legislature who in turn selected the senators. The President was removed three steps from the people; members of the Electoral College were chosen by the state legislatures. The judges were removed four steps from the people; they were appointed by the President for life.

c. THE REPRESENTATIVE PRINCIPLE. The Constitution did not create a democracy, but a representative government. Once the people chose their representatives, those representatives made and executed laws with little heed to the popular will. The framers probably realized that congressmen would be more conservative than the people who elected them.

2. The Democratic Constitution of Today. Since 1787 the Constitution has gradually been transformed into a democratic instrument.

a. TRANSFORMATION THROUGH AMENDMENT. Few changes

have been made in the Constitution. Of the twenty-two amendments, the first ten (the Bill of Rights) were part of the original document, while the Eighteenth and Twenty-First amendments cancel each other. Thus only ten amendments have been necessary. Several of these (providing for the direct election of senators, extending the franchise to women, etc.) have helped make the government more democratic.

b. TRANSFORMATION THROUGH CUSTOM. Democracy has been achieved more through custom than through formal change. Thus the rise of the two-party system has outmoded the Electoral College, giving the people a direct voice in the selection of the President. The Constitution, by proving itself flexible, has been able to endure as an instrument for self-government through the many years of its existence.

ADDITIONAL READING

The evolution of political thought during the Revolutionary era is admirably described in Clinton Rossiter, *Seedtime of the Republic* (1953). The influence of the conflict between democratic and elite elements on state constitution-making is described in E. P. Douglass, *Rebels and Democrats* (1955), and on national constitution-making in Merrill Jensen, *The Articles of Confederation* (1940). The same author's *The New Nation* (1950) is the best history of the Confederation period. Shay's Rebellion is pleasantly described in M. L. Starkey, *A Little Rebellion* (1955). General accounts of the Constitutional Convention include Carl Van Doren, *The Great Rehearsal* (1948) and Broadus and L. B. Mitchell, *A Biography of the Constitution of the United States* (1964), although R. L. Schuyler, *The Constitution of the United States* (1923) is still readable and informative. The challenging view of the motives of the framers advanced in Charles A. Beard, *An Economic Interpretation of the Constitution of the United States* (1913) has been attacked in R. E. Brown, *Charles Beard and the Constitution* (1956), and more tellingly in Forrest McDonald, *We the People: The Economic Origins of the Constitution* (1958). Reasons for opposition to the Constitution are intelligently appraised in Jackson T. Main, *The Antifederalists* (1961). Essential biographical studies of the framers are: Irving Brant, *James Madison: The Nationalist, 1780-1787* (1948) and *James Madison: Father of the Constitution, 1787-1800* (1950), C. P. Smith, *James Wilson* (1956), and J. C. Miller, *Alexander Hamilton* (1959).

CHAPTER VI

The Federalist Period
1789-1800

ℂ THE ERA OF CONSERVATISM

With the adoption of the Constitution, the new nation entered upon a period of conservative domination which lasted until the election of Thomas Jefferson in 1800. The most influential leader during this era was *Alexander Hamilton,* whose aristocratic prejudices convinced him that the common people were incapable of self-rule. To Hamilton the ideal government was not a democracy but an aristocracy, administered by men of property whose wisdom would benefit all. His devotion to this ideal eventually carried him too far; in the end Americans grew suspicious of his monarchical designs and in a bloodless revolution at the polls displaced his concepts with those of the more liberal Jefferson.

I. LAUNCHING THE NEW GOVERNMENT

A. Beginnings of the Washington Administration

1. Inauguration of Washington. *George Washington,* who had been unanimously elected President, was inaugurated at New York on April 30, 1789. *John Adams* was chosen Vice-President.

2. Establishing Governmental Precedents

a. USE OF TITLES. Many Federalists wished to bestow high-sounding titles on the federal officials, hoping in this way

86

to impress the people with the power of the government. Although Anti-Federalists defeated Senate bills to call the President "His Excellency" or "His Elective Majesty" many of the ceremonial procedures used in Congress today date to this period.

b. ORIGINS OF THE CABINET. Congress created three executive departments to which Washington appointed *Thomas Jefferson* as Secretary of State, *Alexander Hamilton* as Secretary of the Treasury, and Henry Knox as Secretary of War.

President

George Washington

Secretary of War
Henry Knox

Secretary of State
Thomas Jefferson

Attorney-General
Edmund Randolph

Secretary of the Treasury
Alexander Hamilton

CHART BY GRAPHICS INSTITUTE, N.Y.C.
From—"A History of Our Country" (revised edition) by Muzzey; Ginn & Co.

When the President began conferring with these men on official matters, the *"cabinet system"* came into being.

c. PRESIDENTIAL RELATIONS WITH CONGRESS. Acting under his constitutional authority to make treaties with the "advice and consent" of the Senate, Washington appeared before that body to ask advice on drafting an Indian treaty. The result was so unsatisfactory that thereafter treaties were negotiated by the executive department, then submitted to the Senate for ratification.

3. Revenue Measures. Two laws were enacted to raise money: 1) a *tariff on imports;* and 2) a *tonnage duty* which levied a heavy tax on foreign vessels and a light duty on American vessels entering ports of the United States.

4. Creation of a Federal Judiciary. A *Judiciary Act* (1789) created a Supreme Court, three circuit courts, and thirteen district courts, as well as defining their jurisdiction and methods of appeal.

5. Adoption of the Bill of Rights. During the ratification contest five states insisted on a Bill of Rights to protect the peoples' liberties from federal encroachment. Twelve amendments for this purpose were adopted by Congress, and of these ten were ratified by December 15, 1791. They guaranteed freedom of speech and press, liberty of conscience, jury trials, and the like.

B. Hamilton's Financial Measures

1. Purpose of the Measures. Hamilton, as Secretary of the Treasury, proposed to Congress a series of laws designed: 1) to restore the government's credit at home and abroad; and 2) to strengthen the national government at the expense of the states.

2. The Financial Measures

a. FUNDING THE NATIONAL DEBT. Government bonds issued during the Revolution were held by: 1) foreign investors or governments ($12,000,000); and 2) domestic bondholders ($42,000,000). All agreed that the foreign debt should be paid in full, but Anti-Federalists insisted that the speculators who held the domestic bonds should be paid off at the current rate of 25 cents on the dollar. Hamilton, seeking to win the support of these speculators, instead pushed through Congress a funding scheme to pay the entire debt at par.

b. ASSUMPTION OF STATE DEBTS. A similar motive led Hamilton to propose the federal assumption of all state debts contracted during the Revolution, for he hoped in this way to place the creditor class under obligation to the national government. Opposition in Congress came largely from southern states such as Virginia which had partially retired their debts by sale of western lands. To win their support, Hamilton made a bargain with Jefferson in which he agreed to favor a southern site for the national capital in return for Jefferson's support for assumption. Hence the capital was located at Washington, while the United States assumed state debts of $18,000,000.

c. CREATION OF THE BANK OF THE UNITED STATES.

I. *Hamilton's Proposal.* Hamilton asked Congress to charter the Bank of the United States, with a capital stock of $10,000,000, one-fifth to be subscribed by the government. The bank would then serve as a depository for federal funds, and would be authorized to issue paper money on the basis of the securities it held.

II. REASONS FOR PROPOSAL. Hamilton wanted the bank because: 1) the business classes would benefit by the use of its facilities; and 2) Congress in chartering the bank would be forced to accept the principle of *implied powers.* On the latter point he reasoned in this way: 1) The Constitution did not authorize Congress to charter a bank. 2) Congress did have power to coin money, borrow money, and raise money by taxation. 3) It also had authority to do anything "necessary and proper" to carry out its delegated powers. 4) A national bank was a "necessary and proper" means of caring for the country's finances. 5) Therefore the Constitution *implied* Congress' right to establish a bank. In this way Hamilton developed the argument for the *loose construction* of the Constitution. His opponents, Jefferson and Madison, argued for a *strict construction* by maintaining that Congress had no powers not actually authorized by the Constitution. When Hamilton persuaded Congress to charter the bank (1791) he greatly enlarged the powers of that body, and of the central government.

d. THE WHISKY TAX. Hamilton proposed to raise money by an excise tax on whisky, knowing that this would fall most heavily on the small farmers of the interior who commonly condensed their corn into this exportable commodity. He hoped in this way to impress them with the powers of the new government. Instead the excise tax aroused opposition which culminated in the _Whisky Rebellion_ (1794). When farmers of western Pennsylvania, after mobbing tax collectors, started to march on Pittsburgh, President Washington sent an overwhelming militia force against them. Opposition melted away as this approached, but from that time on the West was wholeheartedly opposed to the Federalists.

C. Beginnings of Political Parties

1. Hamilton vs. Jefferson.   By 1790 Hamilton's financial measures were dividing Washington's followers into two factions: 1) the Hamiltonians or _Federalists_ who looked forward to an industrialized America governed by a strong national government under aristocratic control; and 2) the Jeffersonians or _Anti-Federalists_ who favored an agrarian America governed by a weak national government under popular control. Although still lacking political organization, the Federalists were supported by the _Gazette of the United States_ (1789), while the Anti-Federalists were upheld by the _National Gazette_ (1791) under the editorship of the poet, _Philip Freneau._ By 1792 the quarrel between these two papers and the factions they represented seriously alarmed Washington, whose ideal was a united government.

2. Significance of Political Parties.   The rise of political parties negated the undemocratic features of the "checks and balances" system of the Constitution. One party could now control all three branches of the government—legislative, executive, and judicial—preventing them from checking each other. As parties became powerful they also allowed the people to express themselves more directly in choosing a President or Congress.

II.   WESTERN PROBLEMS OF THE WASHINGTON ADMINISTRATIONS — 1789 - 1796

A.   Indian Relations in the Northwest

1. Causes of Indian Unrest.   Two factors were responsible for unrest among the tribes north of the Ohio River: 1) the continued encroachment of frontiersmen on their lands; and 2) the presence of British agents at Detroit and other Northwest Posts who, while not inciting the natives, created the impression that aid would be forthcoming in case of war.

2. Indian Warfare in the Northwest

a. BEGINNING OF WARFARE. War broke out in 1790 as Indians attacked the advancing settlers. The first two expeditions sent against the natives ended in failure. General *Josiah Harmar* (1790) returned after his force had done nothing more than destroy a few abandoned villages along the Maumee River. General *Arthur St. Clair* suffered a disastrous defeat (1791) that cost the lives of 600 of his men.

b. EXPEDITION OF "MAD ANTHONY" WAYNE. After carefully training his army, Wayne moved into the Indian country during the fall of 1793. His force wintered at the newly built Ft. Greenville. During that winter two significant events occurred: 1) Lord Dorchester, governor of Canada, told an Indian conference that an impending war between England and the United States would allow the British to fight on their side; and 2) the English built *Ft. Miami* on the lower Maumee to protect Detroit from Wayne. Hence when Wayne began his advance in 1794 the Indians were confident of victory. Instead they were decisively defeated at the *Battle of Fallen Timbers* (August, 1794), fought just south of Ft. Miami.

3. Treaty of Greenville (1795).

Wayne gathered the defeated Indians at Ft. Greenville where he forced them to sign a treaty ceding to the United States most of southern Ohio and a triangle of land in southeastern Indiana. For the next fifteen years the Northwest was at peace.

B. Spanish-American Conflicts in the Southwest

1. Indian Warfare in the Southwest.

During the Confederation period the Creek Indians under Chief *Alexander McGillivray* were goaded by the Spanish into attacking the southwestern frontier (see pp. 75-76). Spain hoped in this way to drive back the advancing Americans far enough to protect Louisiana and the disputed Yazoo Strip.

2. The Treaty of New York.

When Georgia (1789) sold much of the Southwest to speculators organized as the Yazoo Land Company, President Washington knew that further Indian retaliation could be expected. Hence he denounced the sale, at the same time inviting Chief McGillivray to New York to talk peace. Knowing that Washington's influence alone would overthrow the Yazoo Company, McGillivray accepted. In the *Treaty of New York* (August, 1790) he accepted peace terms, receiving in return financial rewards and a salary of $1,800 yearly as a brigadier general in the American army. Two years later McGillivray repudiated the treaty when Spain offered him $3,000 a year. War continued until Tennesseans under James Robertson and John Sevier defeated the natives in 1793 and 1794.

C. Advance of Settlement in the West

1. Admission of New States.   Congress had sufficient power to satisfy the western demand for statehood. *Vermont,* which had been seeking admission since 1777, became the fourteenth state in 1791, followed by *Kentucky* (1792) and *Tennessee* (1796).

2. Revision of Western Policy

a. INDIAN POLICY. An *Indian Intercourse Act* (1796) ruled that: 1) no settlers should occupy land not previously ceded to the United States by the Indians; and 2) Indian traders must be licensed and bonded. Another law provided for government-operated *trading factories* (1796) where natives could be supplied with trading goods at low cost.

b. LAND POLICY. A *Land Act* (1796): 1) raised the price of land to $2 an acre; and 2) allowed one year's credit on one-half the purchase price. Passed over western opposition, this measure perpetuated the eastern principle of using the public domain as a source of revenue.

III. FOREIGN PROBLEMS OF THE WASHINGTON ADMINISTRATIONS — 1789 - 1796

A. The French Revolution and the United States

1. American Reaction to the Revolution.   Americans, viewing the French Revolution as a continuation of their own struggle for liberty, were united in its support from 1789 to 1793. With the execution of Louis XVI and the entrance of England and Spain into a war against the Revolutionists

(1793), opinion divided. Anti-Federalist agrarians, whose strength lay in the South and West, not only continued strongly pro-French, but formed Republican Clubs to advocate war against English Canada and Spanish Florida. Federalists, on the other hand, increasingly viewed England as the defender of property rights against "French anarchy and atheism." This division not only complicated foreign relations, but gave an emotional basis to party differences.

2. Mission of Citizen Genêt

a. THE PROBLEM OF NEUTRALITY. News that the Revolutionists were sending a minister to the United States forced President Washington to face the problem of neutrality. The *Treaty of 1778* still bound the two nations in an alliance that committed each to aid the other in time of war. Jefferson maintained that the treaty was between nations and still binding; Hamilton that the treaty had been with the French king and was no longer valid. Washington accepted Jefferson's interpretation, but decided that the treaty forced the United States to aid France only in a defensive war. Hence he: 1) issued a *proclamation of neutrality* (April, 1793); and 2) formally *recognized the French Republic*, thus establishing the principle of recognizing new governments as soon as they were able to maintain themselves.

b. PROJECTS OF GENÊT. The French minister, Edmond Genêt, reached Philadelphia in April, 1793, after landing at Charleston and traveling northward through the back country. Not realizing that he had visited the most violently pro-French section of the United States, he interpreted his enthusiastic reception to mean that he could ask for anything. Hence he: 1) began organizing two *"revolutionary armies"* of frontiersmen under such leaders as *George Rogers Clark* to attack Spanish Florida and Louisiana; and 2) fitted out privateers in American ports to send against British shipping. When, even after Washington had warned him against this violation of neutrality, he ordered the conversion of a captured vessel into a privateer called the *Little Democrat*, the President asked for his recall.

c. RESULTS OF THE GENÊT MISSION. Genêt not only embarrassed the United States but lessened good feeling between the two nations. Another result was the *resignation of Jefferson* as Secretary of State (December, 1793). From that time on Washington's government was entirely Federalist.

B. Relations with England

1. Problem of Neutral Commerce

a. EXTENSION OF AMERICAN COMMERCE. The strained relations already existing between England and the United States (see p. 75) were complicated by the entrance of American shippers into the trade between France and the French West Indies. This was not only welcomed by France whose own merchant marine was driven from the seas by England, but proved highly profitable.

b. ENGLISH RETALIATION.

I. STATUS OF INTERNATIONAL LAW. The United States maintained that three principles of international law legalized this trade: 1) "free ships made free goods" (a neutral ship could carry goods of any sort without interference by a belligerent); 2) contraband (which could be legally seized by a warring power when on the way to its enemy) was limited to materials of war; and 3) a blockade had to be effectively enforced to be legal. Differences between England and the United States developed when: 1) England refused to recognize these rules of international law; and 2) British war vessels stopped American merchantmen on the high seas to *impress* into the royal navy English deserters (and sometimes American subjects) found serving in the crews.

II. THE "RULE OF 1756." England announced (June, 1793) that it would enforce the "Rule of 1756": trade closed to a nation in time of peace could not legally be opened in time of war. Under this rule the British navy confiscated some 150 American vessels engaged in trade between France and the French West Indies.

2. The Diplomatic Settlement

a. EARLY NEGOTIATIONS WITH ENGLAND. The Washington government opened negotiations to settle the conflict over the Northwest Posts (see p. 75) in 1791 when a near war between Spain and England over the right of English traders to operate in the Pacific (the *Nootka Sound Controversy*) made the latter conscious of the need for American friendship. The minister sent at that time, George Hammond, was powerless to settle the controversy as he had no authority to surrender the Northwest Posts, while the United States would negotiate only on that basis.

b. THE JAY MISSION.

I. *Course of Negotiations.* As commercial conflicts intensified antagonism between England and the United States, President Washington made a last bid for peace by sending *John Jay* to London with instructions to: 1) secure the Northwest Posts; 2) win compensation for American shippers whose cargoes had been illegally confiscated; and 3) obtain a satisfactory commercial treaty. In the preliminary conversations, Jay won many concessions. England's retreat at this time was due to: 1) fear that Wayne (who was then advancing northward) would attack Detroit; 2) the collapse of the European confederation that had been fighting the French revolutionists; and 3) threats of the *League of Armed Neutrality* to enter the war against Britain to protest the invasion of its members' neutral rights. Hence Britain could not risk the enmity of the United States. The favorable influence of these factors was offset by Alexander Hamilton, who assured the English minister that the Federalists would prevent any war with Britain. Thus assured, the English negotiators refused to make further concessions.

II. *Jay's Treaty.* The final treaty, signed in November, 1794, provided that: 1) the British would evacuate the Northwest Posts by June 1, 1796; 2) commissions would settle boundary disputes and establish the amount due American shippers for loss of goods; 3) England's contentions that food was contraband and "paper blockades" (unenforced blockades) legal be accepted; 4) American ships under seventy tons could trade in the British West Indies, but could not carry molasses, sugar, coffee, and cotton from the West Indies or the United States to any part of the world. This last article was so unfavorable to the United States that it was stricken from the treaty before ratification.

III. *Ratification of the Treaty.* Jay's Treaty was so unfavorable to the United States that Senate ratification was secured by only one vote (June, 1795). House appropriations needed to carry the treaty into effect were voted only after an impassioned oration from *Fisher Ames,* a New England Federalist. The treaty, however, temporarily settled differences with England.

C. Relations with Spain

1. Reasons for American Success

a. THE EUROPEAN SITUATION. Spain showed no willingness to settle its long-standing differences over ownership of the Yazoo Strip and navigation of the Mississippi until 1795. By that time its armies had been so badly defeated in the war with France that a separate peace treaty was signed (July, 1795). Spain feared English retaliation for this desertion, especially after news of Jay's Treaty showed that England and the United States had settled their differences. Friendship with the United States was needed to forestall an Anglo-American attack on Louisiana.

b. FAILURE OF SPANISH FRONTIER POLICY. Spain had sought to strengthen and expand her holdings in the Mississippi Valley by: 1) carrying on intrigue with frontiersmen to separate Kentucky and Tennessee from the Union; 2) encouraging migration to Louisiana; and 3) building up Indian alliances to hold back the aggressive Americans. By 1795 all these devices had failed; the intrigue won few supporters, almost no Americans migrated to Louisiana, and the Indians were untrustworthy. Thus discouraged, the Spanish were ready to abandon plans for an expanded empire in the Mississippi Valley.

2. Pinckney's Treaty.

Thomas Pinckney was sent to Madrid in time to take advantage of this situation. Pinckney's Treaty, or the *Treaty of San Lorenzo* (October, 1795) provided: 1) for a southern boundary at the 31st parallel, giving the United States all the Yazoo Strip; and 2) that Americans could navigate the Mississippi freely and have the "right of deposit" at New Orleans for three years.

3. French Retaliation.

The French were angered by Jay's and Pinckney's treaties. When the strongly pro-French minister at Paris, *James Monroe,* attempted to sooth their feelings by hinting that after the election of 1796 things would be different, he was recalled by Washington. France refused to receive C. C. Pinckney, the arch-Federalist sent in his place. Ill feeling was strong as Washington's administrations drew to a close.

IV. THE ADMINISTRATION OF JOHN ADAMS
1797 - 1801

A. The Election of 1796

1. The Opposing Parties. By this time the two parties were well enough organized to present candidates. The Anti-Federalists, or *Jeffersonian Republicans*, selected as their nominees *Thomas Jefferson* for President and Aaron Burr of New York for Vice-President. The *Federalists*, realizing that Hamilton was too unpopular to be elected, nominated *John Adams* and Thomas Pinckney. In his anger Hamilton tried to throw the election to Pinckney. Although he failed, the resulting conflict hurt the party.

2. The Election of John Adams. The Republicans might have won had not the French minister resigned his office to campaign openly for Jefferson. Resentful of this foreign interference, the electoral college chose Adams by a vote of 71 to 68. Jefferson, who received more votes than Pinckney, became Vice-President.

B. Conflicts with France

1. The X Y Z Affair. Adams took office amidst a demand for war against France following that nation's refusal to accept C. C. Pinckney as minister. In a final bid for peace, the President sent C. C. Pinckney, John Marshall, and Elbridge Gerry to Paris (June, 1797) with instructions to settle the disputes in any way possible. Talleyrand, the French foreign minister, refused to see them until paid a sizable bribe. Outraged by this insult, they returned home, where they laid their correspondence before Adams, substituting X, Y, and Z for the names of the French agents with whom they had negotiated. When these letters were published the whole nation demanded a war of revenge.

2. The Naval War of 1798

a. PREPARATIONS FOR WAR. Congress responded to the popular demand by: 1) authorizing construction of new warships; 2) ordering merchantmen to arm themselves; 3) issuing papers to 400 privateers that were sent out to raid French shipping; and 4) commissioning the President to raise an army of 10,000 men. Over Adams' objections, Alexander Hamilton was named commander of the army. The appointment of this unpopular conservative, together with the realization that higher taxes would be needed to support the army, cooled the ardor of the people rapidly.

b. THE WAR ON THE HIGH SEAS. For two years war raged on the seas. During this period nearly ninety French ships were captured, while an equal number of American ships surrendered to enemy war vessels or privateers.

3. The Convention of 1800.
Talleyrand, who had no liking for an American war, informed Adams that a new minister would be hospitably received. The President responded by sending a commission of three to Paris (February, 1799) over Hamilton's objections. By the time the commissioners reached France (March, 1800), Napoleon Bonaparte was in control. As he was anxious for peace while he consolidated his position, he readily agreed to the *Convention of 1800* which provided: 1) abrogation of earlier treaties between the two powers; 2) acceptance of the principle that free ships made free goods; and 3) that the United States should not seek indemnities for vessels illegally seized by France. When the Convention was ratified (July, 1800) peace was restored.

C. The Election of 1800

1. The Alien and Sedition Acts

a. PASSAGE OF THE ACTS. The French naval war strengthened the Federalists, whose policies of conservatism and national consolidation seemed more acceptable in time of war. Seizing on this shift in opinion to protect themselves against future Republican victories, they adopted a series of acts designed to perpetuate their control:

I. THE ALIEN ACTS (1798). Designed to weaken the political influence of immigrants who were normally Republican, these laws: 1) lengthened the period of residence required for naturalization from five to fourteen years; 2) gave the President power to deport dangerous aliens; and 3) authorized the President in time of war to imprison aliens who refused to leave the country.

ii. THE SEDITION ACT (1798). This measure, which was designed to suppress hostile criticism of the Federalists, provided that: 1) any combination or conspiracy to oppose the legal measures of the government could be punished by a fine of $5,000 and five years imprisonment; and 2) any person publishing a false or malicious statement which would bring the President or Congress into disrepute could be imprisoned for two years and fined $2,000. If enforced, this law would have ended all criticism of the government.

b. REACTION AGAINST THE ACTS. Noting that those punished under the laws became public martyrs, the Republicans determined to capitalize on this sentiment before the election of 1800. With this in view, the Republican-dominated legislatures of Virginia and Kentucky adopted the *Virginia and Kentucky Resolutions* for circulation among the legislatures of other states. The Virginia Resolution simply stated that states could legitimately object when Congress exceeded the authority delegated to it by the states, but the *Kentucky Resolution* (written by Thomas Jefferson went beyond to assert that in such a case the states could refuse to obey the law. This was the first expression of the *doctrine of nullification* which was later employed in the slavery controversy.

2. The Election of Thomas Jefferson. The Federalists were so discredited by the Alien and Sedition Acts and so disrupted by the conflict between Adams and Hamilton that *Jefferson* secured 73 electoral votes to 65 for John Adams. Only New England, Delaware, and New Jersey remained predominately Federalist.

3. Dispute Over the Vice-Presidency. The framers of the Constitution, not forseeing the rise of the two-party system, had ruled that each elector should cast two votes. As all Republican electors voted for Jefferson and *Aaron Burr,* his vice-presidential candidate, each had the same number of votes for the presidency. This threw the election into the Federalist-dominated House of Representatives. After a number of dead-locked votes, Hamilton cast his support to Jefferson, winning him the presidency.

V. ENDURING CONTRIBUTIONS OF THE FEDERALISTS

A. A Stabilized Government. Despite their unpopularity, the Federalists made a number of enduring contributions: 1) their program of centralization provided a basis for the future expansion of federal power at the expense of the states; 2) their efficiency and conservatism endowed the new republic with a firm financial system; and 3) their emphasis on a diversified economy prepared the way for the industrial civilization of the nineteenth century.

B. The Federalists and Democracy. The people were wise when they elected Federalists at a time when order and efficiency were needed to place the new nation on its feet; they were equally wise when they repudiated the party as soon as the republic was established. Hamilton and his followers belonged to the aristocratic past rather than the democratic future. Their defeat demonstrated that any party, to enjoy success in America, must be concerned with the welfare of the many rather than the few.

ADDITIONAL READING

The best survey is J. C. Miller, *The Federalist Era* (1960), but Nathan Schachner, *The Founding Fathers* (1954) has useful information. A readable interpretation is included in Marcus Cunliffe, *The National Takes Shape, 1789-1837* (1959) which is brief. Useful biographical studies are: J. C. Miller, *Alexander Hamilton* (1959), Nathan Schachner, *Alexander Hamilton* (1946), Marcus Cunliffe, *George Washington* (1958), and Page Smith, *John Adams* (1962). Opposition to the Federalists is appraised in N. E. Cunningham, *The Jeffersonian Republicans* (1957) and Gilbert Chinard, *Thomas Jefferson* (1939). Adrienna Koch, *Jefferson and Madison: The Great Collaboration* (1950) is interpretative. Foreign policies are discussed in A. B. Darling, *Our Rising Empire* (1940) and more expertly in P. A. Varg, *Foreign Policies of the Founding Fathers* (1963). Alexander De Conde, *Entangling Alliance* (1958) and L. M. Sears, *George Washington and the French Revolution* (1960) deal with special aspects. A fine discussion of the Alien and Sedition Acts is in J. M. Smith, *Freedom's Fetters* (1956).

CHAPTER VII

Jeffersonian Democracy
1800-1815

❰ THE PHILOSOPHY OF THE JEFFERSONIANS

The election of 1800 was no revolution, for despite their espousal of democracy and their belief in the improvability of man, the Jeffersonians were not ready to turn the government over to the people. Until the masses could be educated for their new responsibilities, Jefferson felt, rule must be entrusted to the agrarian upper class whose interests paralleled those of the small farmers making up the bulk of the population. Hence the sole effect of the election was to shift control from the mercantile aristocracy of the Northeast to the agrarian aristocracy of the South and West. Yet Jefferson's faith in the perfectibility of mankind, his insistence on strong local governments to check monarchial trends in the national government, and his belief that each generation should remake its laws and constitutions proved a stimulus to democracy. European conflicts that kept the United States constantly embroiled prevented Jefferson from translating his liberal theories into practice, but his administrations paved the way for the democratic gains of the next generation.

I. THE FIRST JEFFERSONIAN ADMINISTRATION
1801 - 1805

A. Domestic Problems of the First Administration

1. Overthrow or Retention of the Federalist Inheritance?

a. JEFFERSON'S APPOINTMENTS. Jefferson's principal appointees were representatives of the agrarian aristocracy ; *James*

Madison as Secretary of State, and _Albert Gallatin_ as Secretary of the Treasury were most prominent. Federalists were retained in most minor offices under the theory that their experience should be used so long as they placed national loyalty above party.

b. FISCAL POLICIES. Gallatin, feeling that a large national debt benefited only upper-class bondholders, affected rigid governmental economies. Loss of revenue suffered through _repeal of the whisky tax_ was offset by customs duties after an English court held in the case of the _Polly_ that American ships might legally carry goods from the French West Indies to France by passing those goods through a neutral port. These duties allowed Gallatin to retire much of the debt.

c. REPEAL OF THE JUDICIARY ACT OF 1801. Just before retiring from office, the Federalist Congress created sixteen new federal judgeships and other minor judicial offices. These were all filled with Federalist appointees by Adams just before his term expired. This act was immediately repealed by the Republicans, who felt that the Federalists were trying to entrench themselves in one branch of the government.

I. _Marbury vs. Madison._ Federalists charged that repeal of the Judiciary Act was unconstitutional, as it deprived judges of their offices when the Constitution guaranteed them tenure during good behavior. To test this issue, one of Adams' "midnight appointees" William Marbury, asked the Supreme Court for a writ of mandamus compelling Madison, the Secretary of State, to deliver his commission. _John Marshall,_ who had been named Chief Justice by Adams, denied this petition on the grounds that the Court, under the Constitution, did not have _original jurisdiction_ to issue such writs (1803). Thus Marshall concluded that the section of the original Judiciary Act of 1789 which granted it that authority was unconstitutional. In this way Marshall wrote into law the _doctrine of judicial review_ which gave the Supreme Court power to declare acts of Congress unconstitutional.

II. _Impeachment of Judges._ Republicans next planned to impeach the more biased Federalist judges. One district judge was removed from office when found to be insane, but the

Senate refused to convict Judge *Samuel Chase* of the Supreme Court on purely political grounds (1805). This established the precedent that partisanship was no crime.

2. Western Policy of the Jeffersonians

a. REVISION OF THE LAND POLICY. As little land had been sold under the earlier laws, the Jeffersonians readily agreed to a revision when this was demanded by *William Henry Harrison,* the congressional representative of the Northwest Territory. Two measures were adopted: 1) The *Land Act of 1800* established land offices in the West, reduced the minimum amount purchasable to 320 acres, and introduced the *credit system* by allowing a purchaser to spread three-fourths of his payments over four years. 2) The Land Act of 1804 further reduced the minimum amount that could be purchased to 160 acres.

b. ADMISSION OF OHIO. The Enabling Act (1802) admitting Ohio: 1) set aside one section of land in each township to aid education; and 2) appropriated 5 per cent of the proceeds from land sales in the state for road building. In return Ohio agreed not to tax federal lands for five years.

c. COMPLETION OF STATE LAND CESSIONS. *Georgia,* after the sale of its western lands to four *Yazoo Land companies* had been revoked (1795), finally agreed to cede its territories (1802) if the United States world: 1) pay the state $1,250,000; and 2) grant 5,000,000 acres .o the Yazoo Land companies. Attempts to set aside this land were blocked in Congress by *John Randolph* of Virginia, who charged that the transaction was fraudulent. His followers, known as the *Quids,* were soon in open warfare with Jefferson on many issues. Not until Randolph left Congress in 1814 were the companies compensated.

B. Foreign Problems of the First Administration

1. Dealing with the Barbary Pirates. Under the Federalists, tribute had regularly been paid the Barbary pirates who frequented the south shore of the Mediterranean. In 1801 one of the Barbary states, Tripoli, declared war on the United States, charging that its share was not large enough. The *Tripolitan War* raged for the next three years as American vessels fought the pirates with fair success, but peace was not secured until an overland expedition from Egypt threatened to invade Tripoli (1805). Tribute was still paid some of the pirate states until 1815.

2. The Purchase of Louisiana

a. THE EUROPEAN BACKGROUND. Spain, which found Louisiana valuable only as a barrier between aggressive frontiersmen and Mexico, was anxious to sell the territory after Pinckney's Treaty (1795) settled differences with the United States. France was equally anxious to buy, as the rise of Napoleon Bonaparte to power awakened visions of a new colonial empire. The transfer was made at the _Treaty of San Ildefonso_ (1800). Then, having made peace with England (Treaty of Amiens, 1802), Napoleon undertook to crush a slave insurrection on Santo Domingo, which would be the center of his American empire. By the time 10,000 of his best troops had failed to subdue _Toussaint L'Ouverture_ and his Negro followers, French interest in empire began to diminish.

b. AMERICAN REACTION TO FRENCH OWNERSHIP. Jefferson, alarmed by the prospect of an aggressive neighbor in Louisiana, threatened to seek an alliance with England to prevent transfer of the territory. His fears seemed confirmed when Spanish officials at New Orleans (who had been left in control there) announced the suspension of the "right of deposit" (1802). As western trade was seriously threatened, Jefferson feared that the frontiersmen would attack New Orleans and precipitate a French war unless he could settle the problem peacefully.

c. SALE OF LOUISIANA TO UNITED STATES. James Monroe was sent as a special agent to join Robert Livingston, American minister at Paris, in an effort to purchase New Orleans. Before Monroe arrived, Napoleon had decided to sell because: 1) the conquest of Santo Domingo had depleted his resources; and 2) he needed money for additional conquests in Europe. Hence he sold Louisiana to the American envoys for $15,000,000 (April, 1803).

d. AMERICAN OCCUPATION OF LOUISIANA.

I. _Transfer of the Territory to the United States._ Jefferson, who had opposed the use of _implied powers,_ was forced to employ them, as the Constitution did not authorize Congress to purchase territory. Despite this, the treaty was ratified without serious opposition except from New England, which feared the creation of new agricultural states. The Ordinance of 1787 was applied to Louisiana (1804), but the demand for self-rule from the territory's 50,000 inhabitants was so strong that they were granted an elected assembly in 1805.

II. *Exploration of Louisiana.* To investigate the resources of his acquisition, Jefferson sent several expeditions westward: 1) The *Lewis and Clark Expedition* (1804-1806) ascended the Missouri to its source, crossed the Rockies, and descended the Columbia to the Pacific. 2) Expeditions under *Zebulon M. Pike* explored the headwaters of the Mississippi (1805) and the southern Rocky Mountain country (1806).

II. DOMESTIC PROBLEMS OF THE SECOND JEFFERSONIAN ADMINISTRATION — 1805 - 1809

A. The Election of 1804

1. Triumph of Jefferson. Jefferson was so popular that he carried nearly every state, receiving 162 electoral votes. His Federalist opponent, C. C. Pinckney, had only 14 votes.

2. The Federalist Plot. Disgruntled Federalists from New England approached *Aaron Burr* of New York, who was angry at Jefferson's refusal to accept him as running mate in the election. Together they laid plans to elect Burr governor of New York, then separate that state and New England from the Union. When Alexander Hamilton heard of the plot, he threw his influence against Burr, causing his defeat. This ended the threat of secession.

B. The Burr Conspiracy

1. Duel with Hamilton. Angry at Hamilton, Burr issued a challenge to a duel. When the two met in July, 1804, Hamilton was killed. The assassination of this respected leader made Burr so unpopular that he could no longer remain in the East.

2. The Burr Expedition

a. AARON BURR'S PLANS. Burr started westward where Hamilton was so hated that his assassin could still enjoy public favor. Before doing so, he approached the English minister with a plan to separate the western states from the Union and form a new republic under British protection. Although the English government refused to listen to this plan, Burr probably still harbored treasonable designs. These were supported by several of his unscrupulous friends, including *James Wilkinson,* governor of Louisiana Territory, who was a party to the conspiracy.

b. WESTERN EXPEDITION. On reaching the West (1805), Burr began forming an expedition at the island home of *Harman Blennerhassett* on the Ohio River. When the force started down the river in flatboats (1806) only sixty men had been secured. James Wilkinson, realizing that the plot had failed, informed Jefferson of Burr's treasonable plans. Learning of this, Burr fled eastward toward Florida, but was captured and sent to Richmond to stand trial for treason.

3. The Burr Trial. Chief Justice John Marshall, who presided over the circuit court that tried Burr, was too prejudiced against Jefferson to administer justice. He found Burr not guilty of treason, holding that he had not been actually present at Blennerhassett Island when the overt act (the start of the expedition) was committed. This narrow definition of treason embarrassed the courts for many years.

III. ORIGINS OF THE WAR OF 1812

A. The Conflict Over Neutral Rights

1. The Conflict with France. Jefferson's second administration began just as England won dominance of the seas (Battle of Trafalgar, 1805), and France supremacy in Europe (Battle of Austerlitz, 1805). As neither could strike directly at the other, each tried to starve its opponent into submission. Napoleon attempted to do this by devising the *Continental System,* embodied in two decrees that would end England's trade with the continent and world: 1) the *Berlin Decree* (November, 1806) which placed the British Isles under a blockade and forbade English ships to enter ports under his control; and 2) the *Milan Decree* (December, 1807) which ruled that any neutral ship that had visited or was bound for a British port, or had been searched by a British boarding party, could be confiscated. Numerous American vessels were captured under these decrees.

2. The Conflict with England

a. INTERFERENCE WITH AMERICAN SHIPPING. In the *Essex Case* (1805), English courts reversed their decision in the *Polly Case* (see p. 102) by holding that goods could not be shipped from the French West Indies to France via the United States. Five hundred American vessels were seized under this ruling. England also issued a series of *Orders in Council* (1807) that: 1) forbade neutral trade between French ports; and 2) placed under blockade all ports occupied by France. These orders closed to Americans all trade with the continent or French colonial possessions.

b. IMPRESSMENT OF AMERICAN SEAMEN. To capture deserters from the royal navy, England searched the crews of American ships stopped on the high seas, impressing: 1) British deserters; 2) naturalized Americans who were still considered Englishmen under that nation's *doctrine of indelible allegiance;* and 3) American seamen taken by mistake. American resentment reached a climax with the *Chesapeake-Leopard Affair* (June, 1807). Four sailors were taken from the *Chesapeake,* an American warship, after that vessel had been fired on by the *Leopard.* The public reaction was so violent that Jefferson could readily have carried the country into war.

3. American Retaliation

a. THE EMBARGO ACT. Seeking to force England to respect American rights by some means short of war, Jefferson pushed through Congress the *Embargo Act* (December, 1807) which prohibited all American trade with foreign ports. Although frequently violated, the act did hurt England before that country opened new trade with South America. France, however, actually benefited, for the embargo helped Napoleon starve Britain into submission. The greatest hardship was suffered by American commercial classes, whose ships rotted at the docks. Sentiment against Jefferson mounted rapidly, especially in New England.

b. ELECTION OF 1808. *James Madison,* Jefferson's successor, was elected by a vote of 122 to 47, but New England was again solidly Federalist. To prevent that party from making further gains, the Republicans were forced to repeal the _Embargo Act_ a few days before Jefferson left office.

c. THE NONINTERCOURSE ACT. To replace the Embargo Act, Congress adopted the _Nonintercourse Act_ (March, 1809) which: 1) reopened trade with all countries save France and England; and 2) provided that if either of those countries would repeal its trade restrictions commerce would be resumed. Alarmed by this, England instructed its minister at Washington, _David Erskine_, to offer to withdraw the Orders in Council if the United States would: 1) reopen trade with Britain but not with France; 2) abide by the "Rule of 1756"; and 3) allow the royal navy to seize American ships trading with France. When Madison refused the last two conditions, Erskine omitted them from a second proposal. On the day this was accepted by Madison (June 10, 1809), 600 vessels sailed for England. News soon arrived, however, that the British had repudiated the _Erskine Agreement._ The net result was to increase Anglo-American bitterness.

d. MACON'S BILL No. 2. As the Nonintercourse Act failed to stop American vessels from trading with the belligerents, it was replaced with _Macon's Bill No. 2_ (May, 1810) which: 1) lifted all restrictions on trade; and 2) provided that if either nation would repeal its commercial decrees, the United States would restore nonintercourse with the other. It was now Napoleon's turn to be alarmed. Deciding on trickery, he sent Madison the _Cadore Letter_ in which he promised that the Berlin and Milan decrees would be repealed by November 1, 1810, "it being understood that, in consequence of this declaration, the English shall revoke their Orders in Council." As there was no chance of this, Napoleon did not intend to repeal his decrees. Madison, however, proclaimed nonintercourse against England (February, 1811).

4. English Capitulation. England was forced to back down because of: 1) protests from its merchants against loss of trade; and 2) the American demand for war that followed the victory of a United States naval vessel over a British warship, the _Little Belt_, which had tried to impress its seamen. Hence on June 16, 1812, the _Orders in Council were repealed._ The action came too late; two days later the United States declared war on England.

B.   Western Demands for War

1.   Reasons for Western Pressure

a. DEPRESSION IN THE OHIO VALLEY.   Pressure for war was strongest in the South and West.   Westerners, who suffered from a depression after 1805, believed that England's trade restrictions were responsible, even though the real cause lay in inadequate trade outlets for western goods.   They felt that a war to win freedom of the seas would restore prosperity.

b. DESIRE FOR CANADA.   Frontiersmen hoped that a war would add Canada to the Union.   This was wanted as: 1) an area for future fur-trade operations; 2) a region needed for eventual expansion of population; and 3) especially as a pawn to force England to end attacks on American shipping. Portions of an easily conquered Canada, Westerners believed, could be offered Britain in return for freedom for American vessels on the high seas.

c. INDIAN WARFARE.   A series of land-grabbing treaties negotiated by *William Henry Harrison*, governor of Indiana Territory (1800-1811) goaded the Indians into rebellion.   Their leader was a gifted chief, *Tecumseh*, who with his brother, The Prophet, welded the tribes of the Northwest into a con-

OPPOSING INFLUENCES—WAR OF 1812

Trade with belligerents

Embargo

Impressment

British incitement of Indians

"War Hawks" wanted Florida, Canada

From—"A History of Our Country" (revised edition) by Muzzey, Ginn & Co.

federation pledged to cede no more land without the consent of all. When Harrison defied the confederation by drafting another treaty with a fragment of a tribe, Tecumseh announced that war would follow if the lands were occupied. Harrison accepted the challenge by leading an army against the confederation headquarters at Prophetstown. The *Battle of Tippecanoe* (November, 1811), fought near the village, was indecisive, but Prophetstown was destroyed. From that time on war raged along the frontiers. Frontiersmen blamed this on England, holding that the Indians were armed and encouraged by officials at *Ft. Malden,* which had been built opposite Detroit. War would give them a chance to destroy this fort.

  2. The Declaration of War. In 1811 and 1812 Westerners sent to Congress aggressive young representatives known as *war hawks,* who demanded an immediate declaration of war. Their leader was *Henry Clay* of Kentucky, who boasted that Canada could be overrun by the militia of his state alone. Unable to resist their pressure, President Madison on June 1, 1812, recommended that Congress declare war on England. The vote was far from unanimous; Federalists and commercial representatives were opposed, while many Republicans hesitated to side with the despotic Napoleon. Votes from the South and West carried the day, however, and on *June 18, 1812, war was declared.*

IV. THE WAR OF 1812

A. The Election of 1812. The election served as a mandate on the war. *Madison* and DeWitt Clinton, the Federalist candidate, divided the votes of the eastern states, Madison receiving 90 and Clinton 89. The five western states gave all their votes to Madison and war. He was re-elected by a vote of 128 to 89.

B. Lack of Preparations for War

  1. Inadequacy of the Army. Enlistments in the army of 35,000 men authorized by Congress were so few that principal dependence was placed on state militiamen, who numbered 10,000. At no time during the war were more than 35,000 in service. To make matters worse, militiamen refused to leave their native states, while the generals were incompetent.

2. Lack of Financial Support. The United States depended for most of its revenue on tariffs, which yielded little before or during the war. An excise tax and stamp act also proved inadequate, forcing the government to depend on borrowing. Even this proved difficult, as the wealthiest men were opposed to the conflict. New England especially contributed little to "Mr. Madison's War."

C. Military Campaigns of 1812

1. The Attack on Canada. Despite its weakness, the United States counted on the easy conquest of Canada. Three attacks were launched in 1812.

a. THE ATTACK FROM DETROIT. No sooner had General *William Hull* crossed the Detroit River with his army of 1500 men than a small British detachment landed at the western end of Lake Erie to cut his supply lines to Ohio. The cautious commander retreated to Detroit, where efforts to reopen communication with Ohio failed. Fearing an attack from Tecumseh's Indians, who had joined the British at Ft. Malden, Hull surrendered his army (August, 1812). At the same time Ft. Mackinac in upper Michigan and Ft. Dearborn in Illinois fell to the enemy.

b. THE ATTACK FROM NIAGARA. American regulars successfully crossed the Niagara River and captured *Queenstown* (October, 1812), but when New York militiamen refused to follow, they were forced to withdraw.

c. THE LAKE CHAMPLAIN ATTACK. General Henry Dearborn, who commanded the largest army, delayed his march northward along Lake Champlain until November, 1812. When he reached the Canadian border his militiamen refused to cross into foreign territory, forcing him to return.

2. The War on the Seas. Although the navy of sixteen ships was outnumbered ten to one, several brilliant victories were recorded. Among these were the triumph of the *Constitution* over the *Guerrière* (August, 1812), the *Wasp* over the *Frolic* (October, 1812); the *United States* over the *Macedonian* (October, 1812), and the *Constitution* over the *Java* (December, 1812), in which it won its nickname of "Old Ironsides." With the spring of 1813, however, the weight of

British numbers turned the tide. By summer nearly all American vessels had been chased into port save the _Constitution_, which roamed the seas for the rest of the war.

D. Campaigns of 1813 and 1814

1. The Invasion of Canada

a. THE CAPTURE OF FT. MALDEN. _William Henry Harrison_, who succeeded General Hull in the western command, realized that Canada could not be invaded until Lake Erie was under American control. A fleet built during the winter of 1812-1813 under the command of _Oliver Hazard Perry_ accomplished this at the _Battle of Lake Erie_ (September, 1813). Harrison then ferried his army across lower Lake Erie, landing a few miles below Ft. Malden. The British commander burned the fort and fled eastward, pursued by the Americans. The two forces met at the important _Battle of the Thames_ (October, 1813) which ended in the defeat of the English and the death of Tecumseh.

b. THE WAR ON LAKE ONTARIO. Toronto, the capital of Upper Canada, was captured by a force under General Dearborn (April, 1813) but soon abandoned, as the British retained control of Lake Ontario. An expedition against Montreal under James Wilkinson failed, as did further attempts to invade Canada through Niagara. In the last of these (June-July, 1814), an American army under General Jacob Brown defeated superior British forces at the battles of Chippewa and Lundy's Lane, but was forced to retreat when reinforcements arrived.

2. Defeat of the Southern Indians.

When the Creek Indians went on the warpath (1813), a frontier army under _Andrew Jackson_ of Tennessee invaded their territory, inflicting a decisive defeat at the _Battle of Horse Shoe Bend_ (March, 1814). This defeat, combined with that at the Battle of the Thames, broke the power and spirit of the Indians. Jackson was able to force the humiliating Treaty of Ft. Jackson on the Creeks (August, 1814), in which they ceded their choicest lands to the United States.

3. The British Offensive, 1814

a. BATTLE FOR LAKE CHAMPLAIN. With Napoleon defeated in Europe, England planned three large-scale attacks against the United States. One army of 11,000 men was sent south along Lake Champlain to isolate the New England states. Although outnumbering their opponents five to one, the British knew that they could not supply their army without naval control of Lake Champlain. An attempt to win this failed when an outnumbered American squadron under Captain Thomas McDonough defeated their fleet at the *Battle of Lake Champlain* (September, 1814). This forced the British army to retire to Canada.

b. THE ATTACK ON WASHINGTON. A second English army landed on Chesapeake Bay near Washington, then marched on the city, overpowering an American force on the way (August, 1814). After burning the government buildings, the British advanced on Baltimore. When an attack on that city failed, they withdrew by sea.

c. THE ATTACK ON NEW ORLEANS. A third force of 10,000 troops under Sir Edward Pakenham landed near New Orleans late in 1814. *Andrew Jackson,* who had been delegated to defend the city, met the invaders at the *Battle of New Orleans* (January, 1815), which cost the British 2000 dead, and the Americans only 13. The battle made Jackson the hero of the West.

E. New England's Opposition to the War

1. Reasons for Opposition. New England's commercial classes opposed the war from the beginning, but opposition did not reach a climax until 1814 when the British blockade was extended to that region. With its trade stagnating, the section's opposition reached near-treasonable heights.

2. The Hartford Convention. Representatives from the New England states met at Hartford (December, 1814) to voice this opposition. Following the pattern of the Virginia and Kentucky Resolutions, they declared that any state had the right to oppose congressional action believed to violate the Constitution. Thus was the *doctrine of states' rights* used by the Federalist minority against Republicans, as it had been by the Republican minority against Federalists. The delegates also recommended several Constitutional amendments to Congress: 1) limiting the power of Congress to make war, admit new states, and impose embargoes; 2) restricting presidents to one term and preventing successive presidents from being elected from the same state; and 3) abrogating the "three-fifths" clause of the Constitution so that Negroes would not be counted in apportioning representation in Congress.

F. The Treaty of Ghent

1. The Peace Delegations. As England's ablest diplomats were busy reshaping the continent at Vienna, subordinates were sent to Ghent to conclude the American peace. On the other hand the United States was represented by a skilled delegation, led by *John Quincy Adams, Albert Gallatin,* and *Henry Clay*. The superiority of these delegates gave them an advantage when negotiations began on August 14, 1814.

2. The Opposing Demands

a. THE BRITISH DEMANDS. In a virtual ultimatum, England demanded that the United States: 1) cede the Northwest Posts and portions of Maine; 2) erect the region north of the Ohio into a perpetual Indian buffer state; 3) allow Canadians the free right to navigate the Mississippi River and Great Lakes; 4) recognize the British interpretation of maritime law; and 5) relinquish the right to fish in Canadian waters.

b. THE AMERICAN DEMANDS. The American delegation was instructed to secure: 1) recognition of their country's interpretation of maritime law; 2) indemnity for ships illegally taken by England; 3) the cession of all or part of Canada; and 4) the exclusion of Canadians from the Great Lakes.

c. THE ENGLISH RETREAT. As compromise was obviously necessary, the American delegates agreed to accept England's contentions on maritime law if that nation would back down on its other demands. The British agents eventually agreed to this because: 1) the English people were tired of war; 2) the defeat of their army at Lake Champlain convinced them that complete conquest would be costly; and 3) the Duke of Wellington advised them that the United States could be subdued only by winning control of the Great Lakes, a long and expensive process.

3. Terms of the Treaty. The *Treaty of Ghent* (December, 1814) provided for the mutual restoration of all conquests, and made no mention of maritime rights or other issues for which the United States had gone to war. It also created several commissions to settle minor points at issue. 1) A _Commercial Convention_ (July, 1815) allowed American ships to trade in all parts of the empire but the West Indies. 2) The _Rush-Bagot Agreement_ (April, 1818) provided for the disarmament of the Great Lakes, laying the basis for the unfortified boundary of today. 3) A _Fisheries Convention_ (October, 1818) "acknowledged" the right of Americans to fish in Canadian waters. 4) A _Boundaries Convention_ (October, 1818) adopted the 49th parallel as the Canadian-American boundary between the Great Lakes and the Rocky Mountains.

V. ENDURING RESULTS OF THE WAR OF 1812

A. Influence of the War on the West. Technically the War of 1812 ended in defeat for the United States; the objects for which war was declared were not attained. Actually the nation benefited greatly. The West gained especially as: 1) the decisive defeats inflicted on the Indians of the Northwest and Southwest at the battles of the Thames and Horse Shoe Bend assured peace on the frontier for a generation; and 2) the amicable settlement of differences with England also contributed to lasting tranquillity on the frontier.

B. Influence of the War on the East. The failure of the United States to win adoption of its interpretation of maritime law proved unimportant, as Europe remained at peace for the rest of the century. During the Civil War, when England was a neutral, the Union benefited from the British interpretation of international law implicitly accepted in the Treaty of Ghent.

C. Influence of the War on Europe. The war allowed the United States to enter upon a long period of uninterrupted development by: 1) convincing Europe that it was no longer a third-rate power whose interests could be ignored; and 2) initiating a period of peace on the continent which lessened the temptation of other powers to meddle in American affairs. For the remainder of the nineteenth century the American people could occupy themselves with the conquest of their own continent.

ADDITIONAL READING

An interpretive survey of this period is in C. M. Wiltse, *The New Nation: 1800-1845* (1965). N. E. Cunningham, *The Jeffersonian Republicans in Power* (1963) emphasizes administrative history, and should be supplemented by biographical studies of Jefferson, the most thorough of which is Dumas Malone, *Jefferson and His Time* (1948-   ), and the most readable C. G. Bowers, *Jefferson in Power* (1936). The period is also expertly surveyed in Irving Brant, *James Madison: Secretary of State, 1800-1809* (1953), and *James Madison: Commander in Chief* (1961). Jefferson's conflicts with the Supreme Court are briefly described in E. S. Corwin, *John Marshall and the Constitution* (1919), and his Louisiana Purchase in A. P. Whitaker, *The Mississippi Question* (1934). The latest book on the exploration of the purchase is R. H. Dillon, *Meriweather Lewis* (1965). Conflicting interpretations of the causes of the War of 1812 are in J. W. Pratt, *Expansionist of 1912* (1925), A. L. Burt, *The United States, Great Britain, and British North America* (1940), Bradford Perkins, *Prologue to War* (1961), Reginald Horsman, *The Causes of the War of 1812* (1962), and R. H. Brown, *The Republic in Peril: 1812* (1964). On the war itself see F. F. Beirne, *The War of 1812* (1949), and P. C. T. White, *A Nation on Trial* (1965). The diplomacy of the war and peace is explored in S. F. Bemis, *John Quincy Adams and the Foundations of American Foreign Policy* (1949), and Bradford Perkins, *Castlereagh and Adams: England and the United States, 1812-1823* (1965). G. G. Van Deusen, *The Life of Henry Clay* (1937) is the best biography of one of the peacemakers.

Chapter VIII

Life and Thought
During the Revolutionary Era

⟨ NATIONALISM AND CONSERVATISM

Between the beginning of the Revolution and the close of the War of 1812 two forces shaped the lives and thought of the American people. One was an intense nationalism; swept along on a mounting tide of patriotism, they sought to write books, paint pictures, design buildings, and even worship God in a distinctly American way. The other was a deep-seated belief in democracy. So persistent was this faith that even during the Federalist period, when the political pendulum swung to the right, the people were busily engaged in recasting their religious institutions, legal theories, and economic practices along more liberal lines. Eventually democratic excesses induced a reaction. As Jefferson entered the White House to inaugurate an era of political liberalism, conservatism again captured control of the popular mind. The period between 1800 and 1815 was one of patrician direction of American life and thought.

I. THE PEOPLE OF REVOLUTIONARY AMERICA

A. Nature of the Population

1. Growth of Population. The population increased from 4,000,000 in 1790 to 9,000,000 in 1815. This rapid growth was not due to immigration, for war-torn Europe sent less than

4000 aliens to the United States yearly. Responsible instead was: 1) a high birth rate normal in a land of great opportunity; and 2) the gradual lowering of the death rate through the introduction of such medical discoveries as *vaccination* (1800). Epidemics of yellow fever still took a terrible toll of the urban population, despite sanitary reforms urged by Dr. *Benjamin Rush* of Philadelphia, the country's leading physician.

2. Distribution of Population. At the close of the Revolution settlement was confined to the region east of the Appalachians, save for a handful of pioneers in Kentucky and Tennessee. During the next three decades these two states were filled with migrating Southerners, while come-outers from New England and the Middle States settled western New York and the eastern Ohio Valley. In 1815, however, most of Indiana, Illinois, Michigan, and Wisconsin were still unoccupied, as were western Georgia, Alabama, and Mississippi.

B. Economic Activities of the People

1. Emphasis on Agriculture. Nine-tenths of the people were still farmers in 1815. Even town dwellers lived in a rural atmosphere, as the principal function of villages was to supply surrounding areas. Farming methods remained crude, with little use of crop rotation, fertilization, or improved machinery. This was because markets were limited by: 1) poor transportation facilities between the interior and seaboard; and 2) the disruption of foreign trade by wars in Europe. Not until after 1815 did expanding markets encourage farmers to increase production.

2. Beginnings of Urbanization. An urban trend, later to become most important, was barely discernible. Philadelphia's population increased from 40,000 to 110,000 (1790-1820), and New York's from 30,000 to 120,000. Other cities and towns grew in proportion, especially in southern New England.

3. The Professions. The ministry remained the principal profession, followed by law. Most lawyers were self-trained; the first law school (at Harvard) was not established until 1817. Doctors were similarly poorly prepared, although medical schools multiplied. Bloodletting and purging remained the principal remedies for all ills.

II. THE CULT OF NATIONALISM IN LITERATURE AND THE ARTS

A. Growth of a Cult of Nationalism

1. Domestic Influences. The intense national pride that shaped the character of American cultural efforts was due to: 1) the decline of provincialism during the Revolution as troop movements made the people aware of the vastness and wealth of their land; 2) popular pride in military and naval victories won during the Revolution and War of 1812; 3) a conscious desire to develop a culture worthy of the new republic; and 4) an effort to sever cultural ties with now-hated England.

2. Foreign Influences. The achievement of cultural independence was made easier as: 1) the opening of commercial and diplomatic relations with other countries allowed Americans to become familiar with non-English modes of life and thought; and 2) the French Revolution was so popular in the United States that the people adopted the thought patterns and customs of France to replace those of England.

B. Patriotism in Literature

1. Growth of the American Language. Patriots who resented having to use even the language of England seriously proposed substituting German or Hebrew. A more practical reformer who acted under this same impulse was *Noah Webster*, a Connecticut educator and editor. Recognizing that a distinct American idiom had developed in the oral form, he produced a number of spelling books and dictionaries designed to incorporate these changes in the written language. By this he hoped to: 1) encourage authors to employ the native idiom in books about America; 2) help children to learn to read so that they could become intelligent voters; and 3) discourage sectional differences by emphasizing the common language of the people. His most important work was *The American Dictionary of the English Language* (1828).

2. The Novelists

a. POPULAR NOVELISTS. Novels, which had been virtually unknown in the colonial period, increased in popularity rapidly as declining religious interests and widening secular activities lessened the social stigmas attached to fiction reading. Highly sentimental works were popular among the uneducated masses. The first American novel, William H. Brown's *The Power of Sympathy* (1789), was followed by dozens of others, including Susanna H. Rowson's *Charlotte Temple* (1790) which went through more than one hundred editions and was a best seller for generations.

b. THE BETTER WRITERS. The first novelist of note was *Charles Brockden Brown,* whose *Wieland* (1798) and other works were not only laid in America but glorified the nation's people and scenery.

3. The Poets. The *Hartford Wits,* a group of lawyers, merchants, and educators living near Hartford, Connecticut, enjoyed a fabulous reputation as poets. Best known among them were Joel Barlow, author of "The Vision of Columbus," and *Timothy Dwight,* whose long poem "Greenfield Hill" exhibited unrestrained patriotism in its descriptions of the Connecticut countryside and people. Within the same tradition were the authors of such patriotic songs as "Yankee Doodle," "Hail Columbia," and "The Star Spangled Banner." The words of the latter were written by *Francis Scott Key* during the War of 1812. The leading poet of the generation, however, was *Philip Freneau* whose inspiration was a love of democracy rather than a love of country.

4. The Historians. Historians and biographers also glorified the new republic in countless works. Among the most popular was *Mason L. Weems,* whose *Life of Washington* (1800) introduced the legend of George and the cherry tree into American folklore, and John Marshall, whose *Life of Washington* (1804-1807) devoted five volumes to proving that Washington was the father of the Federalist party.

5. Newspapers and Periodicals

a. RISE OF POLITICAL JOURNALISM. The number of newspapers published increased from 40 in 1783 to 350 in 1815. Most were weeklies, although daily papers multiplied after the appearance of the *Pennsylvania Packet* (1784). Editors were violently partisan, devoting more of their space to attacks on rival politicians than to news.

b. MAGAZINES. Magazines played little part during this generation. The only successful periodical launched at the time was the _North American Review_ (1815) which was printed in Boston.

C. The Fine Arts

**1. Patriotic Painters.** Artists, like historians, devoted themselves to glorifying their country and its leaders. Outstanding was _Gilbert Stuart,_ whose portraits of Washington and other Revolutionary heroes displayed unusual talent. John Trumbull eulogized the United States in such canvases as "The Signing of the Declaration of Independence" and "The Battle of Bunker Hill." Charles Willson Peale was only slightly less known than Stuart as a painter of contemporary patriots. Their works, which appealed to the people on patriotic grounds, helped break down prejudices against painting.

2. Classical Influences in Architecture

a. THE ROMAN REVIVAL. Architects utilized classical forms because: 1) they wished to identify their country with the republics of the ancient world; and 2) they were influenced by a classical revival then sweeping Europe. At first Roman examples were imitated by such architects as _Thomas Jefferson_ who designed the capital building at Richmond (1789) and the campus of the University of Virginia (1818). In the North _Charles Bulfinch_ employed modified Roman forms in numerous buildings, including the Massachusetts State House in Boston. These influences also predominated in the new capital city of Washington, which was planned by a notable French architect, Major Pierre l'Enfant.

b. THE GREEK REVIVAL. In the 1820's builders turned to ancient Greece as their inspiration because: 1) a Greek revival in Europe centered attention on this style; and 2) Americans were watching with approval the course of the Greek struggle for independence from Turkey. _Benjamin Latrobe_ was the leading architect of this school.

**3. Music and Drama.** Little progress was made in these two fields of culture. Singing societies continued to multiply, but few other opportunities for musical enjoyment existed. Theaters, which had long been frowned on as immoral time wasters, were introduced in eastern cities, but remained unpopular. The leading playwright was *William Dunlap,* whose patriotic dramas attracted such favorable interest that some of the prejudice against the theater diminished.

III. EXPANSION OF THE ENLIGHTENMENT
1776 - 1800

A. Reasons for Expansion

1. *Continuing Impact of the European Enlightenment*
Philosophers of the European Enlightenment had long taught that man: 1) should rebel against excessive authority; 2) was entitled to certain natural rights; and 3) could better himself by improving the environment in which he lived. As these concepts were the very ones used to justify the Revolution, they gained great popularity in the United States.

2. *Changes in the Class Structure.*   The conservative upper class, which had opposed the liberalism of the Enlightenment in both Europe and America, was driven from the United States by the *exodus of the Tories* during the Revolution. With the conservative influence thus diminished, the people were unrestrained in their efforts to secure political, social, and economic democracy.

3. *The French Revolution.*   As the French Revolution was based on the same theory of natural rights that inspired the American Revolution, the American people were encouraged to make even greater efforts in their struggle for liberty and equality, knowing that men elsewhere were rebelling to secure these ends.

B. Trend Toward Religious Liberalism

1. *Rise of the Cult of Deism*
   a. THE EUROPEAN BACKGROUND. European scholars, who had been taught by the Enlightenment to question all past authorities, subjected religion to a rational scrutiny during the eighteenth century. As a result they rejected the Biblical story of the creation, miracles, the sacraments, the doctrine of salvation by grace, and the concept of a personal God who constantly intervened in the universe. Those who held these beliefs were known as *deists.* They believed in God as a benevolent Creator who allowed the universe to operate by natural laws.

Prominent among European deists were Rousseau and Voltaire in France, and Lord Bolingbroke in England.

b. BEGINNINGS OF AMERICAN DEISM. Deism gained little popularity in America until the Revolution when: 1) French ideas were popularized by the military alliance with that country; and 2) officers from France helped spread the belief among American soldiers. By the close of the war many prominent men were deists, including Benjamin Franklin and Thomas Jefferson. During this phase only a few leaders succumbed; the great mass of the people still embraced orthodoxy.

c. POPULARIZATION OF DEISM. During the postwar years, deism became a fad among the masses, reaching the height of its influence in the 1790's. This was because: 1) many believed that religious orthodoxy was a tool of the few to oppress the many; 2) the propaganda of such writers as Ethan Allen who wrote *Reason the Only Oracle of Man* (1784) and *Thomas Paine,* the author of *The Age of Reason* (1794) won thousands of converts; and 3) the efforts of *Elihu Palmer* who organized deistical societies in many cities helped popularize the movement. So popular was deism for a time that orthodox religion seemed seriously threatened.

2. Growth of Liberal Sects

a. UNIVERSALISM AND UNITARIANISM. Many intelligent men refused to embrace deism because of its lower-class nature, yet were unwilling to worship in existing churches. Two liberal sects sprang up to meet their needs: 1) The *Universalist Church,* organized at Gloucester, Massachusetts (1779) by the Reverend *John Murray,* rejected the divinity of Christ and the belief in human depravity, emphasizing instead the fatherhood of God, the brotherhood of man, and universal salvation. 2) The *Unitarian Church,* formed at Boston (1785) by the Reverend *James Freeman,* stressed freedom of conscience, the discovery of God through reason, and the universal salvation of man.

b. CONFLICTS WITH ORTHODOXY. The new sects, and especially Unitarianism, gained converts rapidly during the 1790's, although their influence was largely confined to New England. By the end of the century Congregationalism seemed near extinction in eastern Massachusetts. Harvard University was lost to orthodoxy when Henry Ware, a Unitarian, was named professor of divinity (1805).

3. Separation of Church and State

a. RELIGIOUS DISESTABLISHMENT. At the beginning of the Revolution the Anglican Church was established south of Maryland and the Congregational in New England. This undemocratic system, which forced nonmembers to support a church in which they did not worship, was first attacked in Virginia where a long struggle led by *Thomas Jefferson* culminated in the adoption of a *Statute of Religious Liberty* (1786) granting complete religious freedom to all people. Virginia's example was imitated by other southern states, but the Congregational Church was supported by the state until Connecticut (1818) and Massachusetts (1833) finally accepted disestablishment.

b. ORGANIZATION OF AMERICAN CHURCHES. Nationalistic Americans were offended by the close ties that united several churches with their European counterparts. The Methodist Episcopal Church of America was organized independently in 1784, the Protestant Episcopal Church of America (formerly Anglican) in 1784-1789, and the Presbyterian Church of the United States in 1785-1788. Even the Catholic Church granted American clergy the right to choose their own bishop (1788).

C. Progress in Science and Technology

1. European Contributions.

As Americans were too materialistic to concern themselves with theoretical science, the principal contributions were made by recent arrivals from Europe, including several refugees from Napoleon's tyranny. Best known was Dr. *Joseph Priestley,* a brilliant English chemist whose Philadelphia laboratory helped inspire American scientists. The emphasis on practical matters was shown by Nathaniel Bowditch, an excellent mathematician from Massachusetts, who is principally remembered for his *New American Practical Navigator* (1802), which was used by seamen for generations.

2. American Contributions

a. THE NATURAL SCIENCES. Because of their interest in agriculture, Americans were more concerned with the natural than the physical sciences. *Thomas Jefferson* in his *Notes on*

Virginia (1782) made a notable contribution, as did _Jedidiah Morse,_ the "father of American Geography," who published numerous geography books after 1784.

b. TECHNOLOGICAL ADVANCES. The practical-minded Americans of this generation made their most important contributions in the field of invention. John Fitch perfected the _steamboat_ (1790) although no workable vessel was constructed until 1807 when _Robert Fulton_ navigated _The Clermont_ on the Hudson River. Oliver Evans revolutionized the design of grist mills by employing laborsaving machinery. _Eli Whitney_ not only invented the _cotton gin_ (1793) but first employed the _principle of interchangeable parts_ which made possible the rise of mass-production industries.

D. The Humanitarian Crusade

1. Progress in Education

a. EFFECT OF THE REVOLUTION ON EDUCATION. Most schools closed their doors during the war, but the Revolution gave a new incentive to education as soon as peace was restored; now the people must be educated to the point where they could vote intelligently. A plan devised by _Thomas Jefferson_ for the free education of all Virginia children (1779) was not adopted, but reformers made some progress in founding new schools.

b. THE SCHOOL SYSTEM.

I. _Primary Schools._ Outside of New England, primary schools remained in the hands of churches or charitable societies. Innovations of this period included: 1) the founding of Sunday schools (1791) to provide secular and religious training for poorer children who worked during the week; 2) the use of the _Lancasterian system_ of instruction through which brighter pupils were taught a lesson, then transmitted their knowledge to other children; and 3) the introduction of American text books, including spellers by Noah Webster and geographies by Jedidiah Morse.

II. _Secondary Education._ Latin grammar schools, which emphasized classical training, were replaced by private or church-supported _academies_ where instruction was provided in English, history, geography, surveying, and other practical subjects. The first *high school* was opened in Boston (1821), but these schools did not become popular until after the Civil War.

III. *College Education.* Nearly all the thirty colleges founded before 1815 were denominational. Classical training was still emphasized, although the sciences and modern languages were studied. The outstanding science teacher of the generation was Benjamin Silliman of Yale University.

2. Protection for the Common People

a. JUSTICE FOR LAWBREAKERS.

I. *Reform of the Criminal Law*. The harsh criminal codes of colonial times failed to distinguish between minor and major crimes; in some states twenty-seven crimes were punishable by execution, while branding, mutilation, and flogging were common. These cruel laws, which discriminated against the poor, were first attacked by *Thomas Jefferson.* His revised criminal code for Virginia (1796) restricted the death penalty to murder and treason, and for other offenses adjusted the severity of punishment to the seriousness of the crime.

II. *Prison Reform.* An important English book, John Howard's *State of the Prisons in England and Wales* (1777) helped show American humanitarians that prisons were breeding grounds for crime rather than institutions to reform lawbreakers. Their efforts resulted in state laws separating hardened criminals from first offenders, segregating the sexes, and otherwise improving jails. Pennsylvania led in this crusade.

III. *Attack on Debtors' Prisons.* Colonial laws allowed a debtor to be imprisoned until he could meet his obligations. Reformers attacked this system, but accomplished little save the passage of laws separating debtors from ordinary criminals.

b. RISE OF THE ANTISLAVERY MOVEMENT.

I. *Attempt to End the Slave Trade*. Within ten years after independence all the states save Georgia had followed the example of Delaware (1776) by forbidding or severely restricting the importation of slaves.

II. *Efforts Toward Emancipation*. Freeing slaves already in bondage proved more difficult except in the northern states where few were held. *Vermont* (1777) prohibited slavery in its first constitution, while in Massachusetts a court decision

(1781) also banned the institution. Other New England states followed these examples. In the Middle States, Pennsylvania set a precedent by adopting *gradual emancipation* (1780) ; further importations were forbidden, while children born in slavery were freed on reaching maturity. In the South economic and social problems involved prevented any action, although all Southerners agreed that slavery was an evil.

c. CHANGES IN INHERITANCE LAWS. Inheritance in the southern states was governed by : 1) *primogeniture* which granted the entire estate of a man dying without a will to his eldest son ; and 2) *entail* which allowed the line of descent for an estate to be regulated for several generations. The attack on these aristocratic measures was led by *Thomas Jefferson* who persuaded the Virginia legislature to abolish entails in 1776 and primogeniture in 1785. Other states followed before 1800.

IV. THE CONSERVATIVE REACTION — 1800 - 1815

A. The Counterreformation in Religion

1. The Reaction Against Liberalism. By 1800 a reaction against the liberalism of the Revolutionary era had begun because : 1) democratic excesses helped convince conservatives that the people were not fit to manage their own affairs ; and 2) a new upper class had risen to replace the loyalists. These conservatives viewed religious orthodoxy as an effective weapon, believing that a respect for religion would restore a respect for authority among the people. With the help of churchmen, they launched an effective counterattack on deism and liberalism.

2. The Great Revival of 1800

a. RELIGION IN THE WEST. The revival of orthodoxy began in the West, where the churches faced the problem of keeping pace with a rapidly expanding population. To meet the problem the newer churches that were less bound by tradition—Methodist, Baptist, and Presbyterian—adopted two new devices that helped launch a religious revival : 1) *circuit riding* (sending a minister on horseback over a regular circuit to preach to the people) ; and 2) the *camp meeting* (an extended outdoor gathering of many people to listen to preaching). Especially influential in establishing these practices was the Reverend *Francis Asbury*, bishop of the Methodist Church.

b. THE CUMBERLAND REVIVAL. Between 1800 and 1803 hundreds of camp meetings were held in the West, one of them (the Cain Ridge Camp Meeting, Kentucky) attracting 25,000 worshippers. The intense emotionalism of these meetings drove those attending to strange physical actions; some fell unconscious, others jerked uncontrollably, barked like dogs, or uttered the "holy laugh." .These "manifestations of divine power" won so many converts that sin vanished from Kentucky and Tennessee, while the whole western country was gripped by the revival spirit.

c. RESULTS OF THE GREAT REVIVAL. The emotionalism of the revival soon died out, but its results were apparent for many years: 1) religious interest remained strong for another generation; 2) Methodist and Baptist churches won so many supporters that they became the leading Protestant sects in the West; and 3) the Presbyterian Church was torn by schisms as conservative eastern theologians objected to the emotional methods employed to win converts; these conflicts led to the formation of the Disciples of Christ and the Christian Church.

3. The Counterreformation in the East

a. REVIVAL OF ORTHODOXY. Stirred by events in the West, eastern ministers renewed their campaign for orthodoxy so effectively that deism died out, church membership increased, and the liberal sects found themselves on the defensive. In New England Congregationalism and Presbyterianism made such gains that Unitarianism was confined to eastern Massachusetts. Even there it was under attack after the orthodox established Andover Theological Seminary (1808) to train clergy in their beliefs.

b. ATTEMPTS TO PERPETUATE ORTHODOXY. Ministers sought to prevent future backsliding by founding societies that would continue to propagate orthodoxy: 1) the American Bible Society (1816) designed to provide every American with a free Bible; 2) the American Tract Society (1825); and 3) the American Home Missionary Society (1826). The American Board of Commissioners for Foreign Missions (1810) was the first of several societies to spread Christianity among the heathen.

B. Conservative Influences in Education

1. Failure to Establish State-Supported Schools. Despite Thomas Jefferson's belief in the improvability of man, the

Jeffersonians made no attempt to found state-supported schools. Instead education after 1800 was increasingly entrusted to *"school societies"* such as the New York Free School Society (1805), which received some state funds but existed largely through charitable contributions. This suggested a distrust of popular government, as no attempt was made to train the people for self-rule.

2. Founding of State Universities. Public funds were used to found five state universities before 1815, indicating a desire to train leaders for the people rather than the people themselves. In addition efforts were made to take over existing private colleges as state-owned schools. Columbia and Pennsylvania were brought under partial state control before the movement was checked by the decision of Chief Justice John Marshall in *Dartmouth College v. Woodward* (1819). The court held that a college charter was a contract which could not be impaired. After this the states were forced to found their own colleges; the number established after 1819 increased rapidly. Outstanding among these was the *University of Virginia*, largely because its advanced curriculum was planned by *Thomas Jefferson.*

V. THE IMPACT OF CULTURAL NATIONALISM AND THE ENLIGHTENMENT

A. The Influence of Cultural Nationalism

1. Stimulus to American Culture. Nationalism greatly stimulated cultural progress. This was because: 1) people who read books or admired paintings for patriotic reasons were introduced to the arts sooner than would have been the case without this impulse; and 2) forms of expression previously considered immoral or wasteful of time (the theater or novel reading) became respectable when they glorified the United States. The audience created in this way was responsible for the cultural advances made by the next generation.

2. Efforts Toward Cultural Independence. American writers and artists did not achieve cultural independence; writing, music, art, and other forms of expression remained essentially European. Yet the emphasis on nationalism hurried the future break with past tradition.

B. The Persistence of the Enlightenment. The conservative gains made during the Counterreformation were temporary. The return to cultural and political liberalism came during Jackson's presidency when reforms demanded by philosophers of the Enlightenment were finally achieved. Before this time, however, the conservatism exhibited by the patrician direction of thought was to find political expression in the Era of Nationalism.

ADDITIONAL READING

An excellent general survey is R. B. Nye, *The Cultural Life of the New Nation, 1776-1830* (1960); in greater detail and with emphasis on cultural rather than intellectual history are E. B. Greene, *The Revolutionary Generation* (1943), and J. A. Krout and D. R. Fox, *The Completion of Independence* (1940), which together span the period 1776-1830. An important study of scientific progress is Brooke Hindle, *The Pursuit of Science in Revolutionary America* (1956), a subject also explored in Daniel Boorstin, *The Lost World of Thomas Jefferson* (1948). Biographies of outstanding scientists include: E. T. Martin, *Thomas Jefferson: Scientist* (1952), I. B. Cohen, *Benjamin Franklin* (1953), and Ernest Earnest, *John and William Bartram* (1940). Religious thought is surveyed in W. W. Sweet, *Religion in the Development of American Culture, 1765-1840* (1952), and the revivalistic aspects of religion in C. R. Keller, *The Second Great Awakening in Connecticut* (1942), and C. A. Johnson, *The Frontier Camp Meeting* (1955). H. M. Morais, *Deism in Eighteenth Century America* (1934) describes the anti-religious tendencies that inspired the Great Revival of 1800. The best study of literary nationalism is B. T. Spencer, *The Quest for Nationality* (1957), but Van Wyck Brooks, *The World of Washington Irving* (1944) should be read by those seeking to recapture the literary flavor of the period. Artistic progress is described against its social background in O. W. Larkin, *Art and Life in America* (1949), and E. P. Richardson, *Painting in America* (1956).

Chapter IX

The Era of Nationalism
1815-1828

❰ NATIONALISM AND CONSERVATISM IN POLITICS

For a generation after the War of 1812 the ideas and practices of the Jeffersonians who occupied the White House were more nearly akin to those of Hamilton than to those of Jefferson; they increased the powers of the national government at the expense of the states, fostered unrestrained individual enterprise, and erected barriers to keep out foreign goods and ideas. This Federalist system was acceptable to the people only because limitless opportunities seemed to await every American. With national unity achieved, a balance established between liberty and order, a virgin continent awaiting exploitation, and a peaceful Europe willing to allow Americans to develop their resources without interference, a conservative political philosophy seemed more acceptable than at any time since the new nation's founding. This conservatism, combined with pride in the country that made such opportunity possible, were the twin forces that dominated politics until the election of Andrew Jackson to the presidency.

I. THE GROWTH OF NATIONALISM

A. Psychological Basis for Nationalism

1. European Influences. The close of the Napoleonic wars launched a period of conservatism and nationalism in

Europe. Reactionary leaders such as Austria's _Prince Metternich,_ capitalizing on the postwar lethargy of the people, prodded rulers into retracting most of the liberal reforms that had been granted since the French Revolution. This wave of reaction greatly affected the United States.

2. Domestic Influences. Nationalism was intensified by: 1) popular pride in the military victories of the War of 1812, especially those on the sea and at New Orleans; and 2) the usual postwar reaction which inclined the people, grown tired of sacrifice, to concentrate on their own problems rather than those of society.

B. Economic Basis for Nationalism

1. Beginnings of Sectional Specialization

a. INDUSTRIALIZATION OF THE NORTHEAST. Although the first textile factory in America had been built as early as 1790 by _Samuel Slater_ at Pawtucket, Rhode Island, industrialization did not spread until the Embargo Act and the War of 1812 cut off imports from Europe. After that time factories increased rapidly, especially in New England, New York, and Pennsylvania. This concentration was due to the presence in the Northeast of: 1) adequate _water power_ provided by the many small streams of the region; 2) _capital_ accumulated by commercial ventures; and 3) a more plentiful _labor supply_ than existed elsewhere. At first workers were women and children who took jobs to supplement meager farm incomes, but after the 1820's, when improved transportation brought New England agriculture into competition with that of the West, thousands of farmers left their sterile fields to work in mills. Within the Northeast, textile manufacturing was centered in New England while Pennsylvania led in the production of iron and iron goods.

b. PLANTATION AGRICULTURE IN THE SOUTH. The invention of the _cotton gin_ by Eli Whitney (1793) allowed cotton growing to spread over the lower South, especially after the crushing of southern Indians during the War of 1812 opened western Georgia, Alabama, and Mississippi to farmers. As cotton could be grown with slave labor, the plantation system expanded rapidly over those states. Increasingly the South became dependent on this one crop for export purposes.

c. DIVERSIFIED FARMING IN THE WEST. Small farming continued to predominate in the West, but as improved transportation facilities allowed the marketing of surpluses, a tendency toward specialization began to appear. Wheat was grown in the northern portions, corn and livestock in the Ohio Valley, and tobacco in Kentucky. As farmers became dependent on sales at distant markets they lost much of their provincialism.

2. Improvements in Transportation

a. THE DEMAND FOR IMPROVED TRANSPORTATION. Sectional specialization stimulated a demand for better roads and canals. The Northeast needed southern cotton for its textile mills and western food for its workers. The South and West required manufactured goods from the Northeast, while the South also demanded food from the West. Internal improvements would allow development of an *internal trade* that would unite the sections and bring prosperity to all.

b. THE TURNPIKE ERA. Between 1800 and 1825 hundreds of turnpike companies constructed paved toll roads between eastern cities. More ambitious was the *Cumberland Road* built by the national government between Cumberland, Maryland, and Wheeling, West Virginia (1811-1818). When completed, this allowed wagon transportation between the seaboard and the Ohio River. It was later extended to Columbus, Ohio (1833), and to St. Louis.

c. THE CANAL ERA. To meet the demand for cheaper freight transportation, the state of New York constructed the *Erie Canal* (1825) between the Hudson River and Lake Erie. This proved so successful that other eastern states attempted to tap the interior waterways. The *Pennsylvania Canal System* (1825-1835) united Philadelphia and Pittsburgh with an elaborate system of canals and inclined planes, while Maryland chartered both the *Chesapeake and Ohio Canal* and the *Baltimore and Ohio Railroad* (1828) to build toward the Ohio River. The former was never completed, while the railroad did not reach the Ohio until 1852.

d. THE STEAMBOAT. Steamboat transportation spread rapidly, especially in the West, where the first vessel was launched on the Ohio River in 1811. Although steamboats were still in their infancy, they were improved so steadily that by 1830 they carried much of the commerce between West and South along the Mississippi River.

C. Social Basis for Nationalism

1. The Great Migration to the West. As frontiersmen were the most nationalistic of all Americans, the rapid expansion of the frontier after 1815 stimulated the growth of nationalism. Migration westward at this time was greater than ever before. This was due to: 1) the damming up of the population by Indian wars for a generation before 1815; 2) the favorable land system that allowed pioneers to purchase farms on credit; 3) the opening of Indian lands following the defeats inflicted at the battles of the Thames and Horse Shoe Bend; 4) the postwar prosperity; and 5) improved transportation routes that assured markets for western produce.

2. Course of the Great Migration

a. OCCUPATION OF THE NORTHWEST. Until 1825 most new settlers came from the South to fill the southern portions of Indiana and Illinois. At the same time a smaller migration from New England peopled the Western Reserve region of Ohio. After the completion of the *Erie Canal* (1825) come-outers from New England and the Middle States moved into northern Indiana and Illinois, and into southern Michigan. Indiana (1816) and Illinois (1818) achieved statehood as a result.

b. OCCUPATION OF THE SOUTHWEST. Western Georgia, Alabama, and Mississippi were settled rapidly from the Southeast, because of the high profits available from cotton planting. Mississippi became a state in 1817, and Alabama in 1819.

D. Legal Basis for Nationalism

1. The Supreme Court and Nationalism. During this period the Supreme Court under Chief Justice *John Marshall* (1801-1835) handed down a number of important decisions that: 1) increased the powers of the national government; or 2) diminished the powers of the states. In this way Marshall sought to perpetuate Federalist principles of centralization in which he believed.

2. Strengthening the National Government

a. CASES EXPANDING THE AUTHORITY OF THE SUPREME COURT. 1) *Marbury v. Madison* (1803) gave the Court the power of *judicial review* (see p. 102). 2) *United States v. Peters* (1809) established the Court's right to coerce a state legislature, by ordering a Pennsylvania district court to carry out its judgment despite a legislative act forbidding such a step. 3) *Martin v. Hunter's Lessee* (1816) confirmed the Supreme Court's right to overrule a state court. 4) *Cohens v. Virginia* (1821) affirmed the same principle more emphatically. In this case Marshall overruled a Virginia court which had fined Cohens for selling congressional lottery tickets within the state, pointing out the dangers of a system where laws would receive as many interpretations as there were states.

b. CASES EXPANDING THE POWERS OF CONGRESS. 1) *McCulloch v. Maryland* (1819) upheld the right of Congress to charter a national bank, thus writing into national law the *doctrine of implied powers.* 2) *Gibbons v. Ogden* (1824) gave the national government undisputed control over interstate commerce by holding invalid a steamboat monopoly chartered by the state of New York.

3. Cases Weakening the States. 1) *Fletcher v. Peck* (1810) established the principle that state laws were invalid when in conflict with the Constitution. 2) *Dartmouth College v. Woodward* (1819), by forbidding the state legislature to alter the college charter, established the principle that corporation charters were contracts which could not be impaired. 3) *Martin v. Mott* (1827) denied a state the right to withhold its militia from service.

II. NATIONALISM IN POLITICS — 1816 - 1824

A. Nationalistic Legislation of 1816

1. National Defense. Despite Republican fears of a standing army, the dangers of unpreparedness had been so clearly illustrated in 1812 that Congress: 1) created a regular army of 10,000 men; 2) allotted money for several naval vessels; and 3) reorganized the West Point Military Academy on a more efficient basis.

2. The Second Bank of the United States

a. THE CURRENCY PROBLEM. After the failure of Congress to recharter the First National Bank (1811), currency needs were supplied by paper money issued by state-chartered banks. As most banks printed excessive quantities without adequate specie reserves, they were unable to withstand the financial strain of the wartime period. All banks outside of New England suspended specie payment, leaving only paper money in circulation. Business interests demanded a sound national system of finance.

b. CHARTERING THE NATIONAL BANK. A bank bill framed by a committee under *John C. Calhoun* of South Carolina (1816) provided: 1) for the chartering of the Second Bank of the United States with a capital stock of $35,000,000, one-fifth to be subscribed by the United States and the rest by private investors; 2) that the charter should run for twenty years; and 3) that the bank could establish branches throughout the country. Support for the measure came largely from the West and South, while New England, which already had adequate state banks, was opposed.

3. The Tariff of 1816.   A demand for a *protective tariff* mounted as the close of the War of 1812 allowed English manufacturers to dump such quantities of low-priced goods in the United States that the infant native industries were threatened. The resulting Tariff of 1816 imposed import duties of 25 per cent. It was supported by *John C. Calhoun* and *Henry Clay,* representing the South and West, while opposition came from *Daniel Webster,* the spokesman of New England's commercial interests. These positions were to be reversed within a few years.

4. The Bonus Bill of 1816.   Nationalists such as John C. Calhoun and Henry Clay argued that federally built *internal improvements* (roads and canals) would bind the nation together and stimulate the growth of a home market, thus helping secure economic independence from Europe. Their program was opposed by strict constructionists, who pointed out that even with a liberal use of implied powers the constitutional power of Congress to appropriate money for this purpose was doubtful. When Calhoun introduced a bill allotting the $1,500,000 bonus paid the government for its charter by the Second National Bank to the construction of internal improvements, the measure was passed by middle-state and western votes, but was vetoed by President James Madison on constitutional grounds.

B. The Era of Good Feelings

1. The Election of 1816. Madison's Secretary of State, *James Monroe*, was nominated by the Republicans. The Federalists were so discredited by their conduct during the War of 1812 that they did not bother to nominate a candidate. Monroe was elected with 183 electoral votes to 34 cast by three New England states for Rufus King of New York. Never had the nation been so united as in the "Era of Good Feelings" that followed. Monroe capitalized on this feeling by selecting strong men for his cabinet without regard to party affiliation; *John Quincy Adams* became Secretary of State, William H. Crawford Secretary of the Treasury, and *John C. Calhoun* Secretary of War.

2. The Panic of 1819

a. POSTWAR PROSPERITY. Between 1815 and 1819 a wave of prosperity swept the nation. Responsible was: 1) the continuation of the wartime boom; and 2) an inflationary expansion of the currency as state banks issued money far in excess of their reserves. This was loaned to speculators who purchased government land so recklessly that sales increased fivefold between 1815 and 1819.

b. COMING OF THE PANIC. Inflation was checked by the Second Bank of the United States which began in 1818 to accumulate notes of state banks suspected of being unsound, then presenting the notes for payment in gold. Banks thus challenged were forced to call in their loans, forcing debtors to liquidate holdings. By 1819 this practice not only stopped inflation, but sent the nation into a panic. Banks closed, business failures mounted, and prices collapsed.

c. EFFECT OF THE PANIC ON THE WEST. About one-third of the Westerners were buying land on credit under the Land Act of 1800. With declining prices they were unable to keep up payments, facing the loss of their land and improvements. Congress came to their aid with: 1) the *Land Act of 1820* which abolished credit buying but lowered the price to $1.25 an acre and the minimum amount purchasable to eighty acres;

and 2) the *Relief Act of 1821* which allowed a farmer to turn back to the government the unpaid-for portions of his land. The way in which these measures allayed western discontent illustrated the strong spirit of national unity.

3. The Controversy Over Missouri

a. APPLICATION FOR STATEHOOD. During the great westward migration after 1815 the Territory of Missouri filled rapidly with Southerners. By 1819 the 60,000 people living there were demanding statehood. A bill authorizing this was introduced in the House of Representatives that year.

b. INTRODUCTION OF THE SLAVERY QUESTION. While the act was being debated, Representative Eugene Tallmadge of New York proposed the *Tallmadge Amendment* to: 1) forbid the importation of slaves into Missouri; and 2) free the children of all slaves already there at the age of twenty-five. Southerners immediately rose in opposition, launching the nation's first debate on this important issue. They took this stand because: 1) the admission of Missouri as a free state would have upset the balance of eleven slave and eleven free states in favor of the North, giving that section control of the Senate as well as of the House; and 2) only two slave territories (Florida and Arkansas) waited admission as states, while five free territories would soon be ready for statehood. In this situation, Southerners felt that Missouri must be kept slave to maintain a political balance between North and South.

c. THE MISSOURI COMPROMISE. The Tallmadge Amendment passed the House but failed in the Senate. When Congress convened again, Maine, which had been part of Massachusetts, was ready to apply for statehood. This allowed Senator *J. B. Thomas* of Illinois to frame a compromise which provided that: 1) Maine should be admitted as a free state and Missouri as a slave state; and 2) slavery should be banned from the portions of the Louisiana Purchase lying north of 36° 30′. This was adopted and signed by the President in March, 1820.

d. THE SECOND MISSOURI COMPROMISE. Missourians adopted a constitution barring the admission of free Negroes into the state. Northerners in Congress objected so violently to this that admission was delayed until *Henry Clay* devised a second compromise providing that: 1) Missouri be admitted; and 2) the state legislature pledge itself never to deny to the citizen of any state the privileges that he enjoyed under the Constitution.

In effect this nullified the section forbidding the entrance of free Negroes.

C. Foreign Problems of the Monroe Administrations

1. The Purchase of East Florida

a. BORDER CONFLICTS IN FLORIDA. After 1808 Spain was too involved in European wars to police the Florida border, which became a center for runaway slaves, outlaws, and warlike Indians. An American expedition under General Edmund P. Gaines (1816) secured temporary relief by destroying *"Negro Fort,"* the outlaws' headquarters, but the outbreak of the *Seminole War* (1817) between the United States and the Seminole Indians of Florida soon reduced the border to a state of turmoil once more. General *Andrew Jackson,* who was assigned the task of restoring order, invaded Florida (1818) long enough to capture the Spanish towns of Pensacola and St. Marks and to execute two British subjects who had been inciting the natives. This warlike step embarrassed the Monroe administration's efforts to secure Florida peacefully, although John Quincy Adams, the Secretary of State, managed to placate Spain's feelings by restoring the two towns as soon as they could be garrisoned.

b. THE FLORIDA TREATY OF 1819. Adams finally convinced Spain that Florida should be sold to the United States. The treaty provided that: 1) Spain cede East Florida in return for $5,000,000 to be paid to American citizens who had claims against that country; and 2) the boundary between the Louisiana Purchase and Mexico begin at the Sabine River, follow the Red and Arkansas rivers westward to the Rocky Mountains, swing northward along the crest of the Rockies to the 42nd parallel, and follow this line to the Pacific. Thus Spain gave the United States her claims to the Oregon Country in return for clear title to Texas. The Spanish government's desire to prevent American recognition of the revolting Latin American colonies delayed ratification of the *Adams-Onis Treaty* until 1821.

2. The Monroe Doctrine

a. INFLUENCE OF THE LATIN-AMERICAN REVOLUTIONS.

I. *Problem of American Recognition.* Spain's Latin-American colonies revolted in 1807, and by 1821 had won their independence, although the Spanish still refused to grant them freedom. Americans watched the revolts sympathetically as they: 1) identified these struggles for liberty with their own Revolution; and 2) were anxious to trade with the Spanish-American republics. Patriots such as *Henry Clay* urged the United States to recognize the independence of the revolting colonies, but President Monroe refused until after Spain ratified the Florida Treaty in 1821. In March, 1822, formal recognition was extended.

II. *Problem of European Intervention.* Europe's reactionary monarchs, under the influence of Prince Metternich, looked with such disfavor on all revolutions that they considered helping Spain suppress its rebellious colonists. This move was frustrated when revolts against the Spanish king broke out at home. Metternich then advanced the *principle of intervention*: the right of all monarchs to suppress revolutions wherever they occurred. Under this principle, France was delegated by the Europeans powers to stamp out the Latin-American revolts (1822).

b. ENGLAND'S DILEMMA.

I. *Division of English Opinion.* George IV and his Tory followers favored suppressing the Latin American rebellions, but the Whigs, represented by *George Canning*, the Foreign Secretary, hoped for independence as a means of capturing South American trade. Canning could not advocate recognition without offending his monarch.

II. *Canning's Solution.* Realizing that his views were those of the United States, Canning wrote *Richard Rush*, American minister to England (August, 1823), proposing a joint declaration in which both nations: 1) disavowed any intention of taking part of South America for themselves; and 2) denied any other power the right to intervene there. This scheme would have stopped French intervention without committing England on recognition.

c. AMERICA'S DILEMMA.

I. *Reaction to Canning's Proposal.* Monroe favored Canning's declaration, but *John Quincy Adams* was opposed because: 1) he realized that England's navy could stop French intervention at any time, making such a joint declaration unnecessary; 2) he feared that a disavowal of intentions to acquire portions of Latin America would restrain the United States from the future acquisition of Cuba or Mexico; and 3) the declaration did not extend to Russia which by 1821 had occupied portions of the Pacific coast as far south as Ft. Ross (1816) near San Francisco.

II. *Statement of the Monroe Doctrine.* Adams finally won Monroe to his view. Hence the President, rather than joining with England, issued his own doctrine in a message to Congress (*December, 1823*). This stated that: 1) the western hemisphere was not open to colonization by any European power; and 2) the United States would not intervene in Europe's wars.

d. IMPACT OF THE DOCTRINE. The doctrine attracted little attention, and had no effect on Russia, which had already begun to withdraw from the Northwest, or on France, which had abandoned plans to intervene in Latin America. Its importance lay in the future, although Monroe's announcement symbolized the emergence of the United States as a power strong enough to prevent European meddling in American affairs.

III. SECTIONALISM AND PARTY POLITICS
1824 - 1828

A. Emergence of a Sectional Pattern

1. Meaning of Sectionalism. The term "section," as employed during this period of history, meant a geographic area devoted to economic enterprises peculiarly suited to the unique environment. Each section, as a result, demanded national laws that would benefit its economy; thus a manufacturing section would favor protective tariffs, while a section producing raw materials for export would favor low tariffs. Antagonism was a basic feature of the sectional concept.

2. The Sections in 1824. Three sections were emerging by 1824, each with its own legislative demands: 1) the *industrial Northeast* which wanted protective tariffs, high-priced public lands to keep labor from migrating, and federally built internal improvements to expand home markets; 2) the *cotton South* which favored low tariffs to facilitate commercial exchange with England, no internal improvements lest the drain of money from the treasury open the way for high tariffs, and high-priced public lands to provide revenue for the government; and 3) the *agricultural West* which demanded low-priced public lands to encourage settlement, protective tariffs to stimulate the growth of a home market, and federally built internal improvements.

3. Political Basis for Sectional Conflicts. The sec-·tional struggles that began after 1824 were precipitated by the political situation. By this time the Federalist party was extinct, leaving the Republicans without opposition. In this situation the party's leaders began quarreling among themselves, forming sectional alliances to increase their own strength. This factionalism was first shown in the election of 1824.

B. The Election of 1824

1. Nomination by State Legislatures. Until 1820 candidates were nominated by a caucus; congressmen from each party agreed on the nominees for national offices. This system was attacked as: 1) undemocratic; and 2) one that upset "checks and balances" by giving Congress too much power over the executive. Hence in 1824 most candidates were nominated by state legislatures.

2. The Rival Candidates. Four candidates contested for the presidency: 1) *William H. Crawford* of Georgia who represented the Old South in his aristocratic beliefs and distrust of a strong national government; 2) *John Quincy Adams* of Massachusetts, an able statesman without political charm, who represented the Northeast; 3) *Henry Clay* of Kentucky, candidate of the upper-class interests of the West, who favored an *American System* of high protective tariffs to make the United States economically independent, and federally supported internal improvements to bind the sections together; and 4) *Andrew Jackson* of Tennessee, representative of the West's lower classes, whose military record and lack of formal statesmanship won support from the masses. Jackson's position was strengthened by *John C. Calhoun* as his vice-presidential candidate.

3. Results of the Election

a. THE VOTE IN THE ELECTORAL COLLEGE. Adams secured the votes of New England and New York, Crawford of Virginia and Georgia, Clay of Kentucky, Ohio, and Missouri, and Jackson of the rest of the states. Only Jackson's vote was drawn from more than one section. He received 99 electoral votes, Adams 84, Crawford 41, and Clay 37.

b. THE VOTE IN THE HOUSE OF REPRESENTATIVES. As no candidate had a majority, the House of Representatives had to make the final selection from among the three highest candidates. This placed Clay, who was speaker of the House, in a strategic position, as his influence was great enough to throw the election to either of his rivals. He decided to support Adams because: 1) the two agreed on a nationalistic program; and 2) Jackson would probably be re-elected in 1828 but Adams was too unpopular to succeed himself, opening the way for Clay to win that election. Adams was chosen President on the first ballot.

c. POLITICAL RESULTS OF THE ELECTION.

I. *The "Corrupt Bargain."* When Clay was named Secretary of State, Jackson's followers charged he was being rewarded for making Adams President. Although the charge was untrue, it helped discredit the Adams administration and hindered Clay politically forever after.

II. *Beginnings of Party Realignment.* Enemies of Adams and Clay began grouping around Jackson as soon as the election was over. They included Martin Van Buren of New York, Thomas Hart Benton of Missouri, and Duff Green, who was brought to Washington (1826) to establish an antiadministration newspaper. Within a few years the Jackson group came to be known as Democrats and the Clay group as Whigs.

C. Problems of the Adams Administration

1. Aid for Internal Improvements. Attempting to carry out Clay's "American System," Adams persuaded Congress to appropriate more money for internal improvements than in all previous history. The sum allotted was too small to construct the network of roads envisaged by the President, while state-built canals were already proving more useful.

2. The Panama Congress. When the Latin American republics called a conference to urge Spanish recognition of their independence, Clay persuaded Adams to nominate a delegate, hoping to increase American influence among them. Congress refused to approve this action because: 1) the President's enemies seized on any opportunity to discredit him; and 2) Southerners feared that the Congress would inspire revolts in Cuba and Puerto Rico with resulting attacks on their own slavery system. Although delegates were sent later, they arrived after the congress was over.

3. The Georgia Indian Controversy. Pressure from Georgia forced the Indian office to negotiate the Treaty of Indian Springs (1825) with a small faction of the Creek Indians, who ceded lands belonging to the entire tribe. When the Creeks protested, Adams ordered the treaty suspended. Georgia refused to abide by this decision and proceeded with surveys of the disputed lands while the President hurriedly arranged a new treaty, the Treaty of Washington (1827) in which the tribe again ceded its lands for larger compensation. He was discredited in the South and West for siding with the hated Indians.

4. The Tariff Controversy

a. AGITATION FOR A PROTECTIVE TARIFF. As manufacturing increased, protectionist sentiment mounted in the Northeast

SOME REASONS FOR AND AGAINST A PROTECTIVE TARIFF

FOR
① ENABLES INFANT INDUSTRIES TO SURVIVE AND GROW
② ENABLES MANUFACTURERS TO PAY HIGHER WAGES
③ CREATES LARGE, DEPENDABLE HOME MARKET
④ FOSTERS SELF-SUFFICIENCY

AGAINST
① MATURE INDUSTRIES REFUSE TO GIVE UP PROTECTION
② HIGHER PRICES MEAN WAGES BUY LESS
③ REDUCES FOREIGN MARKETS FOR SURPLUS PRODUCTION
④ DISCOURAGES TRADE AND CAUSES HOSTILITY

CHART BY GRAPHICS INSTITUTE, N.Y.C.

and Middle states. A higher tariff measure was defeated in 1820 by southern votes, but a similar bill was adopted as the *Tariff of 1824.* Protectionists, who were still dissatisfied, called a meeting of delegates from thirteen states at Harrisburg, Pennsylvania (1827), to draft a program for still higher duties. This was presented to Congress with strong support.

b. THE TARIFF OF ABOMINATIONS. Jackson's supporters in Congress seized on the opportunity to win support for their leader. They drafted a new bill which placed high duties on all items but particularly heavy duties on raw materials. This measure, they believed, would be defeated by northeastern manufacturers, southern cotton growers, and commercial interests. Then they could claim credit in the North and West for having introduced a high-tariff act, and in the South for defeating it. Instead the *Tariff of 1828* was adopted, largely because New England's industries were becoming so important that that section gave more votes than anticipated for the measure. This badly framed bill further discredited Adams, helping assure his defeat in the election of 1828.

IV. LASTING RESULTS OF THE ERA OF NATIONALISM

A. Domestic Problems

1. The Problem of Sectionalism. The Adams administration made a few far-seeing people aware of the dangerous problem that would soon face the nation: how could men with varying economic interests live together in harmony? For the next thirty years they sought an answer to that question in debate, compromise, and finally civil war. Only when that war was over did they find the solution. This was to endow the national government with sufficient authority to prevent the sections and states from warring among themselves.

2. The Problem of Political Parties. Statesmen of the Era of Good Feelings took pride in the fact that party differences had vanished. Yet they were soon to learn that Americans could not live long under a one-party system. As Republicans fell apart in their scramble for the presidency, they laid the basis for the two new parties, Whig and Democratic, that were soon to coalesce. This was typical of the people's wishes at all periods in our history. They have been wise enough to recognize that two parties are necessary to provide the criticism essential in a successful democracy.

B. International Problems. The nationalistic spirit that produced the Monroe Doctrine launched the United States on a period of comparative isolation from Europe lasting until the Spanish-American War of 1898. Yet those who believed that this independence was the result of their nation's newly developed power were mistaken. Instead they were left free to concentrate on their own affairs only because Europe was at peace during the nineteenth century. As the twentieth century was to show, the United States could never remain aloof from any major world conflict.

ADDITIONAL READING

An excellent survey is G. W. Dangerfield, *The Awakening of American Nationalism, 1815-1828* (1965); the same author's *The Era of Good Feelings* (1952) deals with the period more intensively. Constitutional developments are described in E. S. Corwin, *John Marshall and the Constitution* (1919), and economic in D. C. North, *The Economic Growth of the United States 1790-1860* (1961), a highly technical but rewarding book. The spread of a transportation network is explained in G. R. Taylor, *The Transportation Revolution, 1815-1860* (1951) which deals generally with the subject, and in L. C. Hunter, *Steamboats on the Western Rivers* (1949), and Carter Goodrich, et. al., *Canals and American Economic Development* (1961). An excellent history of agriculture is P. W. Gates, *The Farmers' Age: Agriculture, 1815-1860* (1960). Biographical studies of note include: C. M. Wiltse, *John C. Calhoun: Nationalist, 1782-1828* (1944), G. G. Van Deusen, *Life of Henry Clay* (1937), Clement Eaton, *Henry Clay and the Art of American Politics* (1957), and Lucius Wilmerding, *James Monroe* (1960). Foreign policy is appraised in Dexter Perkins, *Hands Off: A History of the Monroe Doctrine* (1941), and S. F. Bemis, *John Quincy Adams and the Union* (1957). One threat to the harmony of the period is described in Glover Moore, *The Missouri Controversy, 1819-1821* (1953).

~~~~~~~~~~~~~~~~~~~~~~~~~~~~~~~~~~

CHAPTER X

Jacksonian Democracy
1829-1840

~~~~~~~~~~~~~~~~~~~~~~~~~~~~~~~~~~

❮ THE RESURGENCE OF DEMOCRACY

The election of 1828 reversed the conservative trend in politics and thought that had been so marked since the Treaty of Ghent. During the next generation the suffrage was broadened, aristocratic institutions discarded, popular controls extended, and cultural life adjusted to the needs of the masses. In one sense the American people were returning during these years to the principles of the French and American revolutions; for the first time they achieved the natural rights to life, liberty, and happiness promised them in the Declaration of Independence. In another sense the period of Jacksonian Democracy looked toward the future by marking out the pattern that has since been used to increase the liberties and freedom of the common people.

I. DOMESTIC PROBLEMS OF THE JACKSON ADMINISTRATIONS — 1829 - 1836

A. The Election of 1828

1. Growth of Democracy at Home and Abroad

a. THE DEMOCRATIC SPIRIT ABROAD. *Andrew Jackson* owed his election to a world-wide democratic spirit that rose in the 1820's and 1830's to challenge the conservatism of the Age of Metternich. In Europe this was expressed by such events as: 1) the _July Revolution_ (1830) in France which toppled the reactionary Charles X from his throne; 2) the successful Belgian revolution (1831) against Dutch rule; 3) liberal uprisings in Hanover, Saxony, and other German states; and 4) the widening of the franchise in England by such measures as the Catholic Emancipation Act (1829) and the _Reform Bill_ (1832).

b. THE DEMOCRATIC SPIRIT AT HOME.

I. _Rise of the Common Man._ Jackson was elected by the votes of _western farmers_ and _eastern workers_. Westerners were able to make their influence felt, as eleven western states had been admitted by 1828, all with liberal constitutions that allowed the poorer people to vote. Eastern workers were strengthened by industrialization and urbanization, which brought them together in groups, thus allowing organization for political action.

II. _Democracy in Political Institutions._ The lower classes were able to express themselves because: 1) by 1828 five of the eastern states had _abolished property qualifications for voting_, while the remainder were moving in this direction; the last to succumb to liberal pressure was Rhode Island (1843) which adopted a new constitution only after a popular uprising known as _Dorr's Rebellion;_ 2) presidential electors were chosen by the people rather than state legislatures in all but two of the states by 1828; 3) new state constitutions adopted in the 1820's and 1830's made most officials (including judges) elective, provided for biennial meetings of legislatures, and granted governors more power than formerly; and 4) the caucus method of selecting presidential nominees was abandoned after 1824. Instead candidates were chosen in 1824 and 1828 by state legislatures, and after 1828 by party conventions.

2. The Campaign of 1828. As in later elections, personalities were more important than issues. Followers of the candidates, _Andrew Jackson_ and _John Quincy Adams,_ resorted to abusive attacks and personal slander; Adams' supporters branded Jackson as an immoral, brawling frontiersman, while Jackson's henchmen stressed Adams' extravagance and the "corrupt bargain" of 1824. The rising democratic tide determined the outcome. Jackson and his vice-presidential candidate, John C. Calhoun, received 178 electoral votes to 83 for Adams.

3. Jackson Enters the White House

a. THE INAUGURATION. Mobs descended on Washington to watch the inauguration of their hero. At the official reception they swarmed into the White House, trampling the expensive carpets and breaking the delicate furniture, joyful that they had taken control of the government. Aware of this support, Jackson looked upon himself as spokesman for the people. Hence he overrode Congress, the courts, or the states when they opposed him.

b. JACKSON'S APPOINTMENTS. Only *Martin Van Buren,* Secretary of State, was outstanding in Jackson's cabinet. Instead he relied for advice on a *"kitchen cabinet"* of close friends such as Amos Kendall and William B. Lewis. Minor government offices were filled with men who had worked for his election. Jackson justified this *"spoils system"* on the grounds that his appointees better represented the popular will than civil servants who had been long in office.

B. Frontier Problems

1. The Georgia Indian Controversy

a. EFFORTS TO REMOVE THE CHEROKEE. After 1825 the federal government attempted to remove all eastern Indians to the Great Plains area of the Far West. The Cherokee Indians of northwestern Georgia, to protect themselves from removal, adopted a constitution (1827) declaring themselves to be wards of the United States and not subject to the laws of Georgia. The state answered (1828) by throwing open the Indian lands to settlement.

b. JACKSON'S REMOVAL POLICY. When the Cherokee sought help from Congress that body only allotted them lands in the West and urged them to move. The Supreme Court, however, in *Worcester v. Georgia* (1832), ruled that they constituted a "domestic dependent nation" not subject to the laws of Georgia. Jackson, who as a frontiersman had no sympathy with the Indians, was so outraged that he refused to enforce the decision. Instead he persuaded the tribe to give up its Georgia lands for a reservation west of the Mississippi (1835).

c. LATER INDIAN REMOVAL. Other tribes were forced to follow the Cherokee westward. This harsh policy led to two wars: 1) *Black Hawk's War* (1832) in the Northwest; and 2) the Seminole War (1837-1842) in Florida. By the end of Jackson's administrations all but a handful of Indians had been removed from the East.

2. Policies on Internal Improvements and Land

a. THE MAYSVILLE TURNPIKE VETO. Jackson had not expressed himself on the constitutionality of federally supported internal improvements. He finally took a stand against such aid when he vetoed a bill allotting support to a turnpike between Maysville and Lexington, Kentucky. His veto message, however, denounced only federal support for local improvements (despite the fact that the Maysville road was one link in a national chain of roads), thus allowing him to win continued favor in the West where internal improvements were popular.

b. CONFLICTS OVER LAND POLICY. The West, which disliked the Land Act of 1820 (see p. 137), urged liberalization of the land policy by either: 1) *graduation,* which would lower the price of lands that did not sell until they were eventually disposed of: or 2) *pre-emption,* which would allow a pioneer who settled on government land the first right to purchase that land when it was finally put up at auction. These proposals were violently opposed by the East, which feared that they would drain workers from factories. The section's attitude was reflected in the *Foote Resolution* (1829) calling on Congress to stop land sales completely for a time. More moderate Easterners favored *distribution,* which was advocated by *Henry Clay.* This provided that proceeds from land sales should be distributed among the states, to be used for internal improvements or other purposes. Both the West and the South opposed distribution, the former because it would keep land prices high, the latter as it would drain money from the treasury and open the way for a higher tariff. Thus a sectional alignment of West and South against East was suggested. This became important after the Panic of 1837 sharpened sectional differences.

C. The Tariff Controversy

1. Southern Opposition to the Tariff of 1828.

a. LEADERSHIP OF SOUTH CAROLINA. The South intensely opposed the high tariffs of 1824 and 1828 which forced it to buy manufactured goods from the Northeast at tariff-protected prices rather than securing them from England in return for cotton exported there. Opposition was centered in the Southeast where worn-out soils hindered cotton production, and especially in South Carolina where the large-planter class enjoyed greater power than in any other state. Moreover the state was the home of *John C. Calhoun,* who was destined to become the leading spokesman for his section in the tariff controversy.

b. THE SOUTH CAROLINA EXPOSITION. Calhoun's views were expressed in the South Carolina Exposition, a document adopted by the state's legislature. In this he argued that: 1) the states had conferred certain powers on Congress through the Constitution; 2) each state could decide for itself when Congress exceeded that delegated authority; and 3) when a state found any law to be in this category the law could be declared null and void within the limits of that state. This was the *doctrine of nullification.*

2. Attempts to Form a South-West Alliance

a. THE WEBSTER-HAYNE DEBATE. Having issued this warning, the South attempted to strengthen its position by allying with the West. Its chance came when the *Foote Resolution* (see p. 150) proposed stopping land sales. Senator *Robert Y. Hayne* of South Carolina denounced the resolution as violently as any Westerner, hoping in this way to win western support on the tariff. He was answered by *Daniel Webster* of Massachusetts, who steered discussion from the land question to the nature of the union. For two weeks (January, 1830) the two antagonists spoke constantly. Webster argued that the Constitution, which had been created by the people, imposed restrictions on the sovereignty of the states, making nullification impossible.

b. FAILURE OF THE SOUTH-WEST ALLIANCE. Although the South supported the West's land policy, the nationalistic West was unwilling to favor nullification. This was shown when the section's principal spokesman, President Jackson, responded to a toast (April, 1830) with "Our Federal Union — it must be preserved." One result was a break between Jackson and Calhoun. The two were already at odds over: 1) the *"Eaton Malaria,"* a social crisis created when Mrs. Calhoun snubbed the wife of the Secretary of War whose father had been a tavern keeper; and 2) Jackson's discovery that Calhoun had been the one member of J. Q. Adams' cabinet who wished to punish him for his Florida raid in 1818 (see p. 139). With the nullification controversy, the President cast Calhoun aside, selecting *Martin Van Buren* as his running mate in the election of 1832.

3. The Tariff of 1832

a. PASSAGE OF THE TARIFF. The Tariff of 1828 produced so much revenue that surpluses mounted in the treasury. Nor could these excess funds be spent, as Jackson's veto of the Maysville Turnpike Bill prevented their use for internal improvements. Hence the President asked Congress to revise the tariff. As protectionists from West and Northeast controlled that body, the resulting Tariff of 1832 was still high, although it did away with some of the worst features of the Tariff of 1828.

b. NULLIFICATION BY SOUTH CAROLINA. A popularly elected convention in South Carolina immediately declared the Tariff of 1832 null, void, and not binding on the people of the state. In this emergency the President: 1) issued a *Nullification Proclamation* calling on the people of the state to show their loyalty; 2) asked Congress to pass a *Force Act* giving him the power to enforce the laws in South Carolina by any means necessary; and 3) sought a peaceful solution by urging modification of the Tariff of 1832. The resulting *Compromise Tariff* (1833), introduced by Henry Clay, provided for a gradual lowering of rates until 1842, when levels would reach 20 per cent.

c. END OF THE CONTROVERSY. South Carolina welcomed the chance to retreat provided by the Compromise Tariff, as other southern states had not followed its lead. Hence its Nullification Ordinance was withdrawn (March, 1833), and the Force Act was nullified. This empty gesture did not conceal Jackson's complete triumph.

D. The Bank War

1. Opposition to the Bank of the United States. The charter of the Second Bank of the United States (see pp. 135-136) was due to expire in 1836. Although the bank was ably run by *Nicholas Biddle,* its conservative president, Jackson and his followers opposed recharter because: 1) all banks were looked upon as tools of the rich to oppress the poor; 2) the bank foreclosed mortgages ruthlessly whenever a debtor fell behind in his payments; 3) it kept state banks from issuing currency or loaning money recklessly by threatening to call their notes at any time; and 4) Biddle, in his effort to win support for recharter, loaned money freely to congressmen and editors who opposed Jackson politically.

2. Defeat of Bank Recharter

a. VETO OF THE BANK BILL. Although the charter did not expire until 1836, Daniel Webster persuaded Biddle to seek recharter before the election of 1832, hoping to create an election issue if the bill were vetoed by Jackson. The measure was passed during the summer of 1832, and promptly vetoed.

b. THE ELECTION OF 1832.

I. *The Rival Candidates.* The election, following on the heels of the bank bill veto, allowed the people to express themselves. Three parties took part: 1) Jackson's followers, who were soon to be called Democrats, nominated Jackson and Martin Van Buren; 2) conservative supporters of J. Q. Adams and Henry Clay, organized as the *National Republican Party*, chose Clay as their candidate and adopted the *first party platform* in history; and 3) opponents of the Masonic Order, which had been under attack since 1826 when one William Morgan of New York disappeared as he was about to reveal its secrets, went before the country as the *Anti-Masonic Party* with William Wirt of Maryland as their candidate and a platform akin to Clay's American system.

II. *Re-election of Jackson.* Jackson received 219 electoral votes to 49 for Clay and none for Wirt. As the issues had been clearly defined, he interpreted his large popular vote as an endorsement of his principles.

c. END OF THE BANK OF THE UNITED STATES. Acting under this mandate, Jackson decided to cripple the bank at once, even though its charter did not expire until 1836. This was done by removing government deposits, which were placed in carefully selected state banks by the Secretary of the Treasury, *Roger B. Taney*. These were labeled *"pet banks"* by Jackson's enemies.

E. Inflation and Prosperity

1. Factors Encouraging Inflation, 1834-1837

a. EXPANSION OF WILDCAT BANKING. The collapse of the national bank encouraged the founding of many new state banks, especially in the West. Between 1830 and 1837 they doubled in number, while money in circulation increased three-fold and loans outstanding fourfold. Inflation was also stimulated by the deposit of federal funds in western state banks; they were used as the basis for paper money which was loaned freely, especially to land speculators. Government sales rose from 4,000,000 acres in 1834 to 20,000,000 in 1836. As the money borrowed by speculators to pay for land was redeposited in pet banks after each purchase, ready to be loaned again, a dangerous *inflationary spiral* was created.

b. THE INTERNAL IMPROVEMENTS CRAZE. Prosperity encouraged the western states to launch an elaborate program of road and canal building (see pp. 133, 142). This was financed by borrowing from eastern banks and English capitalists. By 1837 total state indebtedness had reached $175,000,000.

c. DISTRIBUTION OF THE SURPLUS. By 1835 the national debt was paid off and a surplus accumulating. Income, which came from land sales and customs duties, could not be reduced without tampering with the Compromise Tariff of 1833, while expenditure of the surplus on internal improvements was impossible since Jackson had vetoed the Maysville Turnpike Bill. Hence the President reluctantly agreed to a *Distribution Bill* (1836) which allotted all money in the treasury in excess of $5,000,000 to the states in proportion to their population. This further stimulated spending and inflation.

2. The Specie Circular.

In an effort to check the inflationary spiral, Jackson issued the *Specie Circular* (1836), which required the use of gold and silver for land purchases. The Circular came too late to check a panic, which began soon after the President left office.

II. FOREIGN PROBLEMS OF THE JACKSON ADMINISTRATIONS — 1829 - 1836

A. Shirt Sleeve Diplomacy

1. Opening the West Indies Trade. The politicians placed in the State Department by the "spoils system" used unorthodox but highly effective methods to win several diplomatic triumphs. One such victory was secured when Jackson informed England that he planned vigorous measures to open trade with the British West Indies. England agreed to open this trade if the United States would stop discriminating against her vessels. When Congress took this step (October, 1830), an English Order in Council (December, 1830) opened colonial ports to American ships.

2. The French Spoliation Claims

a. THE CONVENTION OF 1831. France had never compensated American shippers for ships illegally confiscated under Napoleon's Continental System. At Jackson's insistence, a Claims Convention (1831) set the sum of 25,000,000 francs, payable in six annual installments, as the amount due the United States.

b. FORCEFUL COLLECTION OF CLAIMS. When the French Chamber of deputies refused to appropriate money for these payments, Jackson (1834) asked Congress for authority to seize French property in America and make other reprisals. This warlike proposal led to a severing of diplomatic relations, but France finally agreed to begin payments if the President would apologize. He refused, announcing to Congress that he had never intended to insult France and so could not retract. When this was accepted by France as an apology, the spoliation claims were paid. Jackson's blunt methods were popular with the people.

B. Relations with Mexico

1. Founding of the Texan Republic

a. OCCUPATION OF TEXAS BY AMERICANS. Occupation began when *Moses Austin* (1820) secured Spain's permission to found an American colony in Texas. On his death a year later the grant was assigned to his son, *Stephen Austin,* by the newly established Mexican government. Several hundred pioneers set-

tled in the Austin colony, but wholesale migration did not begin
until a Mexican colonization law (1825) introduced the *empre-
sario system*. This offered large land grants to empresarios in
return for importing several hundred families. As the empresarios sold their land at far less than the $1.25 an acre charged
in the United States, some 20,000 Americans lived in Texas
by 1830.

   b. CAUSES OF THE TEXAN REVOLUTION. Most of the settlers remained loyal to the United States. Moreover, their dissatisfaction with Mexican rule was heightened by: 1) their lack
of self-government, as Texas was part of the Mexican-domin-
ated state of Texas-Coahuila; 2) a decree banning further immigration from the United States (1830); 3) conflicts over
customs duties on goods imported from the United States; and
4) the abolition of slavery by Mexico (1829).

   c. THE TEXAN REVOLUTION. These grievances came to a
climax when the Mexican president, General *Santa Anna,*
abolished local rule by setting himself up as dictator (1835).
When the Texans retaliated by establishing a provincial government, Santa Anna led an army against them. After declaring
their independence (March, 1836), they suffered a defeat at the
Alamo (a mission in San Antonio), then won a decisive victory
at the *Battle of San Jacinto* (April, 1836). Mexico made no
further effort to reconquer the region.

   2. The United States and Texas. The Republic of
Texas, which was formed with *Sam Houston* as president, immediately asked to be annexed to the United States. Jackson
was afraid to take this step, despite his desire for Texas, because: 1) war with Mexico would probably follow; and 2)
many Northerners disliked adding more slave territory to the
United States. Hence he refused annexation, but officially
recognized the existence of the Texan republic (1837).

III. DEPRESSION AND PARTY CONFLICTS
1836 - 1840

A. The Election of 1836
1. Emergence of Political Parties
   a. THE DEMOCRATIC PARTY. As a result of the conflicts of
the Jacksonian period, two new political parties had coalesced

by 1836. The Democratic party commanded the loyalty of: 1) western small farmers; 2) farmers and small planters of the South; and 3) eastern workers. It attempted to please the masses rather than the classes, stressed nationalism, and catered to the desires of frontiersmen.

b. THE WHIG PARTY. By 1836 the National Republicans were calling themselves Whigs to suggest affinity with Revolutionary radicals who had revolted against King George as they were revolting against "King Andrew." The party was composed of: 1) industrialists and merchants from the Northeast; 2) wealthier farmers from the West; and 3) southern planters. It was less united than the Democratic party, as its southern wing opposed the high tariffs, national banks, and centralized federal authority desired by its eastern and western followers. The Whigs were held together only by such strong leaders as Daniel Webster, Henry Clay, and John C. Calhoun.

2. Results of the Election. The Whigs were so disorganized that they did not nominate a candidate, hoping instead that the vote for the four nominees of the party would be so scattered that the election would be decided in the House of Representatives. Instead Jackson's popularity was so great that his successor, *Martin Van Buren* of New York, secured 170 electoral votes to 124 for all his opponents.

B. The Panic of 1837 and Its Problems

1. The Panic of 1837. The inflationary spiral of the 1830's ended when English bankers, alarmed by the growth of speculation, began to call in their loans to American firms. These firms were unable to secure specie to make these payments, as the banks had just depleted their gold supplies by distributing funds to the states under the terms of the Distribution Act. Hence business failures multiplied, banks closed their doors, and farm prices declined rapidly. By May, 1837, the nation was gripped by a serious panic.

2. The Independent Treasury Plan

a. VAN BUREN AND THE DEPRESSION. The President asked Congress to: 1) repeal the Distribution Act; 2) authorize the issue of treasury notes to meet a government deficit; and 3) pass an Independent Treasury Bill which would allow the government to keep its funds in vaults, or subtreasuries, rather

than banks, and to make all payments for services in specie.
The first two measures were adopted, but the "divorce bill" (to
divorce government from banking) aroused greater opposition.

b. WHIG OPPOSITION TO THE PLAN. The Whigs argued
that: 1) the panic was caused by wildcat banking and could
be ended only by rechartering the Bank of the United States;
and 2) the subtreasury plan would ruin all state banks, thus
forcing the nation on a specie basis, with a depressing effect
on business. These arguments were used by Henry Clay, Daniel Webster, and other Whigs so effectively that the Independent
Treasury Bill was defeated in 1837 and 1838.

c. PASSAGE OF THE BILL. Principal support came from
eastern workers in the Democratic party, known as *loco-focos,*
who blamed the panic on the reckless policies of the Bank of
the United States and state banks. They favored the abolition
of all banks and the use of metallic currency alone. Gaining
strength during the depression years, they were able to push
the Independent Treasury Bill through Congress in 1840, after
John C. Calhoun and his followers had returned to the Democratic party.

3. Effect of the Panic on the States

a. BANKING REFORM. New York led the way with two
innovations that were imitated by other states to check abuses
that had helped precipitate the panic: 1) banks were required to
deposit bonds or securities in a "safety fund" which could be
used to redeem the notes of any defaulting bank; 2) instead
of chartering each bank individually (thus allowing incompetent political favorites to become bankers), a *"free banking"*
system was inaugurated. This allowed any individual or group
to open a bank on meeting certain conditions established by law.

b. REPUDIATION OF DEBTS. Several western and southern
states repudiated all or part of the debts they had contracted
by building internal improvements. This created ill feeling
among European creditors that lasted for a generation.

C. The Election of 1840

1. The Log Cabin Campaign. The Democrats, who
were blamed by the people for the panic, renominated *Martin
Van Buren* without enthusiasm. The Whigs, sensing victory,
passed over Henry Clay, whose views on controversial issues

were too well known, nominating instead *William Henry Harrison,* the military hero of the War of 1812. *John Tyler* of Virginia was named vice-presidential candidate to attract southern votes. The campaign was a noisy one, as the Whigs attempted to depict their candidate as a log-cabin-born frontiersman who stood for the common people. Torchlight processions, slogans, songs, and parades were used freely.

2. Election and Death of Harrison. Harrison was elected by a vote of 234 to 60, but died only a month after taking office. *John Tyler,* who became President, was a states-rights aristocrat who opposed a national bank, protective tariffs, government-supported internal improvements, and other measures favored by the Whigs. His administration was marked by continuous conflict within the party.

D. The Whig Legislative Program

1. Henry Clay as a Policy Maker. Clay hoped that Tyler could be forced into line. Hence he asked Congress (May, 1841) to: 1) repeal the Independent Treasury Bill and charter the *Third Bank of the United States;* 2) adopt a new *protective tariff;* and 3) provide for the *distribution* of proceeds of land sales among the states to be used for internal improvements.

2. Conflicts Over Clay's Program

a. DEFEAT OF THE BANK BILL. The Independent Treasury Bill was repealed (August, 1841), but an act to establish a Third National Bank was vetoed by Tyler on constitutional grounds. This split the Whigs and virtually drove Tyler from the party.

b. THE PREEMPTION-DISTRIBUTION ACT. Both the South and West opposed Clay's Distribution Bill, the *South* because distribution would deplete the treasury and open the way for higher tariffs; the *West* because states receiving benefits would be bribed to keep land prices high. Clay had to make concessions to both to secure enough votes. The final act provided (1841) that: 1) proceeds from land sales should be distributed among the states only so long as the tariff remained below 20 per cent; and 2) any settler could preempt 160 acres of the public domain, then have the first right to buy at $1.25 an acre.

c. THE TARIFF OF 1842. After Tyler twice vetoed bills allowing distribution while the tariff was over 20 per cent,

Clay gave up the struggle to secure both distribution and a high tariff. An act of 1842 restored levels to those of 1832, thus ending all chances for distribution. After 1842 the Whigs were so divided that no further legislation was enacted.

E. Relations with Great Britain, 1837-1842

1. The Canadian Insurrection of 1837. Americans, who believed all revolutions were inspired by their own, looked with favor on a Canadian rebellion against British rule that began in 1837. Men, money, and supplies were smuggled to the insurrectionists. Late in 1837 a Canadian-chartered vessel used in smuggling, the *Caroline,* was boarded by English troops while tied to the American shore of the Niagara River. One man was killed and the ship burned. Van Buren demanded reparations, which were refused by England. While feeling was still high (1840) Alexander McLeod, a Canadian, boasted in a New York saloon that he had been the member of the boarding party responsible for the killing. McLeod was arrested and tried for murder in the New York courts. England, taking the stand that it alone was responsible, threatened war if he was executed. Fortunately he was acquitted, allowing the incident to be settled by an exchange of notes.

2. The Maine Boundary Dispute. Due to vague terms used in the peace treaty of 1783, some 12,000 square miles lying between Maine and New Brunswick were claimed by both England and the United States. After attempts at settlement by compromise failed, the situation became acute when lumberjacks from the two nations clashed in the disputed territory (1838). This *Aroostook War* convinced both contestants that the dispute must be settled to avoid a serious conflict. Negotiations between Daniel Webster, American Secretary of State under Tyler, and Lord Ashburton, English ambassador, resulted in the *Webster-Ashburton Treaty* (*August, 1842*). This: 1) awarded seven-twelfths of the territory to the United States; 2) confirmed an earlier inaccurate survey of the 45th parallel as the boundary between the Connecticut and St. Lawrence rivers; and 3) defined the boundary between Lake Superior and the Lake of the Woods.

3. Conflicts Over Slavery

a. THE SLAVE TRADE. Since 1807 the English navy, in attempting to suppress the slave trade, had stopped slavers of all nations on the high seas. This led to conflicts which were finally settled in the Webster-Ashburton Treaty; both nations agreed to keep squadrons in African waters to cooperate in running down slavers.

b. THE CREOLE AFFAIR. As slavery was banned in the British West Indies, slaves carried by American coastal vessels that took refuge from storms in West Indian ports were always freed by the authorities. This aroused protest from their owners, who demanded compensation. The conflict reached a climax when slaves aboard the _Creole_ mutinied, killed a member of the crew, and sailed the vessel into a West Indian port where they were declared free (1841). The United States protested so strongly that England agreed not to interfere with American ships in the future.

IV. AN APPRAISAL OF JACKSONIAN DEMOCRACY

A. Emergence of Political Democracy. For the first time during the Jacksonian period the common people gained control of their government. This transformed the nature of politics and political parties.

1. Transformation of Political Campaigns. The campaign of 1840 opened a new era politically. Realizing that the common man was in power, politicians: 1) began stressing circus tactics rather than issues; and 2) sought to present their candidates as of, rather than above, the people. From that date until the present emotionalism has been stressed in campaigns.

2. Transformation of Political Parties. To reach down to the level of the people, parties began building organizations on the ward and county level. As the minor local politicians who became increasingly important to the parties were interested in winning elections rather than in national issues, agreement on broad policy became more and more difficult. Hence parties tended to obscure rather than crystallize important problems facing the people. Since that day parties have seldom taken clear-cut stands that would allow voters to express themselves on vital issues.

B. Importance of Executive Leadership. Andrew Jackson
was the first president to realize that strong leadership was
needed to secure action from a Congress in which many divergent views were represented. The impressive legislative record
that resulted contrasted strongly with the unimpressive record
under Van Buren or Tyler, who did not exert themselves to control Congress. Every outstanding president from that day to
this — Abraham Lincoln, Theodore Roosevelt, Woodrow Wilson, and Franklin D. Roosevelt — has employed executive leadership to secure adoption of a progressive legislative program.

ADDITIONAL READING

G. G. Van Deusen, *The Jacksonian Era, 1828-1848* (1959)
expertly surveys the period; more interpretive and friendly to
Jackson is A. M. Schlesinger, Jr., *The Age of Jackson* (1945).
Biographies of the President are numerous, but Marquis
James, *Andrew Jackson: Portrait of a President* (1937) remains
the most readable.   Varying interpretations of his administra-
tion are in Marvin Meyers, *The Jacksonian Persuasion* (1957),
J. W. Ward, *Andrew Jackson: Symbol of an Age* (1955), and
Lee Benson, *The Concept of Jacksonian Democracy* (1961).
R. V. Remini, *The Election of Andrew Jackson* (1963) is de-
tailed, as is L. D. White, *The Jacksonians* (1954) which con-
centrates on administrative problems.   Biographical studies
of those about Jackson include: G. G. Van Deusen, *Thurlow
Weed* (1947), W. N. Chambers, *Old Bullion Benton* (1956),
C. G. Sellers, Jr., *James K. Polk, Jacksonian* (1957), M. L.
Coit, *John C. Calhoun* (1950), and T. P. Govan, *Nicholas
Biddle* (1959).   Bray Hammon, *Banks and Politics in America
from the Revolution to the Civil War* (1957) is essential to any
understanding of the Bank War.   The sectional conflicts
emerging at this time can be followed in F. J. Turner, *The
United States, 1830-1850* (1945), C. S. Sydnor, *The Develop-
ment of Southern Sectionalism, 1819-1848* (1948), and Clement
Eaton, *Growth of Southern Civilization, 1790-1860* (1961).
The history of the later years of this period can be traced in
R. V. Remini, *Martin Van Buren and the Making of the Democratic Party* (1959), Freeman Cleaves, *William Henry Harrison*
(1939), and O. P. Chitwood, *John Tyler* (1939).   Foreign
policy is brilliantly discussed in S. F. Bemis, *John Quincy
Adams and the Union* (1957).   The final political contest of the
era of the theme of R. G. Gunderson, *The Log-Cabin Campaign*
(1957).

CHAPTER XI

The Age of the Common Man

❨ THE EMERGENCE OF SOCIAL DEMOCRACY

As the common man gained control of the nation's political institutions during the age of Jacksonian Democracy, he found himself able to reshape America's life and thought to his own needs. Why not, he asked himself, use this new power to stamp out the last relics of aristocracy inherited from the colonial past, recast religion in a more democratic mold, rewrite literature in terms understandable to all, and provide opportunities for self-improvement that would allow the humblest commoner to scale the highest social peaks? With this as their goal, the ordinary people of the United States launched a social and intellectual revolution of more lasting importance than the political revolution of that same day.

I. TRANSFORMATION OF THE NATIONAL ECONOMY

A. Changing Population Trends

1. Rapid Growth of Population. The population increased from 12,800,000 in 1830 to 23,200,000 in 1850. This growth was due partly to natural causes and partly to *foreign immigration;* some 2,000,000 foreign-born reached the United States during those years. Most were from Ireland or Germany, where disastrous potato blights ruined crops in the 1840's. The *Irish* settled largely in the Northeast where they found jobs in factories. The _Germans_ occupied the upper Mississippi Valley, becoming farmers. A number of Scandinavians also drifted to the same region. All contributed to American development, but the German contribution was most notable, due largely to able leaders (such as Carl Schurz) fleeing from oppression after the liberal revolutions of 1848 failed.

2. Distribution of Population. By 1850 nearly half the people lived west of the Appalachians, in contrast with only 5 per cent in 1790. _Cities_ also attracted an increasing number; in 1830 only 5 per cent lived in towns of 8000 inhabitants or more; in 1850 the figure was 16 per cent. New York was the largest city, with 300,000 population, followed by Philadelphia, Baltimore, and Boston.

B. Changing Economic Activities

1. The Revolution in Transportation

a. Expa: sion of the Canal System. A "canal craze" followed the success of the Erie Canal (1825). Many were built in the East, but the most important connected the Great Lakes with the interior river system and were constructed by tne western states. Ohio built the Ohio and Erie connecting Cleveland and Portsmouth (1825-1832), and the Miami and Erie from Toledo to Cincinnati (1825-1835); Indiana built the Wabash and Erie (1832-1843); and Illinois built the Illinois and Michigan (1832-1848). By 1850 canal mileage reached 3200.

b. Improvements in Water Transportation. _Steamboats_ revolutionized western transportation; by 1840 they could travel between Louisville and New Orleans in five days, carrying tons of freight. Americans also gained world supremacy in ocean transportation with the development of the _clipper ship_ during the 1840's. These sleek craft, carrying a vast amount of sail, could cross the Atlantic in only thirteen days. In an effort to recapture the Atlantic trade, English builders concentrated on steam-driven ships. One, the _Great Western_, made the crossing in fifteen days (1838), but clippers dominated the seas until just before the Civil War.

c. The Coming of the Railroad. Railroads remained in the experimental stage before 1840. After that date a number of improvements were made: 1) heavy iron rails were laid; 2) steep grades and sharp curves were eliminated; 3) four-wheel trucks were perfected to allow cars to round curves; and 4) coal-burning locomotives were introduced. Hence mileage increased from 3000 in 1840 to 9000 in 1850. Difficulties in financing kept most lines small; thus the eight separate end-to-end roads that connected New York and Albany in 1842 were not consolidated into the New York Central Railroad until 1853. As different gauges of tracks were used, frequent transshipment of goods was necessary. Despite this, railroads provided far better facilities by 1850 than canals or roads.

2. Agricultural Expansion

a. IMPACT OF IMPROVED TRANSPORTATION ON FARMING. Railroads and clipper ships allowed the upper Mississippi Valley to become the granary of the Atlantic basin, especially after 1846 when England repealed her Corn Laws (tariffs on grain) and allowed the world to feed her industrialized population. For the first time farmers had a chance to sell in a world market.

b. EFFECT ON WESTERN AGRICULTURE. This opportunity led to: 1) A *rapid expansion of the frontier* as Easterners moved westward over the Erie Canal to fill Michigan (1837), Iowa (1846), and Wisconsin (1848). By 1850 the region east of the Mississippi was occupied. 2) *Emphasis on specialization* as farmers sought to expand their output by concentrating on crops best suited to natural conditions. A wheat belt spread westward from northern New York to Wisconsin, a corn and livestock belt from Ohio to Illinois, and a tobacco belt from Kentucky to Missouri. 3) The *invention of farm machinery* to allow greater production. The first steel plow was built by *John Deere* of Illinois (1837), the *reaper* by *Cyrus Hall Mc-Cormick* of Virginia (1831), and the thresher by John and Hiram Pitts of Maine (1836).

3. The Industrial Revolution

a. REASONS FOR GROWTH OF INDUSTRY. Rapid industrial expansion was caused by: 1) the opening of new domestic markets by railroads and canals; 2) the steady growth of population; 3) the influx of immigrants, especially from Ireland, who formed the largest labor pool in the nation's history; and 4) American ingenuity which produced laborsaving machinery that allowed machine-made goods to undersell handmade goods. Important inventions included the *telegraph* (1836) by *Samuel*

F. B. Morse; the *sewing machine* (1846) by Elias Howe; vulcanized rubber (1839) by Charles Goodyear; the repeating revolver (1836) by Samuel Colt; and the rotary printing press (1846) by Richard M. Hoe.

b. NATURE OF INDUSTRIAL PRODUCTION. The *textile industry* was concentrated in New England, the *iron industry* in Pennsylvania and the Middle states, especially after the 1830's when anthracite coal was used in smelting, and *extractive industries* in the West where such cities as Chicago, St. Louis, and Cincinnati became centers for the production of flour, cereals, and livestock. Cincinnati, in the center of the livestock belt, was known as *Porkopolis* because so many hogs were slaughtered there. Most industries remained small, and were owned by individuals or partners.

4. Beginnings of Labor Organization

a. THE PLIGHT OF THE WORKER. The rise of the factory system placed such a gulf between employers and employees that the former no longer took a personal concern in the welfare of the latter. As competition among manufacturers was keen and the labor supply steadily increasing through foreign immigration, they were able to inflict intolerable working conditions on laborers. *Hours of labor* were from thirteen to fifteen a day, six days a week, while *wages* were so low after the Panic of 1837 that a family could exist only if all worked. Hence *child labor* was common. Factories were usually unsanitary, poorly lighted, and with no protection provided from dangerous machinery. Security was unknown; workers were fired whenever sickness or age impaired their efficiency. As neither society nor the government was concerned with these conditions, the workers were forced to organize to protect themselves.

b. ORIGINS OF TRADE UNIONISM.

I. *Political Activity.* The first effective organization was the *Mechanics Union of Trade Associations* (1827), a city-wide association of Philadelphia workers. A year later this merged into the *Workingmen's Party* which soon spread into fifteen states to press for laws setting a ten-hour day, establishing free schools, and abolishing imprisonment for debt and mechanics' liens. It won no victories, but the Democratic party adopted portions of its program.

II. *Use of the Strike*. A few strikes were attempted before the Panic of 1837, but most were defeated by hostile courts that branded all labor combinations as illegal "conspiracies" against employers. Not until 1842 did a Massachusetts court in *Commonwealth v. Hunt* rule that efforts to advance wages were not criminal. The Panic of 1837 allowed owners to smash the infant unions and the Workingmen's Party.

c. IDEALISTIC PANACEAS. Middle-class intellectuals, alarmed by the plight of the workers and fearing that the decline in economic democracy would threaten political democracy, proposed two devices to restore equilibrium to the social order: 1) *Land reform* was agitated by George Henry Evans, who formed the *National Reform Association* (1844) to urge the government to grant free land to all settlers. In this way, he hoped, so many workers would be drained westward that employers would have to pay high wages to the remainder. Horace Greeley, influential editor of the *New York Tribune*, was a prominent supporter of the plan, which finally culminated in the Homestead Act (1862). 2) *Communal colonies* were suggested by Robert Owen, who founded the colony of *New Harmony* in Indiana (1825), and *Charles Fourier*, a French social philosopher, whose ideas were transmitted to America by Albert Brisbane's *The Social Destiny of Man* (1840). More than forty *Fourier Phalanxes* were founded, the best known that at *Brook Farm*, Massachusetts, which attracted the support of New England's intellectuals.

d. LABOR'S GAINS. Despite the failure of both strikes and communal experiments, labor made some gains: 1) the *ten-hour day* was adopted in *New Hampshire* (1847) and other states; 2) imprisonment for debt was abolished in the North by 1840; and 3) laws regulating machinery and working conditions were passed in a few states.

II. HUMANITARIAN CRUSADES

A. Forces Underlying Reform

1. Intellectual Forces. Humanitarianism was strengthened by a revival of interest in the ideals of the French Revolution and by the preaching of European liberals such as *Jeremy Bentham,* an English philosopher who taught that laws should be constantly changed to meet social needs and interpreted by the courts to assure "the greatest good to the greatest number."

2. Social Forces. Reform was stimulated by: 1) the rise to political power of the common people, who were most aware of existing evils; 2) the concentration of workers in cities, making organization for reform possible; and 3) the rapid growth of the nation, encouraging reformers in their belief that perfectibility for man and his institutions was possible.

3. Religious Forces

a. THE DOCTRINE OF PERFECTIBILITY.

I. *Expansion of Rationalistic Religions.* The *Unitarian Church,* under the leadership of the Reverend *William Ellery Channing,* made such rapid gains in the Northeast that Congregationalism seemed doomed. This might have followed had not the Reverend *Horace Bushnell* and other liberal clergymen led a movement to liberalize the church's theology. Other traditional churches were forced to revise their teachings in the same way. Hence worshippers came to believe in a benevolent Deity, anxious to help man achieve perfection on earth and happiness throughout eternity. Their desire for self-improvement was strengthened by the belief that divine help would be theirs.

II. *Expansion of Evangelical Religions.* Emotionalism in religion was stimulated by the "New Measures" revival of the Reverend *Charles G. Finney* and his disciples. Converts accepted Finney's belief that every man, through faith, could obtain divine help in improving himself. Thus the prospect of perfectibility was held out to all.

b. APPLICATION OF THE DOCTRINE OF PERFECTIBILITY. The strong desire for perfection was shown in the formation of such new religious sects as: 1) the Perfectionists, under *John Humphrey Noyes,* who believed in sexual freedom, a communal society, and democratic cooperation between God and man; 2) the Millerites, who held with their prophet, *William Miller,* that the millenium would occur in 1843; 3) the Spiritualists, who believed in communication with the dead; and 4) the *Mormons,* whose prophet, *Joseph Smith,* led his followers from New York to Illinois in an effort to escape persecution.

B. The Crusade for Free Public Schools

1. The Demand for Public Schools. Reformers argued that free schools were necessary to train intelligent voters. As the state would benefit most, the state's duty was to support such schools. These demands were bolstered by *organized labor,* which wanted schools to: 1) educate the children of all classes as a means of blurring class lines; 2) remove children from industrial employment, thus creating more jobs for adults; and 3) afford their own children an opportunity to better themselves socially and economically.

2. Founding the Public School System. The principal reformer was *Horace Mann of Massachusetts,* who helped create the state Board of Education (1837), then served as its secretary for many years. During his administration: 1) state control of schools was established; 2) the first normal school founded (1839); 3) educational appropriations vastly increased; and 4) the school year lengthened. His example was imitated in other states, until by 1850 the principle of tax-supported primary schools had been accepted everywhere in the North.

3. Nature of the School System

a. THE PRIMARY SCHOOLS. Instruction was improved by better teachers and texts. Among the latter the most important were: 1) the Peter Parley series on geography, history, etc., from the pen of Samuel G. Goodrich that sold 7,000,000 copies; and 2) the McGuffey Readers, written by William H. McGuffey of Miami University, which ultimately sold 120,000,000 copies.

b. SECONDARY SCHOOLS. Most secondary education was provided by private *academies,* demonstrating that primary education had not yet reached the point where public high schools were in demand.

c. COLLEGES AND UNIVERSITIES. Although the older colleges stagnated during the period, two significant developments were: 1) the beginning of higher education for women with the founding of Mt. Holyoke College (1836) and coeducational Oberlin College (1833); and 2) the growth of state universities in the West. Twenty were established before 1860, with the University of Michigan (1837) most prominent.

4. *Adult Education.* Improved schools for children created a demand for adult education. This was partially met by: 1) the multiplication of subscription libraries, which existed everywhere by 1850; and 2) the *lyceum movement,* which brought a series of prominent speakers to each town during the winter season. The first lyceum was held in Massachusetts (1826), while regular lyceum speakers included such prominent figures as Ralph Waldo Emerson and Louis Agassiz.

C. The Abolition Crusade

1. *The Institution of Slavery*

a. SPREAD OF SLAVERY IN THE SOUTH. Slavery spread westward with the cotton plantations which by 1850 blanketed the lower South from South Carolina to Texas. This expansion so increased the demand for slaves that the price of field hands rose from $400 to $1,000 (1820-1860). Most were imported from the upper South by slave traders, who marched their chattels southward in chains to be auctioned off to the highest bidders. By 1860 the number in bondage rose to 4,000,000. Most were owned by small planters who not only worked with the slaves but treated them well. On larger plantations, where overseers were in charge, cruelty was not uncommon, especially as the law allowed owners to inflict all punishment for crime.

b. CHANGING SOUTHERN ATTITUDE TOWARD SLAVERY. Southerners who had looked on slavery as a necessary evil during the Revolutionary period rapidly changed their opinion as the institution became economically indispensable. By the end of the 1830's they viewed slavery as a positive good, essential to the well-being of the entire South.

2. *The Northern Attack on Slavery*

a. THE EARLY ANTISLAVERY MOVEMENT. Before 1830 Southerners were willing to free their slaves but hesitated to do so because: 1) the cost of compensating owners was prohibitive; and 2) they were committed to a policy of "white supremacy" and hesitated to face the social problems created by the presence of a large number of free Negroes. To solve the latter problem they formed the *American Colonization Society* (1816) to encourage emancipation, then send the freed slaves to Africa. During this early period the antislavery movement was primarily southern.

b. THE RISE OF ABOLITIONISM.

I. *Character of Abolitionism.* Abolitionism, which was a product of the reforming zeal of the 1830's, differed from the earlier antislavery movement in its emphasis on *racial equality*. Abolitionists wanted to free the slaves, by force if necessary, then educate them to take their place in society. This program was certain to lead to opposition in the South, which was determined to maintain "white supremacy."

II. *Beginnings of Organization.* Organized abolitionism originated in: 1) *New England,* where *William Lloyd Garrison* founded *The Liberator* (1831), a vitriolic newspaper that demanded immediate abolition, and helped form the New England Anti-Slavery Society (1832); and 2) the *West,* where James Birney and *Theodore Dwight Weld* launched a campaign for gradual emancipation to be achieved through a process of religious persuasion. With the backing of two wealthy New Yorkers, Arthur and Lewis Tappan, they converted Oberlin College into a training ground for abolitionists, who gradually won the West to their point of view. Westerners dominated the meeting that formed the *American Anti-Slavery Society* (1833) and controlled this important society during the next decade of rapid expansion.

III. *The Abolitionist Program.* Organized abolitionists: 1) set up an *"underground railroad"* that smuggled some 2000 slaves yearly to Canada and freedom; 2) showered Congress with abolitionist petitions, despite the adoption of a *"gag rule"* (1836) which ordered all such petitions to be laid on the table without debate; and 3) entered politics with the formation of the *Liberty Party* (1840) which nominated James G. Birney for the presidency. These activities attracted such favorable attention in the North that sentiment for abolitionism was sweeping the region by the 1840's.

3. The Southern Reaction to Abolitionism

a. ATTACKS ON ABOLITIONISTS. When a slave rebellion, the *Nat Turner Insurrection* of Virginia (1831), coincided with the appearance of *The Liberator,* Southerners became convinced that abolition literature must be kept out of the South.

At first mobs burned mail sacks containing attacks on slavery, but postmasters soon refused to deliver such materials. Abolitionists were threatened with death if they crossed the Mason and Dixon Line.

b. DEFENSE OF SLAVERY. As the abolitionist attack mounted, Southerners rose to the defense of their institution. Writers argued that slavery was: 1) ordained by God, sanctioned in the Scriptures, and traditional in the ancient world; 2) essential to the southern economy; 3) preferable to the "wage slavery" of the North; and 4) beneficial to the Negro who had been allowed to trade the barbarism of Africa for the blessings of security and Christianity. This *"proslavery argument"* was believed by all Southerners by the 1840's, and was echoed by such statesmen as John C. Calhoun. The resulting division between North and South provided an emotional basis for all later sectional conflicts.

D. The Battle for Women's Rights

1. Changing Status of Women. Women were considered so inferior to men that they were not allowed to receive an education, vote, or control their own property. Improvement was made possible by: 1) the democratic spirit of the Jacksonian period, which caused reformers to rebel against the disenfranchisement of half the population; 2) the industrial revolution which allowed women to demonstrate that they could care for themselves by entering gainful occupations; and 3) the rise of the reform movements which gave them a chance to crusade for abolitionism and other improvements side by side with men.

2. Organized Feminism. When women delegates were denied admission to a World's Anti-Slavery Convention in London (1840), Lucretia Mott and Elizabeth Cady Stanton determined to devote their lives to securing rights for women. By 1848 they could stage the world's first *Women's Rights Convention* at Seneca Falls, New York. Similar conventions were held annually thereafter. The only tangible gains secured were: 1) the right to enter a few advanced schools such as Oberlin on an equal basis with men; 2) admission into the professions; and 3) the right to control their own property in Mississippi (1839) and some other western states. Other legal

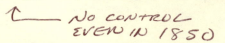
NO CONTROL EVEN IN 1850

gains, including the franchise, had to wait until after the Civil War.

E. Temperance Reform

1. The Demand for Temperance. Excessive drinking was so common among all classes of Americans that reformers in the 1820's began demanding moderation or abstinence from hard liquor. Societies to further this cause sprang up rapidly, the most prominent being the American Society for the Promotion of Temperance (1826), formed at Boston by Lyman Beecher. In 1833 these merged into the *United States Temperance Union.*

2. The Demand for Total Abstinence. After 1840 total abstinence became the objective of reformers. Their most effective instruments were: 1) the *Washington Temperance Societies* made up of reformed drunkards who persuaded other drunkards to take the pledge; and 2) a flood of propaganda typified by Timothy Shay Arthur's famous novel, *Ten Nights in a Bar-Room* (1853). As self-imposed abstinence proved impossible, the demand for legal prohibition mounted during the 1850's. The first such law was adopted by *Maine* (1846) under the prodding of *Neal Dow.* A dozen other states adopted similar laws before the Civil War.

F. Humane Treatment for the Unfit

1. Care of the Insane. The unfortunate condition of the insane, who were treated as ordinary criminals, was revealed by *Dorothea Dix* after investigating conditions in Massachusetts (1841) and other states. Her terrifying revelations shocked eleven states into transferring the insane from jails to asylums before 1854.

2. Reform in Legal Codes. Laws were gradually humanized by: 1) reducing the crimes punishable by death; 2) abolishing public hangings; and 3) abandoning flogging and other cruel punishments.

3. Prison Reform. Jails were breeding grounds for crime as hardened criminals were cast with first offenders. The concept that they should be used to regenerate criminals was first tested with the *Auburn System* (used at Auburn, New York), which kept the men working together by day and separated at night to prevent contamination. The _Pennsylvania System_ was also tried. Criminals were kept in solitary confinement but given work under the theory that they would repent if they had nothing to do but think of their sins. Crude as these systems were, they indicated a growing concern with the reform of lawbreakers.

III. DEMOCRATIZATION OF INTELLECTUAL LIFE

A. Reasons for the Intellectual Renaissance

1. Influence of Democracy. Editors, writers, and artists, aware that a large audience had been created by the educational revolution, made a conscious effort to please this group rather than the cultured few. As a result: 1) cultural progress was stimulated by the larger audience; and 2) efforts to cater to the masses whose tastes were distinctly American encouraged the growth of native schools of writing, painting, and music.

2. Influence of Industrialization. Industry: 1) created the wealth and leisure necessary for cultural progress; and 2) concentrated people in urban units where they could be trained culturally by better schools, newspapers, libraries, and the like. The intellectual pre-eminence of New England during this period was partly due to the rapid industrialization of that section.

B. Newspapers and Magazines

1. Rise of Popular Journalism. The extension of the franchise allowed newspaper editors to exert great influence politically. To extend their audiences, and hence their power, they: 1) lowered the price of their papers to one penny, a step inaugurated by the _New York Sun_ (1833); and 2) made their papers more sensational, a policy introduced by _James Gordon Bennett_ of the _New York Herald_ (1835). As other newspapers followed these examples, editors such as _Horace Greeley_ of the _New York Tribune_ (1841) became nationally famous.

2. Rise of Popular Magazines. Hundreds of magazines catered to every taste. At first the most popular were _Graham's Magazine_ (Philadelphia, 1826-1858), the _Knickerbocker Mag-_

azine (New York, 1833-1865), the *Southern Literary Messenger* (Richmond, 1834-1864), and *Godey's Lady's Book* (1830). In the 1850's these older publications were challenged by *Harper's Monthly Magazine* (1850) and the *Atlantic Monthly* (1857).

C. The Literary Renaissance

1. The Middle States. During the first part of the period the Middle States dominated the literary scene; *Washington Irving* produced his *Astoria* and *Life of Washington* at the time, *William Cullen Bryant* much of his verse, and *James Fenimore Cooper* his *Leather-Stocking Tales.* The two greatest works of the generation, *Herman Melville's Moby Dick* (1851) and *Walt Whitman's Leaves of Grass* (1855) were products of this section.

2. The South. Despite its boasted culture, the South produced few authors during the slavery period. The most prolific writer was *William Gilmore Simms* of South Carolina who published more than one hundred novels, stories, and poems modeled after those of Sir Walter Scott. The South's greatest author, *Edgar Allen Poe,* died at the age of forty (1849) virtually without recognition.

3. New England's Golden Age.

a. Rise of Transcendentalism. The father of New England's Golden Age was *Ralph Waldo Emerson,* a philosopher and writer of Concord, Massachusetts. Accepting from Kant the belief that the realm of the spirit transcended the world of experience, Emerson taught that every man could achieve near-perfection by sharing in the universal "over soul" that was God. This optimistic faith, which was spread by the Transcendental Club and its magazine, *The Dial* (1840), did much to remove the blight of Calvinistic theology from New England, preparing the way for a flood of literary production.

b. The New England Writers. Among the outstanding writers were: 1) *poets* such as James Wadsworth Longfellow and James Greenleaf Whittier; 2) such *novelists and essayists* as Nathaniel Hawthorne, whose *Scarlet Letter* and *House of Seven Gables* were minor classics, Oliver Wendell Holmes, the author of the *Autocrat of the Breakfast Table,* and James Russell Lowell, who contributed the _Biglow Papers_ to the cause of abolitionism; and 3) a number of _historians_ including _George Bancroft,_ whose twelve-volume _History of the United States_ (1834-1875) reflected the nationalism of the day, William H. Prescott, who won fame by writing of the Spanish Empire, John L. Motley, who traced the _Rise of the Dutch Republic_ (1856), and especially _Francis Parkman,_ author of numerous epic volumes describing the conflict between France and England for North America.

D. The Fine Arts

1. Growth of Interest in Music. Mounting interest was shown by: 1) the founding of the first philharmonic orchestras in the 1840's; and 2) the popularity of European artists such as Ole Bull, a Norwegian violinist, and _Jenny Lind,_ whose first American tour (1850) was promoted by P. T. Barnum, a leading showman. The only native composers of note were _Lowell Mason,_ author of hymns sung today, and _Stephen Collins Foster,_ an eccentric genius who composed many folk classics before his untimely death in 1864.

2. Beginnings of the Popular Theater. Sentiment against the theater was receding by the 1840's, allowing actors such as Edwin Forest and Edwin Booth to become nationally prominent. Shakespeare's plays had such an appeal to this oratorical generation that native playwrights were discouraged. A turning point in the history of the theater occurred in the 1850's when the dramatization of Harriet Beecher Stowe's _Uncle Tom's Cabin_ attracted thousands who would not have attended a less moral play.

3. Nationalism in Painting, Sculpture, and Architecture. A group of New York painters, known as the _Hudson River School,_ became famous for their local landscapes. Although still dominated by European influences, their emphasis on the native scene helped foster a national spirit in painting. Both sculptors and architects still slavishly imitated classical examples. Among the former the best known was Hiram Powers, whose "The Greek Slave" was widely discussed, largely because it depicted the nude female figure. Builders modeled everything from state capitols to farmhouses after Greek temples until the 1850's, when a revolt against classicism launched the *Gothic Revival* with its excessive ornamentation and bad taste.

E. Scientific Progress. Theoretical science was still neglected, while the natural sciences attracted far more attention than the physical sciences. Among the leading natural scientists were: 1) *Louis Agassiz,* a geologist and biologist who taught at Harvard after coming to the United States from Switzerland in 1846; 2) *J. J. Audubon,* author of the classic *Birds of America;* and 3) Asa Gray, an outstanding systematic botanist. A noteworthy discovery of the era was that of *anesthesia* by *Dr. Crawford W. Long,* a Georgia physician (1842). Before he published his finding, two New England dentists — W. G. T. Morton and Horace Wells — made parallel discoveries.

IV. SOCIAL AND INTELLECTUAL CONTRIBUTIONS OF THE JACKSONIAN ERA

A. Enduring Contributions of the Period. The remarkable progress made during the era: 1) emphasized that cultural gains were accelerated during periods of greatest democratic progress; 2) demonstrated that the American people of all classes were capable of rapid improvement, with resulting benefits to the nation; and 3) helped sever the cultural connections with Europe that had hindered the growth of a distinctive type of expression. The rapid cultural progress made after the Civil War rested on these foundations.

B. The End of the Era of Progress. Each period of progressive gain in American history has ended in war. This has been no accident; the high idealism bred in the people during such eras has made them ready to fight for causes that would have aroused little enthusiasm at other times. The age of the common man was no exception. Swept along on a wave of humanitarianism and reforming zeal, the American people were ready to take such firm stands for or against slavery during the next decades that civil war was inevitable.

ADDITIONAL READING

An interpretation of the period is in Carl Bode, *The Anatomy of American Popular Culture, 1840-1861* (1959), and compact surveys in R. H. Gabriel, *Course of American Democratic Thought* (1940), and Merle Curti, *Growth of American Thought* (3rd edn., 1964). C. R. Fish, *Rise of the Common Man* (1927), and A. F. Tyler, *Freedom's Ferment* (1944) are thorough general treatments. Literary currents are appraised in Van Wyck Brooks, *The Flowering of New England* (1936) and F. O. Matthiessen, *American Renaissance* (1941). Norman Ware, *The Industrial Worker* (1924) is still the best description of working conditions; the utopian experiments that these inspired are explained in A. E. Bestor, *Backwoods Utopias* (1950). Scientific progress is traced in two fine volumes: A. H. Dupree, *Asa Gray* (1959), and Edward Lurie, *Louis Agassiz* (1960). The relations between religion and reform are explained in W. R. Cross, *The Burned-Over District* (1950), and T. L. Smith, *Revivalism and Social Reform in Mid-Nineteenth Century America* (1957). For specific religious developments see: B. W. Weisberger, *They Gathered at the River* (1958) (revivalism), F. D. Nichols, *The Midnight Cry* (1945) (Millerism), F. T. O'Dea, *The Mormons* (1957), and R. A. Billington, *The Protestant Crusade* (1938) (Nativism). Two fine books on the antislavery movement are Louis Filler, *The Crusade Against Slavery* (1960), and D. L. Dumond, *Antislavery* (1961); readable biographies of a leading abolitionist are R. B. Nye, *William Lloyd Garrison and the Humanitarian Reformers* (1960), and J. L. Thomas, *The Liberator: William Lloyd Garrison* (1963). On the crusade for women's rights, A. S. Blackwell, *Lucy Stone* (1950), Otelia Cromwell, *Lucretia Mott* (1958), and Alma Lutz, *Susan B. Anthony* (1963) are essential biographical studies. The crusade is popularly described in Eleanor Flexner, *Century of Struggle* (1959). J. A. Krout, *Origins of Prohibition* (1925) is still standard on early temperance, and E. H. Marshall, *Dorothea Dix* (1937) on humanitarian reform.

CHAPTER XII

Slavery and Expansion
1840-1850

❡ THE DECADE OF EXPANSION

During the decade of the 1840's the United States virtually doubled its territory. Texas was annexed, the Oregon country secured after a dispute with England, California occupied, and the Southwestern Territories wrested from Mexico by war. To Americans who gloried in the fulfillment of the "manifest destiny" of their nation, the next few years were disheartening. For expansion reopened the slavery controversy in such violent form that civil war was necessary to resolve the conflict between the sections.

I. CAUSES OF AMERICAN EXPANSION

A. Expelling Forces

1. Economic Factors

a. EXHAUSTION OF GOOD LANDS. By 1840 the southern Mississippi Valley was well settled between Missouri and Louisiana. In the northern valley much of Iowa, Illinois, and Wisconsin remained to be occupied, while Minnesota was still a virgin territory. Hence the southern valley was the source of migration during the decade. There younger sons or unsuccessful pioneers believed that they could succeed only by moving westward in search of good soil.

179

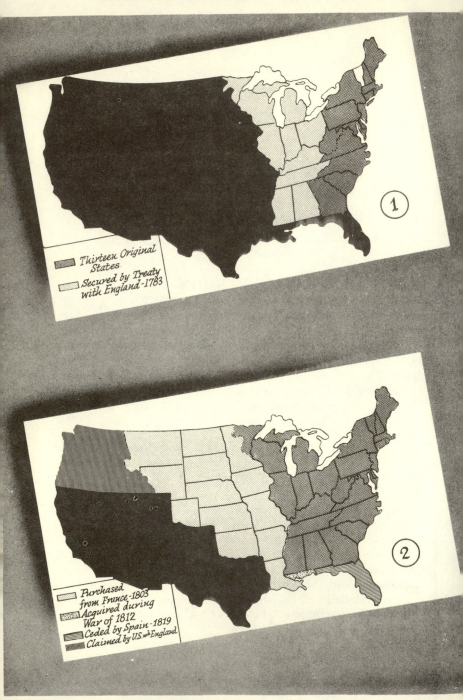

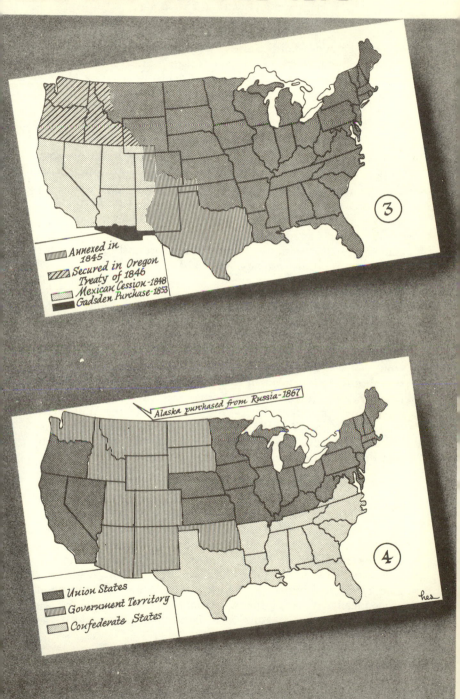

TED STATES 1783-1870 ★ ★ ★

Annexed in 1845
Secured in Oregon Treaty of 1846
Mexican Cession-1848
Gadsden Purchase-1853

③

Alaska purchased from Russia-1867

Union States
Government Territory
Confederate States

④

hes

b. EFFECTS OF THE PANIC OF 1837. Hard times after 1837 encouraged migration because: 1) low prices for farm produce did not allow farmers to meet mortgage payments or complete purchase of their lands; 2) the heavy debts incurred by Mississippi Valley states during the internal improvement craze of the 1830's doomed their citizens to years of high taxes; and 3) the collapse of the canal-building programs meant that farmers would continue to have difficulty marketing crops.

2. Psychological Factors. The intense democratic faith of the Jacksonian era convinced Americans that their country was the most perfect in the world. As God did not want such perfection to be narrowly confined, it was their *"manifest destiny"* to move ever onward until the less fortunate people of the Far West, Canada, Mexico, and Central and South America could enjoy the blessings of their democratic institutions. This bumptious faith drove many westward.

B. Attracting Forces

1. The Geography of Expansion. Lying west of the first tier of states beyond the Mississippi was the treeless Great Plains province which had been branded by early explorers as the "Great American Desert." During the 1830's this region, which was thought to be unsuited to white occupation, was allotted to transplanted Indian tribes from the East. Hence pioneers were forced to leap across this barrier to the black soil regions of eastern Texas, the rich lands of the Willamette Valley of Oregon, and the fertile fields of the Sacramento Valley of California. These attractive areas served as magnets that drew frontiersmen westward.

2. Advertising the Far West

a. THE SANTA FE TRADERS. Traders from the West brought back news of the region's attractiveness. Prominent among these were merchants who visited Santa Fe, New Mexico, after trade with that Mexican town was opened in 1821 by *William Becknell.* Each year thereafter caravans of wagons journeyed between Missouri and Santa Fe, returning with furs, gold, silver, and mules. Although the trade was not important economically, it paved the way for future expansion by: 1) demonstrating that wagons could be used in plains travel; 2) showing pioneers how to organize under elected leaders for the dangerous journey westward; and 3) proving the weakness of Mexico's hold on its northern provinces, thus whetting the American appetite for more territory.

b. THE MOUNTAIN MEN. Under the "rendezvous system" of trading established by the Rocky Mountain Fur Company in the 1820's, hundreds of individual trappers roamed over the Rocky Mountain country and beyond. Once each year they gathered for the "rendezvous" at a designated spot where they met wagons loaded with trading goods sent out by the company from St. Louis. The traders, or "mountain men," explored all the Far West in their search for beaver. One, *Jedediah Strong Smith,* led parties from the Great Salt Lake through the Southwest, California, and the Oregon country (1826-1827). These explorations revealed to Easterners the rich lands and navigable rivers of the West, as well as the *South Pass* of Wyoming that allowed easy passage through the Rockies.

II. EXPANSION INTO OREGON BEFORE 1844

A. Early Interest in the Oregon Country

1. The China Traders. James Cook, an English navigator who investigated the Oregon coast in 1778, found that sea otter furs were highly prized in China, where they could be traded for exotic oriental goods. Within a few years New England merchants were sending their ships around South America, securing furs in Oregon, crossing the Pacific, trading for tea and other luxuries in China, and completing the circumnavigation of the globe. A ship captain on one of these expeditions, Robert Gray, discovered the Columbia River (1792). English competitors were forced to withdraw during the Napoleonic Wars, allowing Americans to monopolize the China trade.

2. Overland Explorers

a. ACTIVITIES OF THE NORTH WEST COMPANY. This Canadian trading company, eager to expand its activities to the Pacific, in 1793 sent Alexander Mackenzie overland to Oregon. Another Northwester, David Thompson, explored most of Oregon and British Columbia during the next few years. These explorations gave England a claim to the region.

b. AMERICAN EXPLORERS AND TRADERS. American claims rested not only on the China trade and the explorations of Lewis and Clark (see p. 105) but on the occupation of Oregon by later traders. *John Jacob Astor,* founder of the *American Fur Company* (1808), established the post of *Astoria* at the mouth of the Columbia River early in 1812. Although his traders under Wilson Price Hunt succeeded in blazing a trail across the continent, the project was doomed to failure by the outbreak of the War of 1812. Astor, knowing that his post could be captured by the British navy, sold his interests to the North West Company, temporarily ending American occupation of Oregon.

3. Period of British Control. After 1812 the contest between the North West Company and the Hudson's Bay Company for control of Oregon grew so intense that the king forced the two companies to merge (1821) under the latter's name. For the next twenty years Dr. *John McLoughlin,* the company's representative, controlled the region. He built *Ft. Vancouver* on the north bank of the Columbia, scattered smaller posts through the area, and began extensive farming operations in the Puget Sound Valley to provide food for his traders. To win Oregon the United States must break this monopoly.

B. American Expansion Into Oregon

1. Rival Claims to the Oregon Country. By this time England and the United States were the only claimants, Spain having withdrawn (1819) when it abandoned claims north of the 42nd parallel, and Russia (1824) when it ceded to the two contestants its rights south of 54° 40'. This restricted the dispute to the region between 42° and 54° 40'. England, however, was ready to settle at any time for the area north of the Columbia River, while the United States wanted only the country south of the 49th parallel. Thus *the triangle of land between the Columbia River and the 49th parallel was the real "core" of the boundary dispute.* As neither nation was ready to assert its claim to this region, a *Treaty of Joint Occupation* (1818) allowed nationals of both countries to trade or settle there.

2. American Attempts to Break the English Monopoly

a. THE COMING OF THE TRADERS. Several individual traders challenged the Hudson's Bay Company's monopoly in the

1820's. Typical was *Nathaniel Wyeth,* a Massachusetts ice dealer, who led an expedition westward, only to be underbid by the Company's agents whenever he tried to buy furs from Indians. Clearly no individual was strong enough to break the monopoly.

b. THE COMING OF THE MISSIONARIES. In 1833 a religious magazine described the alleged visit of a group of Flathead Indians to St. Louis to ask that missionaries be sent to Oregon. This created great excitement among the orthodox. The Methodists (1834) responded by sending the Reverend *Jason Lee* and a small party to found a station in the Willamette Valley. Two years later the Reverend *Marcus Whitman* established a Presbyterian mission at the junction of the Columbia and Snake rivers; Catholic missions under Father Pierre de Smet were also functioning before 1840. All these missionaries carried back news of the riches of the Willamette Valley.

c. THE COMING OF THE PIONEERS. Beginning in 1841 caravans of settlers began following the *Oregon Trail* westward from Independence, Missouri, through South Pass to Ft. Vancouver. By 1843 more than 1000 yearly were treking westward, nearly all to the Willamette Valley. In that year they set up a provisional government, at the same time demanding annexation by the United States. As the Hudson's Bay Company firmly occupied the region actually in dispute — north of the Columbia River — a dangerous controversy was developing.

III. EXPANSION INTO CALIFORNIA BEFORE 1844

A. Spanish Occupation of California. Spain occupied California after 1769, when forts and *mission stations* were scattered along the coast from San Diego to San Francisco. Until 1821, when Mexico won its independence, the principal occupants were Indians who had been converted and civilized by the mission fathers. After that date land was granted to ranchers and farmers. Among the few non-Mexicans given land was Captain *John A. Sutter,* whose fort on the lower Sacramento later became a haven for American pioneers. As the ranchers increased in influence, they demanded the secularization of the missions, hoping to obtain the land that was allotted the Indians. They won this battle in the 1830's, with the result that cattle ranches soon blanketed all of California.

B. American Beginnings in California. From the 1820's on, *hide and tallow traders* from New England regularly visited California to buy leather for shoe factories and tallow for candles. Agents of the traders first called attention to California's rich soil and pleasant climate. Mountain men also visited there occasionally, and similarly advertised the region. Hence overland migrations began in 1841 when the first covered wagons blazed the *California Trail* westward. This branched from the Oregon Trail at Ft. Bridger, followed the Humboldt River across Nevada, and scaled the Sierra Nevada Mountains to emerge near *Sutter's Fort.* By 1844 several hundred Americans lived in the lower Sacramento Valley.

C. Early Attempts at Annexation. These Americans wanted to add California to the United States. Their most active spokesman was *Thomas O. Larkin* of Monterey, who in 1844 became United States consul. Larkin hoped to stir up a Mexican-American revolution against Mexico that would lead to annexation. Thus by 1844 the situation was growing as tense as that in Oregon.

IV. THE ELECTION OF 1844 AND ITS RESULTS

A. The Problem of Texan Annexation

1. British Interest in Texas. After the United States refused to annex the Texan Republic (see p. 156), England became interested in keeping Texas independent. This would: 1) allow British manufacturers to buy cotton in a region where payment could be made in manufactured goods, as it could not in the tariff-protected United States; and 2) give humanitarians a chance to persuade the Texans to free their slaves. Hence England persuaded Mexico to grant Texas an armistice (1843) and even sought to arrange a treaty (1844) guaranteeing the republic's independence.

2. American Interest in Texas. British interest in Texas aroused new American sentiment for annexation. President Tyler (1843) instructed his Secretary of State, A. P. Upshur, to draw up a treaty for this purpose, but Upshur died before this was done. John C. Calhoun, his successor, completed the treaty (April, 1844), then asked ratification on the grounds that annexation would frustrate England's efforts to free the slaves there. The Senate refused to ratify because: 1) Calhoun's message offended antislavery leaders; 2) others refused to take a step that might lead to war with Mexico; and 3) still others hesitated to act until the people had expressed themselves in the election of 1844.

B. The Election of 1844

1. The Whig Campaign. The leading candidate of the party, *Henry Clay,* issued a statement opposing annexation, but after he was nominated attempted to straddle the issue. As a result many northern Whigs deserted to the antislavery Liberty party.

2. The Democratic Victory. The Democrats passed over Martin Van Buren because he opposed annexation, choosing instead *James K. Polk* of Tennessee. Both Polk's speeches and the party platform favored adding Texas to the Union. The popularity of this stand was shown when he was elected with 170 votes to 105 for Clay. The Democrats also won control of both houses of Congress. This was a clear mandate for manifest destiny.

C. Fulfillment of Manifest Destiny

1. The Annexation of Texas. Tyler determined to annex Texas before he left the White House. Knowing that a treaty could not command the two-thirds majority needed for ratification, he proposed a *joint resolution* inviting Texas to join the United States. This was adopted and signed by the President on March 1, 1845. Texas was admitted in December, 1845.

2. The Oregon Treaty

a. AMERICAN DEMANDS FOR OREGON. In December, 1845, Polk asked Congress for authority to terminate the Treaty of Joint Occupation and take any steps necessary to secure Oregon. As the hunger of the Democrats for expansion had been partially satisfied with Texas, and as the commercial-minded Whigs did not want war, the harsh demand for Oregon submitted to England (April, 1846) was accompanied by a strong suggestion that a friendly settlement was desired.

b. ENGLAND'S SURRENDER. This was made possible when the Hudson's Bay Company moved Ft. Vancouver from the

Columbia River to Vancouver Island. This step was taken because: 1) the Company realized that control of the Columbia was not essential to the interior trade; 2) the price of furs was declining in Europe; and 3) officials were afraid that hostile Americans in the Willamette Valley would raid the fort, destroying the valuable trading goods there. In effect the Hudson's Bay Company informed England that it no longer wanted the disputed territory. Britain was glad to surrender, as the repeal of the Corn Laws (1846) made her dependent on American grain. Hence the government agreed to a treaty extending the 49th parallel to the Pacific. This was signed in June, 1846.

V. THE WAR WITH MEXICO

A. Causes of the War

1. American Grievances Against Mexico. Weak governments in Mexico aroused American antagonism by: 1) delaying the drafting of a commercial treaty desired by the people of both nations; 2) failing to protect the lives of Americans during frequent revolutions; and 3) refusing to compensate American citizens for property destroyed during these disturbances. President Polk felt war justified under existing international law on the basis of these grievances alone.

2. Mexican Grievances Against the United States

a. THE TEXAN BOUNDARY DISPUTE. Texas claimed the Rio Grande River as its southern and western boundary. This claim had no basis, as the extreme limit of Texas when a Mexican province was the Nueces River. Polk, however, insisted that this disputed region was now part of the United States.

b. EFFORTS TO ACQUIRE CALIFORNIA.

I. *British Interest in California.* Official American interest in California developed rapidly during the 1840's because: 1) a British consul who was sent there in 1842 began working for annexation by England; and 2) Mexico in 1846 offered California to England as security for a loan. Neither Britain nor France had any designs on the region, but this was not known at the time.

II. *American Interests in California.* The United States, on the other hand, was actively interested in annexing California.

This was revealed to Mexico by: 1) the capture of Monterey in 1842 by an American naval commander who mistakenly believed that war had begun; 2) the activities of Thomas O. Larkin, consul at Monterey, who assured Californians that the United States would welcome them if they won their independence; and 3) the appearance of an official American explorer, *John C. Fremont,* with a large military party, in the fall of 1845. Fremont was allowed to winter near Monterey, but exhibited belligerent intentions before leaving for Oregon in the spring of 1846. These things convinced Mexico that the United States was plotting the seizure of California.

   3. The Slidell Mission. In a last effort to settle differences peacefully, President Polk sent John Slidell to Mexico City (November, 1845) with instructions to: 1) assume all claims of American citizens against Mexico in return for the Rio Grande boundary; 2) buy New Mexico for $5,000,000; and 3) purchase California for $20,000,000. So intense was the anti-American sentiment of the Mexican people that the government did not dare receive Slidell.

   4. The Declaration of War. Polk decided on war as soon as he heard of Slidell's failure. In hopes of provoking Mexico into striking the first blow, he sent troops under General *Zachary Taylor* into the disputed region between the Nueces and Rio Grande rivers (January, 1846). By May 9, 1846, the President was so tired of waiting that he told his cabinet he had decided to ask Congress for a declaration of war on the basis of Mexico's refusal to meet its international obligations. Before this message was sent, news reached Washington that a Mexican force had attacked Taylor's army. Polk redrafted his message, claiming that war was justified by Mexico's invasion of the United States. Congress declared war on *May 12, 1846.*

B. The Conquest of Mexico

   1. Opposition to the War. The Northeast viewed the war as a conspiracy of slaveholders to secure more territory. Even western Whigs shared this belief; *Abraham Lincoln* gained momentary fame with his *"Spot Resolutions"* asking Polk to name the spot where American blood was spilled on American soil. This opposition hindered military preparations, for when Congress asked for 50,000 enlistments almost none volunteered from the Northeast and few from the Southeast. The expansionistic Mississippi Valley alone supported the war.

2. Conquest of the Northern Mexican Provinces

a. CAMPAIGNS OF GENERAL ZACHARY TAYLOR. A threefold campaign was planned against Mexico, New Mexico, and California. Taylor's force started southward from Texas to capture Monterrey (September 21-23, 1846) and *Buena Vista* (February 22-23, 1847). In the latter battle the main Mexican army under General *Antonio Santa Anna* was decisively defeated, opening the way to Mexico City. Polk, however, feared that Taylor's increasing popularity would give the Whigs a presidential candidate by 1848. Hence he ordered him to remain at Buena Vista until the northern provinces were subdued.

b. THE ARMY OF THE WEST. Colonel Stephen W. Kearny led 1700 volunteers over the Santa Fe trail to subdue that city without a battle (August, 1846). After proclaiming New Mexico a part of the United States, Kearny moved westward with 300 men to aid in the conquest of California, while another force under Colonel A. W. Doniphan started south to join Taylor.

c. THE CONQUEST OF CALIFORNIA. Even before the Mexican War began, Americans in California were encouraged to declare their independence by John C. Fremont, who had returned with his exploring party after starting for Oregon. This *Bear Flag Revolt* was only two weeks old when news of the outbreak of war arrived. Fremont, leading a battalion of Bear Flaggers, marched east from the Sacramento Valley to join an American naval force that had captured Monterey (July, 1846). The combined armies drove the Mexican defenders southward, where they were joined by Colonel Kearny in inflicting a final defeat near Los Angeles. By January, 1847, the northern provinces had been won.

3. The Attack on Mexico City.

An army under General *Winfield Scott* sailed to Vera Cruz, then fought its way up the mountain passes that led to Mexico City during the summer of 1847. Advancing to the gates of the city, the Americans stormed the heavily fortified hill of Chapultepec (September

13, 1847) and the next day entered Mexico City. Santa Anna had no choice but surrender.

C. The Peace Negotiations

1. Mission of Nicholas P. Trist.   Polk was so confident of victory that he sent Trist, chief clerk of the State Department, with Scott's army to draft the peace treaty. When Scott and Trist quarreled, Trist was ordered back to Washington. Fortunately for Mexico he refused to return; had he done so harsher terms might have been inflicted, as the easy victory had stimulated a popular movement in the United States to take over all Mexico.

2. Treaty of Guadalupe   Hidalgo. The treaty (February 2, 1848) provided that: 1) Mexico cede New Mexico and California as well as accepting the Rio Grande boundary for Texas; and 2) the United States pay Mexico $15,000,000 and assume claims of American citizens against that country to the sum of $3,250,000. The treaty was ratified by the Senate (March 10, 1848) by a vote of 38 to 14.

3. Effect of the Treaty on the Mormons. One unforeseen result of the war was to bring the Mormons back into the United States. The persecuted members of this church had been led by *Brigham Young* to the shores of Great Salt Lake (1847) in an effort to find a spot where they could worship as they pleased. Although the Utah settlement prospered, the Mormons were destined to undergo further persecution before they were accepted by their fellow Americans.

VI.   RENEWAL OF THE SLAVERY CONFLICT

A. The Wilmot Proviso

1. The Sectional Impasse.   *David Wilmot,* a Pennsylvania Democrat, in August, 1846, moved to amend an appropriation bill before the House to ban slavery from all territory taken from Mexico. This proviso launched the nation on a four-year debate in which the sections drifted wide apart.

2. Arguments of the Sections

a. THE SOUTHERN ARGUMENT. Southerners, led by *John C. Calhoun,* argued that Congress had no legal right to ban slavery from the territories. They held that the territories were the common property of the states. The Constitution guaranteed each citizen protection for his property (Fifth Amendment). Hence any citizen could take his property (in slaves) anywhere within the United States. This stand was pressed vigorously because the South would lose control of the Senate (as it had the House) unless New Mexico and California entered the Union as slave states to offset Minnesota and Oregon which would soon be admitted as free states.

b. THE NORTHERN ARGUMENT. Northerners held that Congress could legally bar slavery from the territories by exercising its constitutional right to "make all needful rules and regulations respecting the territory" of the United States.

c. THE COMPROMISE VIEW. Moderates advanced two compromise proposals during the debate: 1) advocates of *squatter sovereignty* led by *Lewis Cass* of Michigan held that the people of each territory should decide for themselves whether they wanted slavery; and 2) others, led by President Polk, favored *dividing the territory* by extending the Missouri Compromise line of 36° 30′ west to the Pacific.

B. The Election of 1848

1. The Rival Parties

a. COMPROMISING ATTITUDE OF THE MAJOR PARTIES. The major parties, which were composed of both Northerners and Southerners, refused to take a stand on the Wilmot Proviso. The *Democrats,* whose strength lay in the South, nominated *Lewis Cass* of Michigan and made no mention of slavery in their platform. The *Whigs,* whose strength lay in the North, selected General *Zachary Taylor,* a Louisiana slaveholder, as their candidate and did not even draft a platform. *Millard Fillmore,* an obscure New York politician, was chosen to run with Taylor.

b. THE FREE SOIL PARTY. Northern antislavery men, unable to follow either party, formed the Free Soil party on a platform favoring the Wilmot Proviso and free land for actual settlers. Its members included: 1) former members of the Liberty party; 2) northern Whigs or "conscience Whigs," and 3) eastern Democrats, or "Barnburners," who deserted their party when Cass was nominated rather than Van Buren. *Martin Van Buren* was the candidate for the Free Soilers.

2. The Whig Triumph. The Free Soil party took enough votes away from the Democrats in New York to allow

the Whigs to win. The thirteen Free Soil representatives elected held the balance of power in the House of Representatives.

C. The Compromise of 1850

1. Need for Immediate Action. While Congress debated the Wilmot Proviso, New Mexico and California were left with no government save military rule. This situation became intolerable when the discovery of gold near Sutter's Fort launched the famous *rush of the '49ers.* Within a year a polyglot population of 100,000 was scattered through the mining camps. Congress could no longer delay in providing California with a government.

2. Drafting the Compromise

a. POLICY OF ZACHARY TAYLOR. Without consulting Congress, Taylor on becoming President advised California and New Mexico to draft constitutions and ask admission. California (September, 1849) and New Mexico (May, 1850) responded by drawing up constitutions that banned slavery. Hence Southerners were in an angry mood when Congress finally assembled in December, 1849. "Fire eaters" such as Robert Toombs of Georgia favored immediate secession. Never had the Union been in such danger.

b. EFFORTS AT COMPROMISE. Fortunately Congress contained moderates as well as extremists. Two of these, *Henry Clay* and *Stephen A. Douglas* of Illinois, attempted to find a solution in a series of proposals that were laid before Congress in January, 1850. These measures, which together became the *Compromise of 1850,* provided for: 1) the admission of California as a free state; 2) the organization of the remaining Mexican territories without any restrictions on slavery; 3) the establishment of the western Texan boundary as it is today (rather than at the Rio Grande River as desired by Southerners) in return for which the United States would assume the $10,000,000 debt of the Texan Republic; 4) the abolition of the slave trade in the District of Columbia but the continuance of slavery there; and 5) the enactment of a more stringent fugitive slave law.

3. Debate on the Compromise

a. ARGUMENTS OF THE EXTREMISTS. *Extreme Southerners* such as *John C. Calhoun* and *Jefferson Davis* opposed the compromise on the grounds that the South would be forced into a minority position which would threaten its institutions. _Extreme Northerners,_ led by _William H. Seward_ of New York, not only demanded that Congress exercise its "constitutional power" to ban slavery from the territories but insisted that a _"higher law_ than our Constitution" made human bondage illegal.

b. ARGUMENTS OF THE MODERATES. Clay and Douglas pleaded for the compromise on grounds of practical necessity, holding that its provisions were fair to both sides and assuring Northerners that no Wilmot Proviso was needed to ban slavery from arid New Mexico. Even more effective was the _"Seventh of March" speech_ of _Daniel Webster,_ whose magnificent plea for union carried great weight among moderates.

c. POPULAR SUPPORT FOR COMPROMISE. Passage of the compromise was made possible not only by arguments of moderates but by: 1) a wave of prosperity following the repeal of the English Corn Laws (1846) which made the people reluctant to make sacrifices for an ideal; 2) the adjournment without action of a Nashville Convention (June, 1850) which had met to consider secession, making Northerners aware that the South was willing to compromise; and 3) the death of President Taylor (July, 1850) and the elevation to the Presidency of _Millard Fillmore,_ a weak politician who favored moderation more than his blunt predecessor.

4. _Passage of the Compromise._ Realizing that an "omnibus bill" embodying all of Clay's proposals could never pass Congress, its supporters divided the measure into a number of bills which were taken up and adopted, the last in September, 1850.

5. _Reaction to the Compromise._ Northerners objected especially to the new _fugitive slave act_ which: 1) denied fugitives jury trial; 2) prevented them from testifying in their own behalf; and 3) allowed them to be returned south on the evidence of their supposed masters. Southerners resented the admission of California as a free state; in South Carolina a majority favored secession on this issue. Yet these extremists' views were overbalanced by those who thought the compromise would end the slavery conflict for all time.

VII. AN APPRAISAL OF A DECADE OF EXPANSION

A. Manifest Destiny or Imperialism?

1. Meaning of Manifest Destiny. Modern critics have frequently branded the United States' policy regarding Texas and Mexico as imperialistic. Is this charge justified? *Imperialism* implied the conquest of colonial peoples who would then be kept in a state of permanent subserviency toward the mother country. *Manifest destiny,* on the other hand, proposed the annexation of adjacent territories whose people would then be elevated to a point where they could enjoy the full benefits of the American Constitution.

2. The Democratic Spirit. Underlying expansion in the 1840's was a belief in the perfection of American democracy. The people of the United States honestly felt that they were acting in the best interests of the Mexican people when they annexed that country's territories. Even those who did not accepted the inevitability of such conquests as part of their God-given destiny. Abolitionists such as Charles Sumner, despite their opposition to adding more slave territory, looked forward to the day when the capital of the United States would be at Mexico City. No other generation has had such faith in its country's democratic institutions.

B. Sectionalism and Party Politics

1. Nature of Political Parties. The behavior of the major parties in the emergency created by the Wilmot Proviso holds lessons for today. Political parties then and now are formed by the merging of numerous class and sectional interests. Thus in the 1840's both Whigs and Democrats had northern and southern wings.

2. Frustration of the Majority Will. This meant that neither party dared take a stand in the election of 1848; both hedged completely on the most important issue of the day. In this way they frustrated the will of the majority by preventing the more populous North from expressing itself. On the other hand, this avoidance of issues delayed the Civil War until 1861. Political parties perform a valuable function in obscuring problems until initial angers have cooled.

ADDITIONAL READING

The best history of slavery is K. M. Stampp, *The Peculiar Institution* (1956), but this should be weighed against the interpretive concepts in Stanley Elkins, *Slavery* (1959). The southern division over slavery is described in Clement Eaton, *A History of the Old South* (1949), and *The Mind of the Old South* (1964); one segment of opinion is revealed in W. S. Jenkins, *Pro-Slavery Thought in the Old South* (1935) R. C. Wade, *Slavery in the Cities* (1964), explores a little known aspect of slavery. The westward expansion that touched off the slavery controversy is described in R. A. Billington, *The Far Western Frontier, 1830-1860* (1956). Commercial motives underlying expansion are appraised in N. A. Graebner, *Empire on the Pacific* (1955) and psychological in A. K. Weinberg, *Manifest Destiny* (1935). Frederick Merk, *Manifest Destiny and Mission in American History: A Reinterpretation* (1963) questions the extent of expansionist sentiment. Popular but authentic books describing the westward movement on the overland trails are: G. R. Stewart, *The California Trail* (1962), David Lavender, *Westward Vision: The Story of the Oregon Trail* (1962), and Wallace Stegner, *The Gathering of Zion: The Story of the Mormon Trail* (1964). Earl Pomeroy, *The Pacific Slope* (1965) has sound chapters on the peopling of the states reached by these trails. On the war with Mexico, R. S. Henry, *The Story of the Mexican War* (1950) is readable, and O. A. Singletary, *The Mexican War* (1960), is brief. The presidential leaders during the period may be appraised in two biographies: Robert Seager, *And Tyler Too* (1946) and E. I. McCormac, *James K. Polk* (1922). Holman Hamilton, *Prologue to Conflict* (1964) is an excellent history of the Compromise of 1850. The California gold rush is briefly described in R. W. Paul, *Mining Frontiers of the Far West, 1848-1880* (1963) and more thoroughly in the same author's *California Gold* (1947).

CHAPTER XIII

The Decade of Controversy
1850-1860

ℂ THE PERSISTENCE OF THE SLAVERY CONFLICT

Despite the earnest hopes of the American people, the Compromise of 1850 did not end the slavery controversy. Instead the prosperity of the 1850's foreordained an early reopening of the conflict, for good times stimulated expansion, and so long as the frontier moved westward the United States would face a constantly recurring problem: should the newly settled areas be slave or free? As that question was debated and redebated the nerves of the people were worn so thin that a peaceful settlement was impossible. Civil war alone could provide the answer.

I. THE PROSPERITY OF THE 1850's

A. Expansion of the Railroad Network

1. Railroad Building. By 1850 railroads had passed their experimental stage and were ready to enter on a period of rapid expansion. During the next decade mileage increased from 9000 to 36,600. Much of this was concentrated in the Northeast, where *four trunk lines were built between seaports and the interior waterways*: the New York Central from New York to Buffalo, the Erie from New York to Lake Erie, the

Pennsylvania from Philadelphia to Pittsburgh, and the Baltimore and Ohio from Baltimore to Wheeling. Even more extensive construction in the _Middle West_ extended these lines to Detroit, Cincinnati, and especially Chicago. In contrast, the _South_ lagged behind, although many short roads linked leading cities. The only major lines joined Richmond with Memphis and the Ohio River with the Gulf of Mexico.

    2. Railroad Financing. State support ended after the Panic of 1837, although cities and counties usually subscribed to railroad stock. Instead principal support came from: 1) private investors; and 2) the federal government. The latter entered the field in 1850 when Stephen A. Douglas, the Illinois Senator, persuaded Congress to grant the Illinois Central Railroad six alternate sections (square miles) of land along the right of way for each mile of track laid. Thereafter most major roads received similar _land grants._

    3. Sectional Significance of Railroad Building. By 1860 railroads of the Northeast and Northwest formed an integrated system over which Westerners could ship their produce to eastern markets. This tended to break the old West-South trade alliance and to unite the two sections into one: the North. The southern railroads, on the other hand, formed a distinct unit having no connection with northern roads. Thus, from the economic point of view, two separate sections — North and South — were taking shape.

B. Growth of Northern Industry

    1. Causes of Expansion of Industry

      a. EXPANSION OF MARKETS. Railroads opened a nation-wide market for northeastern manufacturers. Equally important were improvements in ocean transportation that allowed sales overseas. Until 1855 American-built clipper ships dominated the Atlantic sea lanes; after that date British-built steam-driven iron vessels captured most ocean commerce, relegating sailing ships to the coastal trade. Their greater speed and lower rates allowed industrialists to broaden markets.

      b. EXPANSION OF CAPITAL. This came largely from the _California gold rush._ Through the 1850's some $50,000,000 in bullion was shipped east yearly, greatly stimulating business activity.

c. EXPANSION OF LABOR SUPPLY. For the first time in history industrialists found workers plentiful. They came from: 1) northeastern farms whose owners were unable to compete with western produce shipped eastward by rail; and 2) Ireland and Germany where disastrous *potato famines* (1845-1848) drove hundreds of thousands of peasants to the New World. The Irish settled largely in the Northeast where they sought jobs in factories; the Germans became farmers in the Upper Mississippi Valley.

2. Nature of Industrial Expansion. Railroads allowed factories to concentrate at strategic points near markets, raw materials, or labor. Hence the Northeast benefited most, although numerous extractive industries centered in the Northwest. A tendency toward consolidation was apparent, but most factories in 1860 were still small, individually owned, and geared to local rather than national markets.

3. Sectional Significance of Industrial Expansion. Industrialization: 1) provided the North with leaders powerful enough to challenge southern plantation owners; and 2) made those leaders increasingly dissatisfied with southern domination of the nation's politics. Particularly disliked were the low tariffs adopted by Democratic congresses: the *Walker Tariff* (1846), which lowered duties generally, and the Tariff of 1857, which dropped levels still more. Northern manufacturers demanded that their section's majority power be used to pass laws favorable to industry rather than to southern agriculture.

C. Spread of the Southern Plantation System

1. Expansion of Cotton Production. Expanding markets and improved textile machinery raised the price of cotton from six cents a pound in 1845 to fourteen in 1857. This encouraged production as the plantation frontier moved westward across Arkansas and Texas. The crop increased from 2,500,000 bales in 1850 to 5,300,000 in 1860 when the United States produced seven-eighths of the world's supply. Tobacco production also doubled during the decade, from 200,000,000 pounds in 1850 to 430,000,000 in 1860. Although the price of slaves and land rose faster than production, the South seemed immensely prosperous.

2. Sectional Significance of Southern Prosperity

Southerners became convinced that slavery was indispensable to their section's continued prosperity, as both cotton and tobacco were grown with slave labor. Hence any attack on the institution was increasingly resented. This attitude was reflected in such books as George Fitzhugh, *Sociology for the South* (1854) which not only defended slavery but the whole system of inequality on which it was based.

D. Expansion of Western Agriculture

1. Agricultural Expansion. New markets for western produce were opened by: 1) railroads, which allowed eastern workers to purchase foodstuffs grown in the West; and 2) the repeal of the English Corn Laws (1846) and the outbreak of the Crimean War (1853-1856), which created an additional demand for American grain abroad. As a result the last unsettled areas of the Old Northwest were occupied and Minnesota added to the Union (1858).

2. Sectional Significance of Agricultural Expansion. Widening markets: 1) made western farmers more aware of world opinion which was hostile to slavery; and 2) convinced them that their welfare was linked to that of the Northeast rather than the South which purchased a smaller portion of their produce.

II. PROSPERITY AND POLITICS, 1850 - 1854

A. The Election of 1852

1. The Compromise of 1850 as an Issue. The *Democrats* nominated a "dark horse," *Franklin Pierce* of New Hampshire, who wholeheartedly endorsed the Compromise of 1850. The *Whigs* selected as their candidate another military hero, General *Winfield Scott*, and without much enthusiasm "acquiesced in" support for the Compromise. The *Free Soil* nominee, John P. Hale, campaigned against the Compromise. Thus voters could choose between complete endorsement, passive acquiescence, and absolute rejection of the measure.

2. The Democratic Victory. The popularity of the Compromise was demonstrated when Pierce received 254 electoral votes to 42 for Scott. The Free Soil vote was only half that of 1848. The Whig Party never recovered from this defeat, remaining hopelessly divided during the next few years.

B. Renewed Emphasis on Expansion

1. Southern Interest in New Slave Regions. The Democrats sought to rekindle interest in expansion as a means of: 1) distracting attention from slavery; and 2) securing more cotton lands.

a. EFFORTS TO ACQUIRE CUBA. President Polk's offer to purchase Cuba (1848) had been curtly refused by Spain. From that time on Democratic leaders stooped to less ethical methods of securing the island: 1) Filibustering expeditions under a Cuban patriot, Narciso Lopez, were allowed to leave New Orleans (1850-1851) in the hope that they would inspire an independence movement that would add Cuba to the United States. 2) When an American ship, the *Black Warrior,* was seized for violating Cuban port regulations, President Pierce issued a virtual ultimatum, but was frustrated when Spain apologized. 3) Disorders in Spain late in 1854 allowed Pierce to order the American ministers to England, France, and Spain to meet at Ostend, Belgium, to formulate a Cuban policy. The resulting *Ostend Manifesto* asserted the right of the United States to seize the island if Spain refused to sell. This accomplished nothing save to lower American prestige in Europe.

b. THE GADSDEN PURCHASE. When surveys showed that a possible railroad route lay south of the Mexican border (the Gila River), the United States purchased a triangle of land there for $10,000,000 (1853).

c. INTEREST IN CENTRAL AMERICA.

i. *The Clayton-Bulwer Treaty.* Expansion centered attention on a possible canal across Central America. The United States secured permission from Colombia to build across the Isthmus of Panama (1846), but England soon obtained similar concessions from Nicaragua, which boasted an even better site. To end a possible controversy, the two nations signed the *Clayton-Bulwer Treaty* (1850) pledging themselves not to seek exclusive control over any Central American canal. Although a triumph for the United States at the time, the treaty became unpopular after the Civil War when it prevented the building of an American canal.

11. *Intervention in Nicaragua.* Rivalry between England and the United States allowed *William Walker* of Tennessee to organize a filibustering expedition which seized control of Nicaragua (1854). Walker ruled the country for two years before being overthrown.

2. Diplomacy of Commercial Expansion

a. EFFORTS TO ACQUIRE HAWAII. The Hawaiian Islands interested the United States as a prospective naval station and port of call for vessels in the China trade. A treaty of annexation was negotiated with the native king (1854) but English protests and the death of the friendly ruler ended efforts to acquire the territory.

b. OPENING TRADE WITH THE ORIENT. American merchants traded with China for many years before 1844 when *Caleb Cushing* negotiated a treaty allowing their ships full privileges in all treaty ports. Japan refused to trade until 1853 when a steam-driven naval squadron under Commodore *Matthew C. Perry* visited that country. Although ordered to leave, he returned in 1854 to sign a commercial treaty that gave Americans limited trading privileges. This was Japan's first contact with the western world.

c. CANADIAN RECIPROCITY. A number of disputes between the United States and Canada were settled by a *Reciprocity Treaty* (1854) which allowed free trade across the border on many items as well as defining fishing and navigation rights in the Great Lakes and certain coastal waters.

C. Persistence of the Slavery Controversy

1. Continued Interest in the Controversy. Despite the prosperity of the 1850's and the belief that the Compromise of 1850 had settled the slavery issue for all time, nearly every event between 1850 and 1854 took on a sectional hue. Thus immigration was denounced by the South because aliens increased the population of the free states, while Pierce's expansionistic efforts were attacked by the North as they threatened to add more slave states to the Union.

2. Northern Defiance of the Fugitive Slave Act. Northerners showed their dislike of this measure by: 1) extending the operations of the underground railroad; 2) forming mobs to rescue slaves being returned to their masters; and 3) passing *personal liberty laws* which forbade federal officials to use local jails, guaranteed fugitives trial by jury, and authorized the use of the writ of habeas corpus in their behalf. These laws, and the refusal of northern states to help capture runaways, made the Fugitive Slave Act inoperative.

3. Continued Spread of Antislavery Propaganda. Thousands of Northerners were convinced that slavery was an evil by Harriet Beecher Stowe's *Uncle Tom's Cabin* (1852), the most effective propaganda work produced during the controversy. After its appearance, only a new issue was needed to raise a demand throughout the North that slavery be abolished. This was provided by the Kansas question.

III. THE STRUGGLE FOR KANSAS — 1854 - 1856

A. The Kansas-Nebraska Act

1. Origins of the Kansas-Nebraska Act

a. FRONTIER EXPANSION. *Stephen A. Douglas* of Illinois, the author of the Kansas-Nebraska Act, knew that the frontiersmen of Missouri and Iowa were anxious to move westward. Before they could do so, the unorganized area west of those states must be divided into territories. This was one of his purposes in introducing the measure.

b. EFFECT OF THE PACIFIC RAILROAD. Douglas was conscious of the growing demand for a railroad to the Pacific that followed the settlement of California. He was also aware that army surveys (1853) showed three possible routes: a northern route, a central route through South Pass, and a southern route. Use of the central route would benefit Douglas' native state, for Chicago would then become the road's eastern terminus. Southerners, however, could argue that a southern route passed through Texas and the territory of New Mexico, while the central route lay in an unorganized area. To offset this argument, Douglas was forced to press for the organization of Kansas.

2. Passage of the Kansas-Nebraska Act

a. FRAMING THE LAW. Knowing that a bill to organize Kansas would be blocked by southern votes, Douglas proposed that: 1) the unorganized lands of the West be divided into two territories, Kansas and Nebraska, one of which would presumably become slave, the other free; and 2) the Missouri Compromise be repealed, with the settlers in each territory deciding for themselves whether or not they wanted slaves — a device known as *popular sovereignty*. This would give the North the free state of Nebraska and the Pacific railroad; the South would receive the slave state of Kansas and repeal of the Missouri Compromise. Moreover Douglas hoped that popular sovereignty would reduce the slavery question to a local issue.

b. PASSAGE OF THE ACT. Southerners in Congress solidly supported Douglas' proposals, while all northern Whigs and some northern Democrats were opposed. After bitter debate, the act was narrowly adopted and signed by the President on May 30, 1854.

B. Effect of the Kansas-Nebraska Act

1. Realignment of Political Parties

a. EFFECT ON THE OLDER PARTIES. The Whig Party, which had been divided since 1852, collapsed completely. Democrats split into *Nebraska Democrats* (defenders of the act) and *Anti-Nebraska Democrats*.

b. RISE OF NEW PARTIES.

i. *The Know-Nothing Party.* Opposition to foreigners and Catholics, which had been mounting since the beginning of foreign immigration, had led to the formation of the *Order of the Star Spangled Banner* (1849), a secret political organization that became known as the Know-Nothing party when members parried all questions by answering "I know nothing about it." The party remained small until the passage of the Kansas-Nebraska Act convinced northern and southern unionists that its program of native white Protestantism would hold the nation together. Then it grew so rapidly that Know-Nothings won control of several states in 1854 and 1855.

ii. *The Republican Party.* Middle-westerners, resentful of the Kansas-Nebraska Act, began forming local parties whose candidates were pledged to *keep slavery out of the territories*. Gradually coalescing as the Republican party, these won surprising victories in the 1854 elections, then in 1855 invaded the East where such prominent ex-Whigs as William Seward became converts. By the end of that year the new party was fast becoming a major political force.

c. SIGNIFICANCE OF PARTY REALIGNMENT. In the past the parties had served as bonds of union, as both had northern and southern wings. Now sectional parties were forming. The Republicans enjoyed strength only in the North, while the Democrats were becoming the party of the South. Only the continued cooperation of southern Democrats and northern Nebraska Democrats held the sections together politically.

2. Failure of Popular Sovereignty

a. THE RACE TO PEOPLE KANSAS. Angry Northerners decided to win Kansas for freedom by sending enough free-state men there to offset the normal proslave migration from Missouri. To accomplish this, they formed emigrant aid societies, the most prominent being the *New England Emigrant Aid Society* under *Eli Thayer*. Although these societies sent few persons to Kansas, which was settled largely from adjacent states, they aroused such resentment in the South that Missourians began organizing secret lodges whose members were pledged to invade Kansas on election days to vote for slavery. Thus the stage was set for a struggle between the forces of slavery and freedom, with Kansas as the battleground.

b. THE FIRST KANSAS ELECTIONS. In an election to name a territorial delegate to Congress (November, 1854), enough Missourians invaded Kansas to select a proslavery candidate. Again in March, 1855, a similar invasion resulted in the election of a proslavery legislature which enacted a drastic slave code. When Governor *Andrew Reeder* protested he was removed from office by President Pierce.

c. THE RIVAL GOVERNMENTS. Realizing the impossibility of winning an election, the antislavery men met at Topeka (October, 1855) to draw up their own constitution for Kansas. This was adopted when the proslavery men refused to vote, and a free-state government was installed. President Pierce refused to recognize its existence. During debate on the issue in Congress *Charles Sumner* of Massachusetts was so severely beaten by *Preston Brooks* of South Carolina that his health was permanently impaired.

d. WARFARE IN KANSAS. As tension increased in Kansas, both sides armed themselves, the Northerners with *"Beecher's*

Bibles," as Sharps rifles were called after a New Haven minister called them a greater moral force than the Bible. Trouble began in May, 1856, when a federal marshal led a mob of Missouri "border ruffians" to Lawrence, where several free-state leaders were arrested and the city sacked. Three days later *John Brown,* a fanatical abolitionist, and a few followers killed five proslavery men in the *"Pottawatomie Massacre."* This touched off a four-month civil war in which 200 persons were killed. *"Bleeding Kansas"* became a national byword.

IV. THE DRIFT TOWARD DISUNION — 1856 - 1860

A. The Election of 1856.   The *Democrats,* with *James Buchanan* of Pennsylvania as their candidate, praised popular sovereignty as the only practical means of settling the slavery conflict. The *Republicans* nominated *John C. Fremont,* the explorer and military leader, who campaigned on a platform calling for congressional prohibition of slavery in the territories and the immediate admission of Kansas under the "Topeka Constitution." As many moderate Northerners refused to vote for Fremont, the Democrats won by 174 to 114. Millard Fillmore, who ran on the ticket of the *Know-Nothing Party,* secured the electoral vote of only Maryland.

B. The Dred Scott Case

1. The Supreme Court's Decision

a. ORIGINS OF THE CASE. Dred Scott, a Missouri slave, had lived with his master in Illinois and Minnesota. On his master's death, abolitionists entered suit in Scott's name, claiming that his residence in the free state of Illinois and the free territory of Minnesota had made him free. When the state court ruled against this plea, Scott was sold to J. F. A. Sanford of New York. This was done to get the case into the federal courts, which were authorized to settle disputes between citizens of different states.

b. OPINION OF JUSTICE TANEY. In the case of *Dred Scott v. Sanford* (March, 1857), Chief Justice *Roger B. Taney* ruled that the Supreme Court could not assume jurisdiction as *Dred Scott was not a citizen.* He was not a citizen, Taney decided, because: 1) he was a Negro, and the framers of the Constitution did not consider Negroes citizens; and 2) he was still a slave. He was still a slave, the justice went on, because his residence in Illinois had not made him free; as a resident of Missouri the laws of any state he visited did not affect his status. Nor was he made free by residing in Minnesota, as Minnesota was not legally a free territory. The *Missouri Compromise was unconstitutional* as it violated the Fifth Amendment which prohibited Congress from depriving any person of his property. In effect the Court ruled that *Congress could not bar slavery from the territories.*

2. Public Reaction to the Decision

a. REPUBLICAN PROTESTS. Republicans, realizing that the decision left them without a platform, denounced Taney's opinion on the grounds that: 1) the Court was too partisan to be judicial, with seven of the nine judges Democrats and five from the South; and 2) all parts of the opinion concerning Scott's status as a slave were *obiter dicta* (gratuitous judicial opinion) which did not have the force of law. Yet Republicans knew that they could negate the ruling only by winning control of the government, then packing the Court with their own appointees who would reverse the decision.

b. DEMOCRATIC SUPPORT. Southern Democrats were jubilant, but northern Democrats were placed in an unfortunate position. So long as they could advocate popular sovereignty as a solution to the slavery question they could support compromise. Many, however, were unwilling to go as far as the Dred Scott decision.

C. Growth of Sectional Tension

1. Continuing Conflict in Kansas

a. THE LECOMPTON CONSTITUTION. The sectional gulf, widened by the Dred Scott decision, was deepened by new conflicts in Kansas. There an election to choose a new constitutional convention was boycotted by the free-state men, allowing the proslavery group to draft a constitution at Lecompton favoring their stand. When this was submitted for ratification, voters were allowed to decide only whether they wished the constitution with or without the further introduction of slaves. As free-staters again refused to vote, this was adopted with a provision for the continued importation of slaves. In the fall of 1857 the antislavery element secured control of the territorial legislature, then resubmitted the Lecompton constitution to the people. This time the slave-staters abstained from voting and the constitution was rejected.

b. BUCHANAN'S EFFORTS TO ADMIT KANSAS. President Buchanan urged Congress to admit Kansas under the Lecompton constitution (1858), but his effort was defeated by northern Democrats under Stephen A. Douglas who charged that this did not reflect the popular will. Southern Democrats then pushed the *English Bill* through Congress. This authorized Kansas to vote once more on the Lecompton constitution; if it was ratified Kansas was to be admitted at once; if not the territory would have to wait for statehood until its population was much larger. Despite this bribe, the constitution was rejected. Kansas did not enter the Union until after the Civil War began.

2. The Panic of 1857

a. THE COMING OF THE PANIC. A serious depression swept the nation in 1857 because: 1) the end of the Crimean War in Europe cut agricultural prices and lowered farmers' purchasing power; 2) speculative activity had reached the breaking point; and 3) many of the state banks issuing currency were unsound. Hard times continued until the outbreak of the war.

b. IMPACT OF THE PANIC ON THE SECTIONS. Northerners, angry that the Democratic administration refused to adopt a high tariff or other measures they deemed necessary for recovery, became convinced that their welfare depended on a Republican victory. Southerners, aware that the panic scarcely affected their section, concluded that their economic system was superior to that of the North.

D. The Disruption of the Democratic Party

1. The Illinois Senatorial Election of 1858

a. THE LINCOLN-DOUGLAS DEBATES. The Illinois Senate seat held by *Stephen A. Douglas* was contested by *Abraham Lincoln* on behalf of the Republican party. During the campaign, Lincoln challenged his opponent to seven debates in as many Illinois cities. In these he succeeded in: 1) making Douglas unpopular with Republicans by forcing him to state that he did not regard slavery as a moral wrong; and 2) making him unpopular with southern Democrats by leading him to pronounce the "Freeport doctrine."

b. THE FREEPORT DOCTRINE. Lincoln asked Douglas whether popular sovereignty was possible under the Dred Scott decision. Douglas (in the debate at Freeport) answered that it was; *the people of any territory, he argued, could keep slavery out by refusing to enact "black codes" and other laws necessary for its survival.* This pleased northern Democrats, who re-elected Douglas to the Senate.

2. Impact of the Freeport Doctrine on the South. Southern Democrats denounced the Freeport doctrine, as popular sovereignty promised their section less than the Dred Scott doctrine. From that time on the northern and southern wings of the Democratic party were hopelessly divided. The last political thread holding the nation together was broken.

E. The Widening Sectional Gulf

1. Legislative Conflicts. Between 1858 and 1860 a number of laws desired by northern business leaders were defeated in Congress: 1) a higher tariff; 2) a homestead bill (to give 160 acres free to every settler); and 3) a Pacific railroad bill. Each defeat drove more northern conservatives into the Republican party.

2. The Raid on Harper's Ferry. Tension was increased when *John Brown* of Kansas, with a few deluded followers, captured the government arsenal at Harper's Ferry, Virginia (October, 1859), as the first step in a plot to arm the slaves and lead a triumphant freedom march through the South. Although he was promptly arrested, Southerners believed that he was the tool of Republicans who wished to incite a slave rebellion. Northerners, on the other hand, elevated Brown to martyrdom after his execution for treason.

3. "The Impending Crisis." Sectional feelings were further inflamed with the publication of Hinton R. Helper's *The Impending Crisis* (1857). Helper, a southern nonslaveholder, argued that slavery had ruined the South economically. The book was almost as influential in the North as *Uncle Tom's Cabin.*

V.   THE ELECTION OF 1860

A.   The Four Candidates

1. Division of the Democratic Party. When the Democrats met at Charleston (April, 1860), Douglas' followers, who were in the majority, voted to include in the platform a plank favoring the Freeport doctrine rather than the Dred Scott doctrine. This so disrupted the convention that it adjourned without nominating a candidate. When it reassembled at Baltimore (June, 1860), delegates from the deep South were absent. The remainder nominated *Douglas on a platform supporting popular sovereignty.* In the meantime southern Democrats, meeting at Richmond, chose as their standard bearer *John C. Breckinridge* of Kentucky. Their *platform endorsed the Dred Scott doctrine.*

2. The Republican Opportunity. The Republicans, sensing victory over a divided opposition, were jubilant as they met in Chicago. To assure the support of moderates they nominated *Abraham Lincoln* of Illinois rather than William H. Seward of New York whose views were too well known. In a further effort to attract a wide following, they promised in their platform to: 1) restrict slavery to the states where it already existed; 2) adopt a protective tariff; 3) pass a homestead law; and 4) provide government support for a Pacific railroad.

3. The Constitutional Union Party. Remnants of the old Whig and Know-Nothing parties met at Baltimore (May, 1860) to form the Constitutional Union party on a platform demanding the preservation of the Union by compromise. *John Bell* of Tennessee was nominated, giving the party its nickname of "Bell ringers."

B.   The Republican Victory

1. The Voting Pattern

a. THE CONTEST IN THE NORTH. The only candidates in the North were Lincoln and Douglas, who differed principally on whether slavery should be barred from the territories by Congressional action or popular sovereignty. Yet voters realized that a larger issue was at stake: should the North inflict its majority will on the South bluntly (as the Republicans demanded) or gradually through continuing compromise (as the

Douglas Democrats proposed) ? That they favored the Republican stand was shown when Lincoln carried every northern state but New Jersey.

b. THE CONTEST IN THE SOUTH. In the South the Breckinridge Democrats advocated protection for "Southern rights" even at the cost of secession. The Douglas Democrats and the Constitutional Union party proposed the preservation of the Union by conciliation. There, as in the North, moderation was in disfavor. Breckinridge carried all states of the lower South. Four border states gave their votes to Bell or Douglas.

2. Results of the Election. Lincoln secured 180 electoral votes, Breckinridge 72, Bell 39, and Douglas 12. Yet Lincoln won only 40 per cent of the popular vote. More significant was the fact that both North and South favored decisive action; Lincoln and Breckinridge together received 2,700,000 votes to 1,900,000 for Bell and Douglas.

VI. AN IRREPRESSIBLE CONFLICT?

Was the Civil War that followed Lincoln's election an irrepressible conflict? Or could moderation have delayed war until the situation solved itself? Historians still fail to agree on the answer.

A. A Repressible Conflict. Those who argue that the war was repressible maintain that: 1) antagonism was primarily the product of emotions aroused by northern abolitionists and southern fire eaters; and 2) if those emotions had been curbed, slavery would eventually have died out in the South.

B. An Irrepressible Conflict. Those who hold that the war was irrepressible emphasize the fact that the conflict was not only over slavery but between two antagonistic economic systems: 1) industrial capitalism based on the wage system; and 2) staple-crop agriculture based on the slave system. They maintain that the former system was destined to gain strength steadily as industrialization proceeded until it could no longer be denied laws favorable to its own interests (tariffs, homestead, and the like). Such laws would not have been acceptable to the South, where the labor system was so inefficient that only favorable legislation kept the economy sound. Hence, historians argue, a clash was inevitable; the emotional conflict over slavery was simply an excuse.

ADDITIONAL READING

A brief survey is in J. G. Randall and David Donald, *The Civil War and Reconstruction* (1961) and an interpretive appraisal in R. F. Nichols, *The Stakes of Power: 1845-1877* (1965). Essential to an understanding of the period are the monumental works by Allan Nevins: *Ordeal of the Union* (1947) and *The Emergence of Lincoln* (1950). A. O. Craven, *Civil War in the Making, 1815-1860* (1959) sums up a lifetime of thought on the subject; the same author treats the problem in greater depth in *The Coming of the Civil War* (1957). The disintegration of the party structure as a cause of war is explored in R. F. Nichols, *The Disruption of American Democracy* (1948). A. O. Craven, *The Growth of Southern Nationalism, 1848-1861* (1953) traces the emergence of secession sentiment in the South. Essential biographical studies are: R. J. Rayback, *Millard Fillmore* (1959), P. S. Klein, *President James Buchanan* (1962), B. T. Thomas, *Abraham Lincoln* (1952), David Donald, *Charles Sumner and the Coming of the Civil War* (1962), C. M. Capers, *Stephen A. Douglas* (1959), and W. E. Parish, *David Rice Atchison of Missouri* (1961). The older work by E. D. Fite, *The Presidential Campaign of 1860* (1911) should be supplemented with Ollinger Crenshaw, *The Slave States in the Presidential Election of 1860* (1945).

CHAPTER XIV

Secession and Civil War
1860-1865

❰ THE PROBLEM OF SECESSION

With the election of Abraham Lincoln, the southern states seceded from the Union one by one, to form the Confederate States of America. Their action brought Lincoln face to face with the most important problem ever faced by a president: should he submit to peaceful secession, or should he coerce the rebellious states? Only his sincere faith in democracy allowed him to find the right answer. Lincoln realized that by their action the Southerners were denying the one right enjoyed by a minority under a democratic system: the right to become a majority. This then was rebellion, and must be suppressed. His decision to employ force plunged the nation into four years of bloody war that only ended when the South, its strength and resources exhausted, lay prostrate before the triumphant North.

I. THE SECESSION OF THE SOUTHERN STATES

A. The Process of Secession

1. Course of Secession.   _South Carolina_ led the way by calling a popularly elected convention (December, 1860) which adopted an "Ordinance of Secession" and issued a "Declaration of Causes." By February, 1861, all other states of the lower South — Mississippi, Florida, Alabama, Georgia, Louisiana, and Texas — had acted. In each, secession triumphed only after the defeat of strong unionist sentiment.

   2. Formation of the Confederacy. Delegates from the seceded states met at Montgomery, Alabama (February, 1861), to form the *Confederate States of America*, with *Jefferson Davis* of Mississippi President and Alexander H. Stephens of Georgia Vice-President. The Constitution that was eventually adopted was remarkably like that of the United States but differed in: 1) protecting slavery in all states and territories; 2) barring protective tariffs or federally supported internal improvements; and 3) limiting the President to one six-year term and allowing the cabinet to sit with Congress.

B. Reasons for Secession

   1. Arguments for Secession

   a. THE EMOTIONAL ARGUMENT. Southerners, who sincerely believed that slavery benefited both master and slave, were convinced that Northerners were not only bent on freeing the slaves but on establishing Negro rule for the South. As they were committed to "white supremacy" they could never accept this.

   b. THE ECONOMIC ARGUMENT. The slave system was so inefficient that the southern economy required favorable national legislation. This would no longer be forthcoming under a Republican president. Instead Southerners thought they were doomed to protective tariffs, a homestead act, and other laws that would impoverish the section.

   2. Validity of the Arguments. Actually slavery was not endangered by Lincoln's election, for the President was no abolitionist, while both Congress and the Supreme Court retained Democratic majorities. Nor would secession protect slavery. Instead the South left the territories (which had been opened to the institution by the Dred Scott case) in the hands of hostile Northerners, and even opened the way for the freeing of all slaves through military conquest and emancipation. Yet sober argument bore little weight; men in both sections were ruled by emotion rather than reason.

C. Northern Reaction to Secession

   1. Reaction of the Public. Most Northerners opposed coercion, believing that the southern states would return to the

Union if a few concessions were made. Others agreed with Horace Greeley, editor of the _New York Tribune,_ that "the erring sisters should depart in peace."

2. _Reaction of President Buchanan._ Buchanan believed that secession was illegal, but that coercion was also. Hence he favored a constitutional amendment guaranteeing protection for slavery in all states and territories to lure the southern states back into the Union. His indecisive attitude was shown when a supply ship, the _Star of the West,_ was fired on while attempting to deliver supplies to the federal garrison of Ft. Sumter in Charleston Harbor (January, 1861). Buchanan did not even bother to protest this act of war.

3. _Reaction of Congress_

a. THE CRITTENDEN COMPROMISE. Congress also took the view that Southerners could be persuaded to return if concessions were made. One proposal advanced by Senator John J. Crittenden of Kentucky would have: 1) prohibited slavery in territories north of 36° 30′ but protected the institution south of that line; 2) guaranteed the continuation of slavery in the

RIVALRIES BETWEEN NORTH AND SOUTH

NORTH WANTED

High tariffs, high prices

To keep the West closed

A strong national bank and a national currency

SOUTH WANTED

Low tariffs, low prices

To open the West — new land needed for development

Local and state banks and cheap money

CHART BY GRAPHICS INSTITUTE, N.Y.C.   From—"A History of Our Country" (revised edition) by Muzzey; Ginn & Co.

District of Columbia; and 3) provided federal compensation for owners of runaway slaves and the repeal of all "personal liberty" laws. The measure was doomed when Republicans refused to compromise on the question of slavery in the territories.

b. THE HOUSE PLAN. A similar compromise plan was worked out by a Committee of Thirty-Three in the House (January, 1861). This would have: 1) guaranteed protection for slavery in the slave states; 2) forced the repeal of all "personal liberty" laws; and 3) admitted New Mexico, which had recently legalized slavery. These proposals proved inacceptable to Southerners.

c. THE PEACE CONVENTION. A peace convention at Washington, called on the invitation of Virginia (February, 1861), proposed constitutional amendments: 1) dividing the slave and free territories at the line of 36° 30'; and 2) forbidding the United States to acquire territory without the consent of a majority of the Senators from each section. The Senate rejected these proposals.

D. Abraham Lincoln's Policy

1. Lincoln's Decision. The failure of congressional compromise meant that the problem of the seceded states was still unsettled when Lincoln was inaugurated (March 4, 1861). He had to decide whether to employ coercion, and if so how to do so without alienating the border states remaining in the Union. His decision to employ force was based on the sensible realization that: 1) the problems of allocating the national debt, handling fugitive slaves, and dividing the territories could never be settled peacefully; 2) the secession principle was dangerous and would lead to further disunion if disgruntled minorities could separate when they chose; and 3) the South, in refusing to abide by the majority will, was denying the whole democratic principle in which he sincerely believed.

2. The Relief of Ft. Sumter. Possibly in the hope of goading the Confederacy into striking the first blow, Lincoln decided to send supplies to the beseiged garrison at Ft. Sumter. When news that this expedition was on the way reached the Confederates at Charleston they opened fire on the fort (*April*

_12, 1861_) forcing its surrender before the ships reached there. The Civil War had begun.

3. Decision of the Border States

a. LOYAL BORDER STATES. Delaware decided to stay in the Union. Kentucky tried to remain neutral, but when a Confederate army invaded the state its indignant citizens retaliated by casting their lot with the United States (December, 1861). Maryland was forced to remain loyal by the presence of federal troops. The northwest counties of Virginia refused to follow that state into the Confederacy, and formed the state of West Virginia (June, 1863).

b. CONFEDERATE BORDER STATES. Lincoln's decision to supply Ft. Sumter convinced Virginia that the North was the aggressor and drove it into the Confederacy. Arkansas, Tennessee, and North Carolina soon followed. In all the border states divided allegiance was common, with members of the same family often fighting on different sides.

II. THE FIRST CAMPAIGNS OF THE WAR
1861 - 1862

A. The Antagonists at the Start of the War

1. Northern Superiority. The North's population was double that of the South, while most of the nation's natural resources, industries, and transportation facilities were also concentrated in that section. This advantage was partially offset by the superior military leadership available to the Confederacy; General _Robert E. Lee_ was the nation's most skilled strategist, while southern officers were generally better trained than northern.

2. Lack of Preparedness. As neither antagonist boasted an effective army, both had to depend on recruits. These were obtained by assigning quotas to each state and community, then appealing to the patriotism of the people to fill the quotas. Lincoln's first call was for 75,000 militiamen to serve three months, while Davis asked for 100,000 volunteers. Although these quotas were filled at once, statesmen on both sides soon realized that longer enlistments were necessary. Congress, when it met in July, 1861, authorized the enlistment of 500,000 men for three years.

B. The Campaign Against Richmond, 1861

1. The Battle of Bull Run.

Popular pressure for an attack on Richmond, the capital of the Confederacy, forced General Irvin McDowell to start southward from Washington before his 36,000 troops were properly trained. Hence they were decisively defeated at Bull Run Creek (July 21, 1861), by a smaller Confederate force under General Pierre G. T. Beauregard.

2. Effect of the Northern Defeat.

The people at last realized that the war was no mere skirmish. Hence: 1) enlisting was put on an efficient basis with some 600,000 volunteers entering the army by the spring of 1862; and 2) General _George G. McClellan_ replaced the over-age General Winfield Scott as commander in chief of the Union forces. McClellan spent the rest of the summer drilling the "Army of the Potomac." In the West, too, General Henry W. Halleck concentrated on whipping an army into shape rather than fighting.

C. The War on the Seas, 1861-1862

1. The Northern Blockade.

Lincoln placed the entire Confederate coast under blockade (April, 1861). Within six months the South was feeling the pinch as needed manufactured goods, ammunition, and medical supplies were cut off. For a time fast _blockade runners_ that slipped into southern ports from the West Indies threatened to meet the South's needs. The United States soon resorted to the _"doctrine of continuous voyage,"_ allowing vessels to be captured on the way to the West Indies if their cargoes were ultimately destined for the Confederacy. This proved so effective that the blockade was the most important single factor leading to a Union victory.

2. Efforts to Break the Blockade

a. THE BATTLE OF THE IRONCLADS. An ironclad steam-driven vessel, the _Merrimac_, destroyed two Union vessels the first day that it was put in service at Norfolk, Virginia (March, 1862). By a coincidence, a United States ironclad, the _Monitor_, arrived at the scene that very night. The two engaged in a furious battle the next day. Although the _Merrimac_ survived, it never again left port. This battle marked the end of wooden sailing vessels in naval warfare.

b. CONFEDERATE PRIVATEERS. The Confederacy purchased several warships from England, the most famous being the

Alabama. Together these destroyed 250 American ships. British yards also constructed two ironclad "Laird rams" designed to destroy blockading vessels (1863), but protests from the United States stopped their delivery.

D. The War in the West, 1862

1. The River War. In January, 1862, _Edwin M. Stanton_ of Pennsylvania was made Secretary of War. One of his first steps was to grant greater authority to General _Ulysses S. Grant,_ who had formulated a plan to drive into the heart of the Confederacy along the highway formed by the Mississippi, Tennessee, and Cumberland rivers. With 17,000 men Grant first captured Ft. Henry on the Tennessee (February 6, 1862), then Ft. Donelson on the Cumberland (February 16, 1862).

2. Capture of Corinth

a. THE BATTLE OF SHILOH. With the road south opened by these victories, Grant advanced with 45,000 troops. The Confederate commander, General Albert Sidney Johnston, awaited him at _Corinth,_ an important railroad center. Before reaching this spot, the Union forces were surprised by Johnston's men while encamped at Shiloh Meeting House near Pittsburg Landing (April 6, 1862). Although the Confederates were beaten off and Johnston killed, Grant's army was too exhausted to follow.

b. EVACUATION OF CORINTH. General Henry W. Halleck, who took over the western army after Grant's defeat at Shiloh, marched southward with 120,000 troops. The Confederates, not daring to resist, evacuated Corinth (May 30, 1862). This cut several important railroad lines needed to supply the eastern armies with western produce. At the same time a naval force under Admiral David Farragut _captured New Orleans_ (April, 1862) and Natchez, but Vicksburg remained in southern hands for another year. During the autumn of 1862 two Confederate counterattacks in the West were beaten off at Perryville, Kentucky, and Corinth.

E. The Eastern Campaigns, 1862

1. The Peninsular Campaign

a. PLAN OF THE CAMPAIGN. General _McClellan_ transported 112,000 troops by water to Ft. Monroe at the tip of the peninsula between the James and York rivers, then started west toward Richmond (March, 1862). At the same time 40,000 Union troops under General *Irvin McDowell* started southward from Washington toward the Confederate capital. This sound strategy was upset by the brilliant generalship of General *Robert E. Lee*, who sent a small army under General *Thomas "Stonewall" Jackson* up the Shenandoah Valley to threaten Washington. Although the city was not in danger, Lincoln ordered McDowell's army to return at once. Thus Lee was free to concentrate his entire force against McClellan on the peninsula.

    b. FAILURE OF THE CAMPAIGN. McClellan advanced slowly westward until June 25, 1862, when he was only a few miles from Richmond. There he was attacked by 65,000 men under Lee and "Stonewall" Jackson, who drove the Union army back to the James River in the *Seven Days Battle*. McClellan wished to move south of Richmond to cut the railroads entering that city, but instead he was ordered back to Washington (August, 1862).

    2. *The Second Battle of Bull Run.* The inefficient General John Pope, who replaced McClellan as commander of the Army of the Potomac, next planned a frontal attack on Richmond, but was decisively defeated at the Second Battle of Bull Run (August 29-30, 1862).

    3. *The Battle of Antietam.* Temporarily freed of attack, General Lee led his army across the Potomac to "liberate" Maryland and isolate Washington. McClellan, who was again in command, started in pursuit, catching the Confederates at Antietam Creek. After a bloody battle (September 17, 1862), Lee was forced to withdraw. Instead of pursuing, the over-cautious McClellan allowed him to escape safely into Virginia.

III.   FOREIGN RELATIONS AND EMANCIPATION

The Battle of Antietam, although hardly a victory, allowed Lincoln to strengthen the Union's position abroad.

A.   Relations with England

    1. England's Attitude Toward the War

    a. SUPPORT FOR THE CONFEDERACY. Most Englishmen favored the Confederacy. The *upper class* adopted this attitude because they: 1) feared the leveling effect of a Union victory on their own disenfranchised masses; 2) felt socially akin to the plantation aristocracy; and 3) looked to the South for cotton needed by textile mills. Many *liberals and lower-class groups* were also favorable, feeling that the war was: 1) a rebellion against northern tyranny; and 2) a struggle to preserve the Union rather than free the slaves. Their support, however, could be transferred to the North by emancipating the slaves.

b. SUPPORT FOR THE UNION. Another large group of English workers and liberals favored the Union cause on the grounds that: 1) a northern victory would lead to emancipation; and 2) northern wheat was more essential to England's welfare than southern cotton.

2. Conflicts Between England and the Union

a. ENGLISH RECOGNITION OF SOUTHERN BELLIGERENCY. On May 31, 1861, Queen Victoria issued a Proclamation of Neutrality, thus recognizing southern belligerency. This aroused great anger in the North.

b. CONFLICTS OVER THE BLOCKADE. England protested the North's use of the "doctrine of continuous voyage" which allowed English ships to be captured on their way to the West Indies when their cargoes were ultimately bound for the Confederacy. Her objections, however, were modified by: 1) her dependence on northern wheat; and 2) the realization that in subsequent wars she would need to apply the same doctrine. This upset the calculations of Southerners who had counted on "*King Cotton*" to secure anything they wished from England.

c. THE TRENT AFFAIR. Ill feeling was heightened when an American warship stopped a British steamer, the *Trent* (November, 1861), to remove two Confederate diplomats (*Mason and Slidell*). England threatened war for this insult unless the United States apologized and released the prisoners. Secretary of State *William H. Seward* did not dare do so in view of inflamed public opinion at home. Finally he freed Mason and Slidell on the ground that the naval commander had been guilty of a technical error when arresting them. This appeased opinion in both countries. The incident, however, increased tensions.

d. CONFEDERATE PRIVATEERS. Hostility was increased when England allowed several Confederate privateers to be built and commissioned in her yards: the *Florida, Alabama,* and *Shenandoah.* Together these vessels did great damage to American shipping.

B. The Problem of Recognition of the Confederacy

1. Attitude of England and France. The Union defeats during 1862 convinced England and France that the Confederacy would triumph. In both nations cabinet meetings during 1862, prepared to recognize the Confederacy, a step that would have weakened the blockade. Only news of the Union victory at Antietam forced a delay.

2. Lincoln's Prevention of Recognition. Lincoln realized that he could prevent English recognition of the Confederacy only by emancipating the slaves, thus swinging liberal support to the North. This step, however, might alienate moderate Northerners who would fight for the Union but not for the slaves. After waiting until the Battle of Antietam demonstrated Union strength, he issued his *Emancipation Proclamation (September 22, 1862).* This stated that slaves in all states still in rebellion were to become free on January 1, 1863. England immediately abandoned all plans for recognition, although France still favored the Confederacy.

3. Reasons for French Attitude. France supported recognition partly because of its own *involvement in Mexico.* Having joined England and Spain in sending troops to collect debts in that country (October, 1861), the French force not only stayed on when the others withdrew (April, 1862) but placed the *Archduke Maximilian* of Austria on the Mexican throne. Although Seward protested this *violation of the Monroe Doctrine,* Maximilian remained in Mexico until the defeat of the Confederacy forced Napoleon III to withdraw his troops or face a war with the United States.

IV. THE FINAL CAMPAIGNS OF THE WAR
1862 - 1865

A. The Eastern Campaigns, 1862-1863

1. Failure to Capture Richmond. General *Ambrose E. Burnside,* who replaced McClellan after Antietam, again advanced on Richmond, but was defeated by Lee at the *Battle of Fredericksburg* (December 13, 1862). His successor, General Joseph Hooker, started south again in the spring of 1863, only to be repulsed at the bloody *Battle of Chancellorsville* (May 2-5, 1863), fought in a tangled wilderness just south of the Rappahannock River. The battle cost the life of the brilliant Confederate leader, General "Stonewall" Jackson.

2. The Battle of Gettysburg. Once more Lee took the offensive, leading 75,000 men into Pennsylvania. There he met a Union force under General *George G. Meade* at Seminary Ridge, just west of Gettysburg. On the last of three days of furious fighting (July 1-3, 1863), Lee ordered 10,000 men under General George F. Pickett to charge the northern center. When *"Pickett's charge"* was repulsed with frightful losses, the Confederate army retreated toward Virginia, with one-third of the men killed or wounded. For the next ten months the eastern front was quiet.

B. The Western Campaigns, 1863-1864

1. Closing the Mississippi River. The western campaigns were less spectacular but more important than those in the East. Their purpose was to cut the Confederacy in two, disrupt rail transportation, and then advance eastward to join in the kill. The first step in executing this plan was taken when Corinth was captured in 1862; the second when General *Grant's* army reduced *Vicksburg* after a long siege (July 3, 1863). From that time on Union gunboats on the Mississippi prevented western foodstuffs from reaching the Confederate forces.

2. The Advance Eastward

a. THE CAMPAIGN AGAINST CHATTANOOGA. The next step in the Union strategy was to subdue the important railroad junction of Chattanooga, which was occupied on September 9, 1863. A fierce Confederate counterattack almost drove Northerners from the city, but when Grant arrived to take control, the Southerners were finally defeated in the *Battle of Chattanooga* (November 24-25, 1863).

b. FROM CHATTANOOGA TO THE SEA. Grant, who was made commander in chief of the Union armies during the winter of 1863-1864, entrusted General *William T. Sherman* with the task of pushing eastward from Chattanooga, while he engaged Lee in the East. Sherman, with 100,000 men, entered Atlanta, Georgia (September, 1864), then began his famous *"March to the Sea"* in which his troops lived off the countryside until they reached Savannah (December 10, 1864). Sherman's destructive tactics were deliberate, for he hated war and wanted to convince the Confederacy that it was beaten.

C. The Eastern Campaigns, 1863-1864

1. Sherman in the Carolinas. Sherman's "march to the sea" isolated the lower South, confining resistance to the strip of coast between Virginia and the Carolinas. There 200,000 Confederates opposed 1,000,000 Northerners. Sherman gradually closed this gap by marching northward from Savannah, reaching Goldsboro, North Carolina, by March, 1864.

2. Grant in Virginia. In the meantime *Grant* started southward from Washington with 120,000 men. Although *Lee* commanded only 65,000 troops, he not only delayed the advance but cut the Union army to pieces in a series of battles known as the *Wilderness Campaigns* (May-June, 1864). After Grant had lost 55,000 men he was forced to change his tactics. Crossing the James, he led his forces into Petersburg, hoping to cut communications between Richmond and the rest of the South. When Lee slipped between the Union army and the Confederate capital, the *seige of Richmond* began. For the next nine months the two forces faced each other with little action. During this stalemate the election of 1864 took place.

D. The Election of 1864

1. Rival Factions

a. THE UNION PARTY. Lincoln's followers, known as the *National Union Party* to emphasize northern unity, renominated the President, with a War Democrat, *Andrew Johnson* of Tennessee, as his running mate.

b. THE RADICAL REPUBLICAN PARTY. Since 1862 extreme Republicans had charged Lincoln with leniency in his prosecution of the war. Organized as *The Committee on the Conduct of the War* in Congress, such leaders as *Benjamin Wade* and Henry W. Davis now demanded his replacement. They nominated *John C. Fremont* for the presidency on a platform calling for suppression of the rebellion without compromise and the confiscation of all "rebel lands."

c. THE DEMOCRATIC PARTY. Extreme Democrats, who were known as *Copperheads,* insisted that the South would return to the Union peacefully if slavery was not molested. They also violently opposed conscription after the passage of a Draft Act (1863). Copperheadism was strongest in Illinois, Indiana, and especially Ohio where the leader of the faction, *Clement L. Vallandigham,* was almost elected governor in 1863. The Democratic convention nominated General *George B. McClellan* on a platform denouncing the war and demanding an immediate negotiated peace.

2. The Re-election of Lincoln. Lincoln seemed certain of defeat in August, 1864, but the tide was turned in his favor by: 1) northern military victories during the autumn; and 2) the withdrawal of Fremont as a candidate. Hence the President received 212 electoral votes to 21 for McClellan, although the popular vote was very close.

E. End of the Civil War. By the spring of 1865 supplies within beleaguered Richmond were nearly exhausted. When Lee failed to break through Grant's attackers at the Battle of Five Forks (April 1, 1865), he knew that his cause was lost. On April 9, 1865, he dispatched an emissary under a flag of truce to ask for surrender terms. These were laid down at a meeting between the two generals at *Appomattox Court House*: officers and men to be released on parole, all arms to be surrendered. The Civil War was over.

V. REASONS FOR THE NORTHERN VICTORY

A. Economic Basis for Northern Victory

1. Prosperity in the North

a. AGRICULTURAL EXPANSION. High agricultural prices and the passage of the *Homestead Act* (1862) led to a rapid expansion of the frontier and to unparalleled farm prosperity. This was due to: 1) unprecedented demands for grain from the armies, prosperous eastern workers, and Europe where crop failures occurred; 2) ideal weather conditions in the West; 3) improved farm machinery which allowed the few men left on the farms to increase production; and 4) scientific advances made possible by the founding of agricultural colleges under the *Morrill Land Grant Act* (1862). This measure endowed such schools with handsome land grants.

b. INDUSTRIAL EXPANSION. Industry enjoyed even greater prosperity because: 1) the government needed manufactured goods of all kinds for its armies; 2) the introduction of labor-saving machinery (such as the sewing machine for uniforms and shoes) and mass-production methods effected such economies that manufacturers' profits soared; 3) the *Morrill Tariff* (1861) and later laws raised levels high enough to afford protection from all foreign competition; 4) resources and capital were constantly replenished; and 5) the extravagant expenditures of wartime profiteers created a large market for luxury goods.

c. WARTIME FINANCE. Prosperity was stimulated by the wartime financial policies. Money was raised by: 1) borrowing through bond sales; 2) excise taxes, a modest income tax, and customs collections; 3) the issue of $400,000,000 worth of *"greenbacks"* or paper dollars; and 4) the *National Bank Act* (1863) which required government-chartered banks to invest one-third of their capital in national securities. These, in turn, could be used as the basis for paper money, or bank notes. Although the unsecured greenbacks depreciated badly in periods of military defeat, the financial structure remained relatively sound.

2. Economic Chaos in the South

a. COLLAPSE OF SOUTHERN AGRICULTURE. Hoping to force England into recognizing the Confederacy, southern leaders not only refused to export cotton during the first year of the war but encouraged crop limitation and even destruction. This policy had little effect on England, where a cotton surplus had developed since the Panic of 1857, but it did ruin the many planters who were dependent on cotton exports. After the first year sales of cotton were doomed by the blockade. So agriculture stagnated throughout the war.

b. FAILURE OF SOUTHERN MANUFACTURING. The South lacked the capital or managerial skill to develop factories when the blockade cut off imports, forcing reliance on home industries.

As these proved inadequate, prices soared, creating dissatisfaction among the people. The collapse of the transportation system also created hardships.

    c. CONFEDERATE FINANCE. As southern resources were inadequate for either taxation or borrowing, the government financed the war by issuing paper money. This depreciated so rapidly that after 1863 finances were chaotic. The South was economically prostrate long before Grant's final victory.

B. Psychological Basis for Northern Victory

    1. Northern Morale. That morale remained high in the North was shown by the way in which the people accepted restrictions on their liberty as well as by their enthusiastic support of the war.

    a. INTERFERENCE WITH PERSONAL LIBERTY. President Lincoln was guilty of several acts of questionable constitutionality: 1) *suspension of the writ of habeas corpus* (1861) despite a Supreme Court decision in *Ex Parte Merryman* (1861) denying him this right; 2) suppression of freedom of speech for such Copperheads as Clement L. Vallandigham who was convicted (1863) for "declaring disloyal sentiments"; and 3) banning newspapers such as the *New York World* and *Chicago Times* for criticizing the war effort. These violations of civil rights were accepted without great opposition, indicating the willingness of the people to make sacrifices for victory.

    b. CONSCRIPTION IN THE NORTH. As enlistments declined, a *Conscription Act* was passed (March, 1863), which authorized any person drafted to escape service by paying $300 or providing a substitute. This measure, which discriminated against the poor, was naturally opposed; a *Draft Riot* in New York (July, 1863) resulted in the death of 500 persons. Yet even such an unfair measure could operate through the rest of the war with no disturbances.

    c. VOLUNTEER AID FOR THE WAR. Enthusiasm for the Northern cause was reflected in the support given such agencies as the *United States Sanitary Commission* (1861), which solicited contributions to care for the sick and wounded. Thousands of dollars were contributed, while additional sums were raised by sanitary fairs held regularly in all northern cities.

    2. Southern Morale. By contrast, Confederate morale declined through the war. So strong was the states' rights spirit that every interference with personal liberty was denounced as tyrannical. When President Davis *suspended the writ of habeas corpus* after receiving Congressional approval (1862) state judges still issued such writs while the Georgia legislature declared his action unconstitutional. Similarly a *Conscription Act* (1862) was so unpopular that most of the 100,000 men who deserted from the Confederate armies were conscripts. Even worse was the strong peace movement that existed through the war and gained strength as military defeats increased. The South was psychologically defeated by the time of Lee's surrender.

VI. THE SIGNIFICANCE OF THE CIVIL WAR

A. Consolidation of American Nationality. The Civil War established the federal government as supreme over the states. Since that time its supremacy has been increasingly asserted, until today the states are largely administrative units, with most vital functions performed nationally.

B. The Consolidation of the Industrial Order. Partly as a result of the Civil War, the agrarian order that had dominated American life and politics before 1860 was displaced by an industrial order after 1865. From that time to the present the people have lived amidst a machine civilization. This important change was made possible by the war which: 1) allowed industrialists to entrench their national influence so securely that they remained predominant thereafter; 2) favored manufacturing with such laws as protective tariffs, thus stimulating the rapid industrialization of the nation in the postwar years; and 3) divided the agrarian forces of the South and West so completely that effective opposition to industry vanished. As a result the nation entered on a new period of history, characterized principally by a continued trend toward industrialization.

ADDITIONAL READING

The course of secession is traced in D. L. Dumond, *The Secession Movement* (1931), while divergent views on the North's reaction to secession are presented in D. M. Potter, *Lincoln and His Party in the Secession Crisis* (1950) and K. M. Stampp, *And The War Came: The North and the Secession*

Crisis (1950). Essential on the whole history of the war is the multivolume work by Allan Nevins, *The War for the Union* (1959-   ). Military events are popularly described in Bruce Catton, *Mr. Lincoln's Army* (1951), *Glory Road* (1952), and *Stillness at Appomattox* (1953), and more technically in K. P. Williams, *Lincoln Finds a General* (5 vols, 1949-1959). Two monumental works by D. S. Freeman describe fighting from the southern point of view: *R. E. Lee* (4 vols., 1934-1935), and *Lee's Lieutenants* (3 vols., 1942-1944). Important biographical studies include B. P. Thomas, *Abraham Lincoln* (1952), J. G. Randall, *Lincoln the President*, (4 vols., 1944-1955), R. W. Patrick, *Jefferson Davis and His Cabinet* (1944), Rudolph Von Abele, *Alexander Stephens* (1946), and B. P. Thomas and H. M. Hyman, *Stanton* (1962). The social and political story is told in such books as T. H. Williams, *Lincoln and the Radicals* (1941), T. H. Williams, *Lincoln and His Generals* (1952), and F. L. Klement, *The Copperheads in the Middle West* (1960). J. H. Franklin is excellent on *The Emancipation Proclamation* (1963). The history of the Confederacy is told in Clement Eaton, *A History of the Southern Confederacy* (1954) and F. E. Vandiver, *Rebel Brass* (1956). Diplomatic aspects are considered in F. L. Owsley, *King Cotton Diplomacy* (1931).

CHAPTER XV

The Reconstruction Period
1865-1877

☾ THE RECONSTRUCTION PROBLEM

A twofold problem faced the United States when General Robert E. Lee's surrender (April 9, 1865) ended the Civil War: 1) how could the eleven Confederate states be restored to their former position in the Union; and 2) how could the economically prostrate South be rehabilitated? Northern politicians were largely responsible for attempts made to solve the first problem, while Southerners were primarily concerned with the second. Hence the story of Reconstruction must be divided into two parts, one dealing with political events, the other with social and economic progress.

I. POLITICAL RECONSTRUCTION. The triumphant North was called upon to decide whether the defeated southern states should be kept perpetually subservient, restored to their full rights in the Union, or readmitted with limited self-government. Divergent opinions among the victors made the solution difficult.

A. Factors Influencing the Formulation of a Reconstruction Policy. The task of restoring the Confederate states to statehood was complicated by several factors:

1. The Constitutional Factor. Northerners before and during the war had held that secession was illegal and that the rebellious states were still in the Union; Southerners had maintained their legal right to secede. With the war over,

Southerners were anxious to return to the United States as soon as possible, yet to do so they must adopt the Northern view. Northerners, on the other hand, wishing to inflict penalties on the Confederates, were forced to accept the South's contention and argue that secession was legal. Both sides found this transition difficult.

2. The Economic Factor. This influenced opinion in two ways: 1) The war had cost the North heavily. The Union war debt amounted to almost $3,000,000,000, and casualties to 360,000 persons. Many Northerners were determined to make the Confederates pay for these losses, while Southerners, convinced that their cause was both legal and just, refused to do so. 2) Northern industrialists, irked by the South's prewar record of aiding agriculture at the expense of manufacturing, were determined to keep the section politically subservient. Only in this way, they felt, could they secure the tariffs, sound-money laws, easy credit, and government bounties needed for business expansion.

3. The Social Factor. Humanitarians in the North viewed political reconstruction as a means of forcing the South to accept the principle of racial equality. Like the industrialists, they favored a program that would allow the federal government to dominate the Confederacy until that section granted political and social equality to the freed slaves and economic privileges to the poor of both races. They also wished to punish the plantation owners for keeping Negroes in bondage.

4. The Psychological Factor. The hatred bred of war did not die easily. Northerners insisted that Southerners be punished; Southerners were in no mood to accept the olive branch from their victorious enemies. Some Confederates fled to Mexico, England, or Canada, while those who remained were suspicious and distrustful. Cooperation under these circumstances was difficult.

5. The Political Factor. The Republican Party viewed the northern victory as its personal triumph. Its leaders felt that their party should be rewarded by perpetual political dominance; the future of America would be threatened, they believed, if the secession-minded Democrats ever regained supremacy. Hence they weighed the political as well as the social effect of each Reconstruction law before Congress, favoring only those that promised to weaken the Democrats and strengthen the Republicans. This narrow policy led to a division within the party, for most Northerners were more concerned with the restoration of the Union than with political quarrels. One faction, the *Moderate Republicans* under the leadership of Presidents *Abraham Lincoln* and *Andrew Johnson,* favored a mild policy toward the South. The other, the *Radical Republicans,* wished to adopt a harsh policy aimed at perpetual political subservience for the section. Its leaders were Charles Sumner, Benjamin Wade, and *Thaddeus Stevens.* The battles between these factions complicated the legislative process throughout the period.

B. The Stages of Political Reconstruction. The story of political Reconstruction falls into four stages: 1) the period before Lincoln's assassination on April 4, 1865; 2) the years between 1865 and 1866 when President Andrew Johnson tried to carry out his own policy; 3) the period from 1866 to 1868 when the Congressional Reconstruction policy was formulated; and 4) the period after 1868 when southern opposition gradually negated the Congressional measures.

1. The Lincoln Reconstruction Plan.

a. FEATURES OF THE PLAN. Abraham Lincoln, whose love of Union transcended sectional hatred, held throughout the war that the southern states could not legally secede, nor did he deviate from this stand as peace approached. Using his power as commander in chief, he issued a proclamation on *December 8, 1863* which established a procedure for political Reconstruction. This provided: 1) that all Confederates except prominent military and political leaders could regain citizenship by taking oath to support the Constitution and the *Thirteenth Amendment* abolishing slavery; 2) that when 10 per cent of the number of people in each state who had voted in the election of 1860 met these requirements they could set up a government which would be recognized by the President. This was the *Presidential Reconstruction Plan,* or *Ten-per-cent Plan.* During 1864 Lincoln used it to set up state governments in Tennessee, Louisiana, and Arkansas.

b. CONGRESSIONAL REACTION. Congress refused to accept the President's moderate program, for the radicals feared that it would not secure equality for the Negroes, punishment for Confederate leaders, or continued victories for the Republicans in southern states. Their reply to Lincoln was the _Wade-Davis Bill_ (July 8, 1864), which provided: 1) Congress rather than the President would administer the Reconstruction program; 2) a majority of the population of each southern state, rather than 10 per cent, must take an oath of allegiance before a government could be established; 3) high Confederate officials and military leaders were disenfranchised; 4) slavery was abolished; and 5) Confederate debts were repudiated. Lincoln disposed of the Wade-Davis Bill by a pocket veto, but Congress answered with the _Wade-Davis Manifesto_ (August 5, 1864), which castigated the President for usurping congressional authority. Lincoln's political skill might have averted the growing conflict, but his assassination on April 14, 1865, ended hope of compromise.

2. The Johnson Reconstruction Plan.

a. CHARACTER OF JOHNSON. Andrew Johnson, a War Democrat who had been Lincoln's running mate in the election of 1864, had neither the political acumen nor the popular backing to battle the congressional radicals. Moreover, the President's murder convinced even moderate Northerners that the South must be punished severely.

b. THE JOHNSON PLAN. Despite these handicaps, the _Johnson Reconstruction Plan_ was based largely on Lincoln's policy. Announced during his first weeks in office, it: 1) proclaimed a general amnesty for all Southerners except Confederate leaders and those whose wealth exceeded $20,000; 2) recognized the governments of Virginia, Tennessee, Arkansas, and Louisiana as constituted under Lincoln's Reconstruction Plan; and 3) informed the remaining southern states that they could re-enter the Union when they had repudiated their war debts, abolished slavery, disavowed their ordinances of secession, and ratified the Thirteenth Amendment. By December 4, 1865, when Congress met, all the southern states save Texas had fulfilled these terms and were ready to be readmitted.

3. *Congressional Reconstruction Policy*. When Congress convened it refused to seat representatives from the reconstructed states, holding that the southern commonwealths had reverted to territorial status by seceding, and were now under complete congressional control. Instead, a radical Republican *Committee of Fifteen*, made up of members of both houses and dominated by Representative Thaddeus Stevens of Pennsylvania, began formulating its own reconstruction policy.

a. EARLY CONGRESSIONAL STEPS.

I. *Freedman's Bureau.* A bill (February, 1866) extended the life of the *Freedman's Bureau*, a wartime agency that had cared for freed slaves. The measure was vetoed by Johnson, but a later bill embodying the same features was passed over his veto on July 16, 1866.

II. *Civil Rights Act*. This measure (April, 1866) forbade the states to discriminate against Negroes, guaranteed persons of color the equal protection of the laws, and decreed that cases rising under the act be tried in the federal courts. It was passed over Johnson's veto.

III. *Fourteenth Amendment.* Fearful lest the Civil Rights Act be declared unconstitutional, radical Republicans

WE, THE PEOPLE OF THE UNITED STATES,

Amendments
ARTICLE THE FOURTEENTH

Citizen if born in United States or naturalized

Reduced representation in Congress for states denying negro vote

Confederate leaders barred from state or Federal office

Forbade payment of Confederate debt; guaranteed United States debt

Chart by *Graphics Institute*, N. Y. C.   From: Muzzey—*A History of Our Country*, New Edition, Ginn & Co.

formulated the _Fourteenth Amendment._ This provided that : 1) all persons born or naturalized in the United States were citizens with full rights; 2) southern states must grant Negroes the vote or suffer the loss of a portion of their congressional representation; 3) former Confederates could not hold office until pardoned by Congress; 4) the Confederate war debt was repudiated; and 5) the measure be enforced by Congress rather than the President or the courts.

b. CONGRESSIONAL ELECTIONS OF 1866. These elections allowed the people to choose between the _Presidential Reconstruction Policy,_ which allowed the southern people to shape their own institutions, and the _Congressional Reconstruction Policy,_ which gave control over the South to Congress.

I. _The Presidential Campaign._ The presidential cause was handicapped by two things: 1) In most districts the choice was between a radical Republican and a copperhead Democrat, forcing even moderate Republicans to vote the radical ticket; 2) Johnson conducted an inept campaign for his candidates, making immoderate speeches and sinking to vituperation rather than stressing issues.

II. _The Congressional Campaign._ The radicals campaigned astutely, appealing to patriotic instincts and hushing basic questions. Moreover, they were aided by three developments in the South: 1) A bloody _race riot_ in New Orleans (July, 1866) convinced northerners that the ex-slaves must be protected. 2) _Black Codes_ adopted in most southern states indicated that Southerners intended to reduce the Negroes to a status resembling slavery. These codes regulated the social and economic status of freedmen, even providing that "vagrants" could be fined $50 and, if unable to pay, apprenticed for six months. 3) The persistence with which southern states elected former Confederate leaders to office demonstrated that the people had not learned the lessons of war.

III. _Results of Elections._ The radical Republicans won a sweeping victory, which they interpreted as a mandate for their program.

c. CONGRESSIONAL RECONSTRUCTION PLAN (March 2, 1867). This measure, adopted after the elections: 1) ruled that no lawful governments existed in any of the southern states save Tennessee; 2) divided the South into five military districts under commanders who were instructed to protect life and property; and 3) decreed that no state could return to civilian rule until its voters, both white and colored, framed a constitution that guaranteed Negro suffrage and was acceptable to both Congress and the people. Each must also ratify the Fourteenth Amendment.

d. ENFORCEMENT OF CONGRESSIONAL RECONSTRUCTION. Recognizing the doubtful legality of their plan, radical Republicans took steps to insure its administration by Congress rather than the courts or the President.

I. *Denial of Court Authority*. An act of March 7, 1868, denied the Supreme Court jurisdiction over the Reconstruction acts. The radicals believed this necessary as the Court had, in two cases, threatened the constitutionality of the measures: 1) in *Ex Parte Milligan* (1866) it had ruled that military trials were illegal in areas where civil courts were functioning; and 2) in *Ex Parte McCardle* (1868) it had accepted jurisdiction in the case of a Mississippi editor who had been convicted by a military tribunal.

II. *Denial of Presidential Authority*. Two acts of March 2, 1867, removed administration of the Reconstruction Act from the President: 1) The *Army Appropriations Act* decreed that military orders could be issued only by the general of the army; 2) The *Tenure of Office Act* prohibited the President from removing any federal officials without Senate consent. Together these laws vested control of the military districts in *Edwin M. Stanton*, a radical Republican who was Secretary of War, and prevented Johnson from dismissing Stanton.

III. *Impeachment of Johnson.* Still fearful of the President, the radicals laid plans to impeach him. Their opportunity came on February 21, 1868, when Johnson dismissed Stanton. Three days later the House voted to impeach Johnson for violating the Tenure of Office Act and for other "high crimes and misdemeanors." He was tried before the Senate, and escaped conviction by only one vote. Although vindicated, Johnson's power was so weakened that he accomplished nothing in his remaining months in office.

e. ELECTION OF 1868. Calling themselves the National

Union Republican Party, the *radical Republicans* nominated General *Ulysses S. Grant* for the presidency, before adopting a platform that lauded congressional reconstruction and promised payment of the national debt in gold. The *Democrats*, seeking a *"New Departure"* to win votes, nominated Governor *Horatio Seymour* of New York, and endorsed the *Ohio Idea.* This promised repayment of federal bonds in "greenbacks," or paper money, rather than in gold, a proposal designed to appeal to debtor elements among eastern workers and western farmers suffering in the postwar deflation that began in 1867. Grant was victorious by an electoral vote of 214 to 80, although his popular majority was only 300,000 votes. The votes of 700,000 Negroes elected him. The result was no mandate for radical policy.

3. Failure of Congressional Reconstruction.

a. ENFORCEMENT OF CONGRESSIONAL POLICY. Even before Grant's election, Johnson faithfully, if unwillingly, carried out the Congressional Reconstruction Act. By the spring of 1868 all states but Texas and Virginia had adopted constitutions. The Mississippi constitution was rejected by the voters, but the other seven states set up governments which ratified the Fourteenth Amendment, and in June, 1868, were readmitted to the Union by Congress. The *Fourteenth Amendment* became effective in *July, 1868*. Thus only three states—Mississippi, Texas, and Virginia—were under military rule when Grant took office. Radicals decided that these states should not be admitted until they had ratified the *Fifteenth Amendment,* which forbade the states to deny the vote to any citizen because of "race, color, or previous condition of servitude." All three did so by 1870.

b. SOUTHERN OPPOSITION TO CONGRESSIONAL RECONSTRUCTION. Between 1870 and 1877 the center of the conflict over Reconstruction shifted to the South. There two factions contested for control of each state: 1) Democrats seeking to re-establish white supremacy, and 2) radical Republicans determined to secure equal rights for Negroes. In this group were Negroes, northern *carpetbaggers* who had come south to lead the freedmen, and southern *Scalawags,* or whites who had deserted to the Republican camp.

This faction was backed by radicals in Congress who were always ready to pass laws for its support.

I. *Reasons for Republican Defeat*. The white Democrats were eventually triumphant in this contest. This was because: 1) The Reconstruction legislatures lost support by accumulating huge debts and by increasing taxes from fourfold to fourteenfold. Many of their expenditures were legitimate, for the cost of physical reconstruction was heavy, interest rates high, and the dollar inflated. Yet tax increases are never popular. 2) Many carpetbaggers and scalawags were corrupt. They, rather than the Negroes they led, were responsible for most of the· dishonesty that discredited the Reconstruction legislatures. 3) The traditions of white rule and local rule were too strong in the South to be broken easily. 4) A rising conservative class, made up of landholders and businessmen, was soon powerful enough to spearhead an attack on radical policies. These *Bourbons* wanted to keep the Negro subjugated in order to assure a cheap labor supply as well as white supremacy. Moreover, knowing they were in the minority, they sought to secure political supremacy for their class by driving a racial wedge between the lower classes.

II. *Form of Southern Opposition*. Opposition to radical rule in the South took two forms: 1) In states where whites were in a clear majority—as Tennessee and North Carolina—Democrats regained control of the state government by legal means; 2) In others, where federal troops remained to enforce racial equality, extralegal devices were employed. Most effective were secret societies—such as the *Ku Klux Klan* and the *Knights of the White Camelia*—to intimidate the Negroes. Their program of terrorism kept Republicans from the polls, allowing the Democrats to recapture the legislatures. Congressional radicals attempted to suppress these societies by passing the *Force Act* (1870) and the *Ku Klux Klan Act* (1871). These gave the President power to: 1) suspend the writ of habeas corpus; 2) supervise congressional elections; and 3) employ troops to assure Negroes civil and political rights. Their enforcement led to the suppression of the secret societies by the end of 1872.

c. END OF CONGRESSIONAL RECONSTRUCTION. By 1872 the United States was tired of radical Reconstruction policies. In the election of that year the Republicans divided, with one faction advocating the end of congressional control of the South. Although the radicals re-elected Grant by a narrow majority, they realized that they must change their program. This was done in 1872 when an *Amnesty Act* restored the franchise to almost all Confederates. As a result, white Democrats gradually regained control of the southern states. By 1877, when *Rutherford B. Hayes* was inaugurated as President, only South Carolina and Louisiana remained in radical hands. In both these states two governments existed, one representing a minority group of carpetbaggers, scalawags, and Negroes backed by federal troops, the other based on white supremacy and supported by nearly all whites. President Hayes, convinced that the radical governments did not represent the majority will, withdrew the troops in *April, 1877*. Democrats immediately seized control. Political Reconstruction was ended, with the radical program completely rejected.

II. **SOCIAL RECONSTRUCTION.** The economic and social rehabilitation of the South was as much a part of Reconstruction as the political revival of the area. That significant progress was made was less the result of the ill-directed efforts of radical Republicans than of the labors of Southerners themselves, principally the freed slaves and small farmers.

A. **The Plight of the South.**

1. The Economic Problem. The South was in a desperate situation when the Civil War ended. Livestock had been slaughtered. Fields were left barren by marauding troops, or neglected because farmers had no seed to plant. Plantations and homes were destroyed, or were decaying away. Many principal cities had been bombarded into rubble. Railroads were torn up, bridges destroyed, and the entire transportation system was in confusion. With the collapse of Confederate money, finances were chaotic. Not a bank or insurance company was solvent, while the securities in which thousands had invested their savings were worthless. All goods had to be imported from the North on credit, at exhorbitant interest rates.

2. The Social Problem. Schools and churches were closed everywhere. Four million freed slaves, suddenly endowed with legal and social privileges for which they had not been trained, must adjust themselves to freedom. Many, intoxicated by release from bondage, wandered about the countryside. Others waited for the government to give them the "forty acres and a mule" that rumor told them would be theirs. For a time all work was at a standstill as Southerners wrestled with the problem of devising a new labor system and an economy suited to freedom.

B. The Economic Revival.

1. Agricultural Readjustment. The first need was to revive agriculture. At first landowners tried to operate plantations with gangs of hired Negro workers, but this was contrary to the whole spirit of emancipation. Gradually, *share cropping* and *tenant farming* were introduced. These methods were necessary in a region where workers lacked means to buy their own farms, but the Negro share croppers were little better off than under slavery. Living in shacks, and working long hours in cotton fields, they were always in debt to landowners and storekeepers.

2. Breakup of Plantations. Gradually, however, the more energetic climbed upward economically as they accumulated capital needed to buy land. Their opportunity came when heavy taxes levied by Reconstruction governments forced plantation owners to throw their holdings on the market. Between 1860 and 1880 the number of farms in the South doubled, while the size of the average farm decreased from 335 acres to 153 acres. This land redistribution benefited the Negro less than the small farmers and former poor whites. During the Reconstruction period this group laid the economic basis for its later political supremacy.

3. Results of Agricultural Changes. The whole South benefited from the displacement of plantation agriculture by small-scale farming. By 1870 the yield per acre was greater than at any time before the war. By 1879 the cotton crop was greater than in 1860, while the value of minor crops now surpassed that of cotton.

C. The Social Revolution. The democratizing influence of land redistribution was paralleled by social gains for the hitherto underprivileged classes in the South, both white and colored. The Reconstruction legislatures were responsible for this improvement. Their Negro members, thirsting for means of self-improvement and conscious of the needs of the lower class, passed dozens of progressive laws. In many states roads were built, public buildings improved, taxation systems modernized, poor relief inaugurated, and land distributed to the needy. More important were their educational innovations. Nearly all "carpetbag" legislatures established compulsory free schools for the children of both races. The program for human betterment outlined during these years has not yet been fully achieved in the South.

III. THE BALANCE SHEET OF RECONSTRUCTION. An assessment of the results of the Reconstruction policies adopted between 1865 and 1877 indicates that the era's legacy to the future contained both harmful and beneficial features:

A. Harmful Results.

1. Less Intelligent Leadership Was Provided for the South. The disenfranchisement of the Confederate military and civil leaders forced members of this well-educated group into oblivion. Their eclipse elevated the former small farmers and poor whites to positions of political and economic supremacy. The vision of these men was cramped by a background of poverty and ignorance, while their hatred of Negroes accentuated the race problem.

2. The Racial Issue Was Sharpened. Southern whites thereafter associated Negroes with carpetbaggers and scalawags whose reign had produced corruption and fraud. Hence they concluded that Negro participation in politics was dangerous, and systematically restricted voting to whites.

3. The South Became Unnecessarily Economy-Minded. Shocked by the expenditures of radical Republican legislatures, Southerners concluded that good government and economy were synonymous, even though social gains must be sacrificed.

4. One-Party Government Was Fastened on the South.
The Reconstruction legislatures convinced southern whites
that the Republican Party was the party of "niggers" and
corruption; thereafter no self-respecting white man would
vote anything but the straight Democratic ticket. From 1876
to 1916 that party was completely supreme below the Mason-
Dixon Line; not until 1928 was there any serious deflection
in the *"Solid South."* The harmful results were noticeable
both locally and nationally:

a. LOCAL RESULTS. One-party rule stifled democracy
in the South. Two competing parties would have bid for
support by broadening the voting lists, promising social legislation, and campaigning for progressive measures dear to
the people. With only one party in control, voting lists were
contracted by depriving Negroes of the franchise, while the
South lagged behind other sections in social legislation, education, and other measures to benefit the masses.

b. NATIONAL RESULTS. These were of two sorts: 1)
One-party rule prevented an alliance of lower-class elements
in the South and West. Hence northeastern industrialists,
with their opposition divided, were able to control the government through the late nineteenth century. 2) The Democratic Party was burdened with a conservative wing which
blocked much progressive legislation, particularly during the
twentieth century when the remaining members of that party
followed a liberal course. This was the case especially as
conservative Southerners, elected time and again without
opposition, gained control of many congressional committees
through seniority, then used their powerful positions to
frustrate the majority will.

5. Sectional Hatred Was Increased. Southerners hated
the North for its radical policies and Negro rule; Northerners hated the South for its insistence on white supremacy.
The wartime wounds would have healed much sooner had
they not been inflamed during the Reconstruction period.

B. Beneficial Results.

1. The Redistribution of Property forced on the South
by the Reconstruction legislatures ultimately benefited the
entire section. Wealth was more equitably spread, crops
diversified, and agriculture placed on a sounder basis.

2. The Educational System and Social Legislation proposed by the radical governments, although not achieved at the time, laid a basis for many of the gains made since.

3. Reconstruction Was Less Brutal Than It Might Have Been. No Confederate leader was executed, almost no land confiscated, and few Southerners punished. Although the radical policies seemed harsh to Southerners, they were far milder than those adopted in other countries following civil wars. As the South awakened to this fact, its resentment was slowly forgotten, allowing the two sections to merge into one during the late nineteenth century. By 1898, when Congress removed the last political disabilities from ex-Confederates, the animosities of the Civil War were all but forgotten.

ADDITIONAL READING

A brief, factual survey of Reconstruction is in James G. Randall and David Donald, *The Civil War and Reconstruction* (revised edn., 1961), and another somewhat more interpretative in Roy F. Nichols, *The Stakes of Power, 1945-1877* (1965). Fuller treatments are in John Hope Franklin, *Reconstruction: After the Civil War* (1961), and Kenneth M. Stampp, *The Era of Reconstruction, 1865-1877* (1965). These books, which stress social as well as political events, reveal the social gains made in the South under the Radicals. Pioneer studies on this theme were Howard K. Beale, *The Critical Year* (1930), and W. E. B. DuBois, *Black Reconstruction* (1935). A stimulating re-appraisal of President Johnson's role is in Eric McKitrick, *Andrew Johnson and Reconstruction* (1960). Paul Buck, *The Road to Reunion* (1937), pleasantly describes the forces helping reunite North and South. Social and economic developments during the period are described in Allan Nevins, *The Emergence of Modern America* (1937).

Examination Questions

Three types of questions are employed in most American history courses: 1) objective questions, 2) identification questions, and 3) essay questions. These are used by instructors in a variety of combinations. Thus one examination may consist entirely of objective questions; another may combine objective questions and essay questions; still another may employ identification questions and essay questions. Usually students are told in advance the kind of questions that will be asked. If not, they should be prepared to deal with all three types. The examples given below will make this preparation easier.

I. OBJECTIVE QUESTIONS

Objective questions are so named because they can be graded objectively — that is, without resort to any subjective judgment on the part of the reader — and rapidly. Hence they are usually employed in large courses. Four types of objective questions are commonly used: 1) true or false, 2) multiple choice, 3) association, and 4) completion.

A. True or False Questions. As with all objective questions, the true or false questions are distributed to students in mimeographed or printed form. Answers are marked directly on the printed pages, which are then returned to the instructor. In this type the student is required to designate whether a large number of brief statements are true or false. Typical questions of this sort follow:

    1. Nathaniel Bacon was a royal governor of Virginia. F

    2. The colonies enjoyed a favorable balance of trade in their relations with England and the British Empire. F

3. Puritanism stifled the intellectual progress of the New England colonies. *F*

4. The triangular trade was essential to the New England economy. *T*

5. The Seven Years' War began in the back country of New York. *F*

6. Parliament before 1763 refrained from legislation touching the "internal affairs" of the colonies. *F*

7. George Rogers Clark was instrumental in defeating the British in the southern colonies. *F*

8. One cause of the weakness of American military operations during the Revolution was the lack of a real authorized government. *T*

9. The Townshend Acts settled the problem of western settlement in 1767. *F*

10. Embargoes and nonimportation agreements served as an important American weapon during the pre-Revolutionary controversy with England. *F*

11. Thomas Paine's *Common Sense* helped stimulate the growth of deistic thought in America after the Revolution. *F*

12. In nearly all the new state constitutions adopted during the Revolutionary period limitations were placed on the powers of the governor. *T*

13. Shays' Rebellion showed the hostility of the interior southern farmers to the tidewater planters. *F*

14. The Northwest Ordinance provided for statehood when the population of any territory equalled the population of the smallest state. *F*

15. The Constitution awarded to the Supreme Court the right of judicial review. *F*

16. The Ordinance of 1785 applied a system of rectangular surveys to the Northwest Territory. *T*

17. The small states favored proportional representation in the Constitutional Convention. *F*

18. The federal Constitution was ratified by the existing state legislatures. *F*

19. The first ten amendments to the Constitution went into effect in 1789 with the new frame of government. *F*

20. One of the first successes of the new government under

the Constitution was the settlement of the land survey problem in the West. *F*

21. Pinckney's Treaty was greeted with enthusiasm by Westerners. *T*

22. Hamilton favored an excise tax on whisky to impress the people with the power of the national government. *T*

23. The French Alliance of 1778 proved valuable to the Federalists in settling American foreign problems. *F*

24. The election of Jefferson to the presidency brought complete democracy to the United States. *F*

25. The Treaty of Ghent gave the United States all of the things for which it had gone to war in 1812. *F*

26. The Rush-Bagot Agreement settled the Maine boundary controversy. *F*

27. Kansas was admitted as a free state under the Missouri Compromise. *F*

28. The Land Act of 1820 ended the use of credit which had stimulated sales since 1800. *T*

29. The First National Bank was chartered in 1816. *F*

30. The Foote Resolution proposed ending land sales in the West. *T*

31. John C. Calhoun sponsored the Force Bill of 1832. *F*

32. The Tariff of 1828 was designed to elect a president *T*

33. Proceeds of the sale of public lands under the Pre-emption Act of 1841 were to be applied to internal improvements *F*

34. The Texans won their independence in 1845. *F*

35. "Manifest destiny" was a term used to describe the United States' right to expand in the 1840's. *T*

36. Slavery interests in Congress supported the Wilmot Proviso. *F*

37. The great period of canal development came after the success of the Erie Canal in 1825. *T*

38. William Lloyd Garrison believed in the gradual compensated emancipation of slaves. *F*

39. Dorothea Dix conducted an "advice to the lovelorn" column in newspapers of the Jackson period. *F*

40. The case of *Commonwealth v. Hunt* (1842) held that combinations of workers were in restraint of trade. *F*

41. The Kansas-Nebraska Act had the effect of invalidating the Missouri Compromise. *T*

42. The Dred Scott decision was popular in the North since it struck a blow against slavery. *F*

43. The "Ostend Manifesto" referred to the South's desire to expand into Cuba. *T*

44. John C. Calhoun's "Seventh of March Speech" contained a classic argument on the position of the states in the federal Union. *F*

45. The Republican party took over one wing of the southern Democrats in 1860. *F*

46. Lincoln was elected by a clear majority in 1860. *F*

47. All the slave states seceded from the Union as a result of the election of Lincoln. *F*

48. Lincoln's principal concern was saving the Union rather than freeing the slaves. *T*

49. The Wade-Davis Manifesto accused the President of usurping the powers of Congress. *T*

50. The influence of the states' rights doctrine weakened the Confederacy during the Civil War. *T*

B. Multiple-Choice Questions. In this type of examination the student is confronted with a series of statements, only one of which is correct. He must designate which one. Typical multiple-choice questions follow:

1. The expansion of Europe began (1) at the time of the crusades (2) in 1592 (3) with Prince Henry the Navigator (4) with the discovery of the compass (5) in 1348.

2. The natural environment forced New Englanders to turn to any, all, or some of the following: (1) fishing (2) fur trading (3) growing rice (4) gold mining (5) trade and commerce.

3. Geography affected the French in America by (1) keeping them on the coast (2) turning them into farmers (3) making them anti-Catholic (4) luring them into the interior (5) forcing them to turn to the sea for wealth.

4. During the seventeenth century the chief source of labor supply came from (1) slaves (2) indentured servants (3) Indians (4) prisoners of war (5) Germany.

5. The first legislative assembly was established in (1) Maryland (2) Massachusetts (3) Virginia (4) Rhode Island (5) Pennsylvania.

6. British mercantilistic policies before 1763 did not arouse opposition in the colonies because (1) there was little unity of interest among the colonists (2) the laws were not enforced (3) the regulations then imposed were not too injurious to colonial trade (4) the colonial trade was so varied that the policy did not fall heavily on any one group (5) for all of the foregoing reasons.

7. The Proclamation of 1763 offended American colonists because (1) it forbade settlement west of the mountains (2) it extended the boundaries of the Province of Quebec to the Mississippi River (3) it subordinated colonial assemblies to the control of Parliament (4) it permitted the use of writs of assistance.

8. Accused of "a long train of abuses" was (1) Governor Berkeley (2) Alexander Hamilton (3) John Adams (4) the southern planters (5) George III.

9. Americans were successful in the Revolution because of any, some, or all of these: (1) they knew the topography (2) the British were forced to fight far from their bases (3) they secured aid from France (4) the British were poor fighters (5) the colonists were better fighters.

10. Writs of assistance were (1) grants of aid to colonial officials (2) enumerated articles (3) blanket military levies (4) general search warrants (5) royal grants made to proprietors.

11. The Treaty of Paris ending the Revolution gave the United States: (1) the Floridas (2) a western boundary at the Rocky Mountains (3) a western boundary at the Mississippi (4) a southern boundary at the 35th parallel (5) the Ohio River boundary.

12. The agrarian elements in power during the Confederation period were interested in (1) legal tender acts (2) "easy" money, stay laws, and a weak central government (3) "hard" money and a strong central government (4) distilling whisky for sale (5) legal tender laws and the payment of all debts in specie.

13. The chief weakness of the Articles of Confederation was (1) lack of compulsive power (2) lack of power to control commerce (3) lack of separation of powers (4) lack of a strong judiciary (5) a unicameral rather than bicameral legislature.

14. The Northwest Ordinance of 1787 framed (1) trade

agreements with England (2) a government policy for the West (3) a system for the survey and sale of western lands (4) an Indian policy for the federal government (5) a method of amending the Articles of Confederation.

15. Which of the following was a fundamental principle of the Constitution of the United States (1) unicameral legislature (2) federal sponsorship of internal improvements (3) the doctrine of popular sovereignty (4) a division of governmental powers (5) right of Congress to levy protective tariffs.

16. The Constitution was ratified by (1) Committees of Correspondence (2) state legislatures (3) the people directly (4) state ratifying conventions (5) all of these methods.

17. The Federalists in the main represented (1) the agrarian elements (2) the propertied classes (3) lawyers (4) great planters (5) Washington and Hamilton.

18. The doctrine of natural rights is best stated in (1) the Bill of Rights of the Constitution (2) the Declaration and Resolves of the Continental Congress (3) the Newberg Addresses (4) Hamilton's Report on Manufactures (5) the Declaration of Independence.

19. As a commercial nation during the Napoleonic Wars, the United States' chief concern in foreign policy was over (1) neutral rights and impressment (2) the acquisition of Florida and Canada (3) the opening of new markets (4) the enforcement of the "rule of 1756" (5) the collection of spoliation claims.

20. The order of the development of transportation facilities in the United States was (1) roads, canals, railroads (2) railroads, roads, canals (3) canals, roads, railroads (4) roads, railroads, canals (5) none of these.

21. Following the War of 1812 American nationalism (1) shifted to become a southern doctrine (2) grew in intensity (3) was replaced by sectionalism (4) decreased (5) was transformed by the impact of the states' rights doctrine.

22. Internal improvements at government expense were championed chiefly by (1) the South (2) the Northeast (3) the West (4) all the sections.

23. The United States adopted its first protective tariff in (1) 1861 (2) 1846 (3) 1828 (4) 1816 (5) 1789.

24. Jackson's view of the presidency emphasized (1) cabinet

leadership (2) the strengthening of the power of the states (3) congressional leadership (4) <u>executive leadership in the interests of the people</u> (5) sectionalism.

25. Jackson's attack on the Second Bank of the United States was caused by (1) the bank's political activities (2) Jackson's views on financial monopolies (3) Jackson's personal dislike of Biddle (4) Jackson's attempt to please western farmers and eastern workers (5) <u>all of these.</u>

26. The Panic of 1837 was the result of (1) overspeculation in land (2) the building of internal improvements (3) loose banking practices (4) an English recession (5) <u>all of these.</u>

27. The Book of Mormon was revealed to (1) William Miller (2) John Humphrey Noyes (3) Brigham Young (4) <u>Joseph Smith</u> (5) none of these.

28. Robert Owen established a communistic community known as (1) New View (2) New York (3) Newport (4) Newton (5) <u>New Harmony.</u>

29. The term "manifest destiny" refers to (1) <u>American expansion</u> (2) southern sectionalism (3) antislavery agitation (4) religious revivalism (5) spread of communistic communities.

30. The "reoccupation of Oregon and the reannexation of Texas" was the campaign slogan of (1) John Tyler (2) Martin Van Buren (3) John C. Calhoun (4) Andrew Jackson (5) <u>James K. Polk.</u>

31. American claims to Oregon were based partly on (1) activities of the Hudson's Bay Company (2) the capture of Astoria during the War of 1812 (3) the Treaty of Ghent (4) <u>the occupation of the area by missionaries and settlers</u> (5) Clay's American System.

32. The message advocating war with Mexico was written by (1) Buchanan (2) <u>Polk</u> (3) Calhoun (4) Taylor (5) Jackson.

33. The leader of the Mexican army in the Mexican War was (1) Santa Cruz (2) Santa Barbara (3) Santa Anita (4) Santa Claus (5) <u>Santa Anna.</u>

34. The Mexican Cession (1) first extended the American boundaries to the Pacific (2) settled all problems with Mexico (3) was approved by abolitionists (4) <u>reopened the slavery controversy</u> (5) ended American territorial expansion.

35. The Compromise of 1850 (1) established slavery in California (2) permitted slavery north of 36° 30′ (3) admitted California as a free state (4) repudiated the fugitive slave law (5) banned slavery in the District of Columbia.

36. The Kansas Nebraska Act was devised by (1) John C. Calhoun (2) Stephen A. Douglas (3) Abraham Lincoln (4) James Buchanan (5) Henry Clay.

37. From 1846 to 1860 the tariff policy of the United States was (1) highly protectionist (2) one of free trade (3) designed largely for revenue (4) none of these.

38. The Dred Scott decision (1) led to Douglas' victory in the election of 1858 (2) aided the abolitionists (3) was favorable to the North (4) decided that slaves were not property (5) caused further agitation on the slavery question.

39. The leading peace Democrat in the North during the Civil War was (1) Charles Sumner (2) Benjamin Wade (3) Clement Vallandigham (4) Edwin Stanton (5) none of these.

40. West Virginia became a state by (1) the Compromise of 1850 (2) the Kansas Nebraska Act (3) the Ordinance of 1787 (4) the Dred Scott decision (5) seceding from Virginia.

C. Association Questions. A student is confronted with a list of names, dates, and events, then asked to associate those that are connected or arrange them in proper sequence. The following examples illustrate this type of question:

1. In the space provided at the left, place the number of the term associated with the man.

(7) Nicholas Biddle
(10) Thomas Hart Benton
(4) Elias Howe
(9) John C. Calhoun
(11) James Buchanan
(16) Stephen A. Douglas
(8) John Tyler
(17) Henry Clay
(2) John Marshall
(14) Ralph Waldo Emerson
(12) Roger Taney
(6) Joseph Smith

1. Abolitionist leader
2. Gibbons v. Ogden
3. Specie Circular
4. Invention of sewing machine
5. "Tippecanoe and Tyler Too"
6. Mormon Church
7. Second Bank of the United States
8. Annexation of Texas
9. Doctrine of Nullification

(5) William Henry Harrison
(13) Dorothea Dix
(1) William Lloyd Garrison
(15) Thomas R. Dew
(3) Andrew Jackson

10. Western leader on land question
11. Lecompton Constitution
12. Dred Scott decision
13. Care of the insane
14. Transcendentalism
15. The proslavery argument
16. Freeport Doctrine
17. The American System

2. Associate the following events and episodes with the administration in which they occurred by placing the proper number in the brackets at the left.

(3) Embargo Act
(1) Second Bank of the United States
(5) Lincoln-Douglas debates
(4) Emancipation of slaves
(6) Mexican War
(2) Acquisition of East Florida
(5) Secession of South Carolina
(1) Treaty of Ghent
(8) Annexation of Texas

1. Madison
2. Monroe
3. Jefferson
4. Lincoln
5. Buchanan
6. Polk
7. Jackson
8. Tyler
9. Pierce

3. Number each of the following in the proper order of occurrence in the space provided at the left.

(4)
(5)
(3)
(7)
(1)
(6)
(10)
(2)
(9)
(8)

1. Stamp Act
2. Townshend Acts
3. End of Seven Years' War
4. First Continental Congress
5. Navigation Act of 1696
6. Intolerable acts
7. Purchase of Louisiana
8. Molasses Act
9. X Y Z affair
10. Northwest Ordinance

D. Completion Questions. The student is presented with a number of statements which must be filled in with the proper date, name, or event. The following examples will illustrate this type of question:

1. _NICHOLAS TRIST_ negotiated the treaty of _GUADALUPE HIDALGO_ for the United States which closed the Mexican War in _1848_.

2. The _DRED SCOTT_ decision, written by _TANEY_ ruled that the Missouri Compromise was unconstitutional and that slaves could be taken anywhere in the territories.

3. Jackson's _SPECIE CIRCULAR_ came too late to prevent the Panic of 1837.

4. The principle of _INTERCHANGEABLE PARTS_, which was first developed by _ELI WHITNEY_, underlies today's mass-production industries.

5. "The Reannexation of Texas and the Reoccupation of Oregon" was a term used by advocates of _MANIFEST DESTINY_ during the administration of _JAMES K. POLK_.

6. The doctrine of _NULLIFICATION_, which had been employed in the _VIRGINIA AND KENTUCKY_ Resolutions, was expressed again by _JOHN C. CALHOUN_ in the "South Carolina Exposition."

7. The British retained the _NORTHWEST POSTS_ from the close of the Revolutionary War until Washington's diplomatic agent, _JOHN JAY_, finally negotiated a treaty that forced their withdrawal in 1796.

8. _LEWIS_ and _CLARK_ made the first explorations of the Louisiana Territory during the years _1804-1806_.

9. The most important result of the Lincoln-Douglas debates was the enunciation of the _FREEPORT_ Doctrine by _DOUGLAS_.

II. IDENTIFICATION QUESTIONS

The student is given a list of names or events, and asked to write a brief note about each. Occasionally a list of well-known quotations is substituted for the names or events. As identification questions are frequently employed to test the student's knowledge of the text or other assigned reading, he should take pains to include in his answer material that could be drawn from those sources only. The answers should be brief and compact, but crammed with information. Typical questions follow:

1. Write brief notes to explain the significance of the following: William Berkeley, John Winthrop, Jonathan Edwards, Philip Freneau, John Dickinson, Thomas Paine, Dorothea Dix, John Humphrey Noyes, Charles Fourier, John Brown.

2. Write brief notes on: the Treaty of Greenville, Battle of Saratoga, Bacon's Rebellion, the Scotch-Irish, Galloway's Plan, the Dominion of New England, *Worcester v. Georgia*, Rush-Bagot Agreement, Macon's Bill No. 2, Freeport Doctrine, the Confederate Constitution.

3. Identify as closely as possible and discuss as fully as you can the significance of the following quotations:

(a) "The judges in every state shall be bound thereby, anything in the constitution or laws of any state to the contrary notwithstanding."

(b) "No state shall . . . coin money; emit bills of credit, make anything but gold and silver coin a tender in payment of debts."

(c) "The geographer shall designate the townships, or fractional parts of townships by numbers progressively from South to North, always beginning each range with No. 1."

(d) "No new state shall be admitted into the Union by Congress, in virtue of the power granted by the Constitution, without the concurrence of two-thirds of both houses."

(e) "All other armed vessels on these lakes shall be forthwith dismantled, and no other vessels of war shall be there built or armed."

(f) "We owe it, therefore, to candor, and to the amicable relations existing between the United States and those European powers, to declare that we should consider any attempt on their part to extend their systems to any part of this hemisphere as dangerous to our peace and safety."

(g) "You are hereby instructed, after the 15th day of August next, to receive in payment of the public lands nothing except what is directed by the existing laws, viz: gold and silver."

(h) "That, as an expressed fundamental condition . . . to the use by the executive of the moneys herein appropriated, neither slavery nor involuntary servitude shall ever exist in any part of said territory, except for crime."

III. ESSAY QUESTIONS

Essay questions are used more widely than any other type, either by themselves or in connection with objective questions or identification questions. As they are the most difficult kind to answer properly, adequate time should be spent in preparation for them. This time can be used intelligently only when the student realizes the *purpose* of an essay question.

An instructor who gives properly prepared essay questions is testing his students' ability to 1) *understand* the material of the course, 2) *organize* that material intelligently, 3) *select* the most important events for discussion, and 4) demonstrate *factual knowledge*. If the student will always remember that his grade will depend on all four of those attributes, he should be able to handle the essay question satisfactorily. They should be kept constantly in mind both when studying for an examination or when writing one.

Understanding of the material is the first requisite of a good answer. A penetrating essay on a phase of history cannot be written from memory alone; the student must immerse himself in the material so thoroughly that he completely masters the subject. This is necessary, as the essay question usually does not test knowledge already familiar to the student (a chapter of the text or a classroom lecture, for example). Instead it forces him to combine information drawn from several sources, arrange that information in an unfamiliar pattern, and draw conclusions that may be new to him. This requires a thorough understanding of the material.

Organization is equally important. Any intelligent essay must be built upon a carefully planned framework; only then will the events unfold in the logical sequence that gives meaning to the past. No instructor is satisfied with a jumbled mass of information, no matter how exact that information may be. Before starting to write an essay question the student should work out an outline in his mind, or perhaps even jot one down on a blank page of his examination book.

Selection of the material to be included in an essay question tests both the student's intelligence and his familiarity with the subject matter. Any well-prepared person would be able to write for an hour or more on most essay questions. To answer them in the limited time available he must choose only the most essential material, eliminating that which is less important. This requires both a thorough knowledge of the subject and a common-sense ability to distinguish between the essential and the nonessential.

Factual knowledge is also needed for a proper answer to an essay question. Many students on an examination may understand, organize, and select their material well. In that case the instructor is certain to give the highest mark to the one whose essay .contains the largest amount of exact information.

With these four points in mind, the student should read carefully the following essay questions, selecting those that fall within the field covered in the portion of the course on which he is to be examined. He will note that some are *general essay questions* covering a wide range of time; these are likely to appear on final examinations. Others are *specific essay questions* dealing with briefer episodes of history. These are used on both final examinations and on the shorter examinations that occur periodically in every course. They have been grouped below to conform to the chapters in this outline.

A. General Essay Questions

1. Does early American history illustrate the truth or falsity of the dictum that the history of religion is one of continuous conflict between the forces of modernism and fundamentalism?

2. Comment fully on the following quotation: "The finer arts of civilization are the product of an aristocratic organization of society and decline proportionately with the rise of democracy."

3. Describe the changing role played by the aristocracy during the colonial and Revolutionary periods.

4. "The issues that brought about the disruption of the British Empire in the American Revolution were the issues which threatened the existence of the Union under the Articles of Confederation." Do you agree? Discuss fully.

5. Trace the development of the coordinancy principle underlying the Northwest Ordinance for the period 1763-1821.

6. The doctrine of states' rights has been described as a shield for the protection of the interests of a minority section against the unfriendly policies of the majority in control of the national government. Illustrate the truth or falsity of this statement for the years 1781-1860.

7. "Despite the inferior vote-getting power of minor parties, they have undoubtedly performed a vital function in our political development." Discuss the truth or falsity of this statement for the years between the Revolution and the Civil War.

8. How did the question of American debts to British merchants influence American history between 1775 and 1802?

9. Trace the effect of the concept of divisible sovereignty on American development between 1787 and 1860.

10. Describe the spread of cotton culture in the lower South, indicating the reasons for this development and the political and economic results.

11. Describe the territorial acquisitions of the United States between 1789 and 1860, accounting as fully as you can for each new burst of expansionistic sentiment.

12. Discuss fully the effect of the rise of internal commerce on the constitutional, political, and diplomatic history of the United States before 1860.

13. Compare Clay and Jackson as exponents of western views in national politics. Which do you think more faithfully represented his section?

14. Compare Calhoun's course in national politics before 1820 with his course thereafter, accounting for any differences.

15. Analyze nationalistic tendencies and sectional cross currents, 1812-1860.

16. Compare the contributions which Washington as President and John Quincy Adams as Secretary of State and President made to American foreign policy.

17. Describe and contrast the policies of Thomas Jefferson and James Monroe as presidents, accounting for any differences.

18. "The end of the War of 1812 marked the beginning of progress toward complete political and diplomatic isolation from

Europe." Do you agree? Discuss in the light of American foreign policy before the Civil War.

19. How do you account for the intense nationalism of the Era of Good Feelings and the equally intense sectionalism of the period immediately following?

20. "The Rise of the New West was the most significant factor in American history in the years following the War of 1812." Do you agree? Discuss fully.

B. Specific Essay Questions

I. *The Colonization of America,* 1492-1660

1. Describe and contrast the English, French, and Spanish colonization of North America, accounting as fully as you can for the greater success of England.

2. How do you account for the dominance of Portugal and Spain in the early colonization of the New World, and of England and France in the later period?

3. Comment fully on the following remarks: "All the world knows that in 1630 the blessings of civil and religious liberty were brought to America with the Massachusetts Bay Charter. The Puritans were in some ways religious bigots, but they were political liberals, and the democratic government they set up in Boston was independent of England."

4. Compare and contrast the early development of Virginia and Massachusetts, politically, economically, and socially. Account as fully as you can for any differences.

5. Why did the Virginia Company lose its charter?

6. Describe the forces leading to the establishment of a theocracy in Massachusetts, the political and religious attitudes and actions of its leaders, and its decline.

II. *The Maturing of Colonial America,* 1660-1703

1. "All Colonies or Plantations do endamage their Mother-Kingdoms, whereof the Trades of such Plantations are not confined by severe Laws, and good execution of those Laws, to the Mother-Kingdom." Discuss England's application of this theory, and show its effect on colonial economic development.

2. Distinguish between royal, proprietary, and chartered colonies, and describe the political organization of each.

3. It has been said that royal governors in the eighteenth century "were in the most unfortunate of all situations: one of responsibility devoid of power." Do you agree? Discuss the effect of this situation on the political development of the colonies.

4. In what ways does the Treaty of Utrecht constitute a dividing line in American colonial history?

5. Why did the Seven Years' War originate in the back country of Pennsylvania rather than in the back country of New York?

6. Do you agree with Pitt's statement that "Canada was won in Germany"?

III. Life and Thought in Colonial America

1. Describe non-English migration to America during the colonial period, and appraise the influence of the newcomers on life and thought.

2. Contrast the land and agricultural systems of the northern, middle, and southern colonies, accounting as fully as you can for any differences.

3. Describe and contrast the intellectual life of the New England and southern colonies during the seventeenth century, accounting for any differences.

4. Were the cultural interests and activities of colonial Americans determined more by the European heritage or by the American environment?

5. "Puritanism was a stifling force which slowed the entire intellectual development of the New England colonies." Do you agree? Discuss fully.

6. Describe the nonpolitical activities of the "many-sided Benjamin Franklin."

IV. The American Revolution, 1763-1783

1. Comment on the following from Professor Whooziz, *School History of the United States*: "All the trouble started in England. Although the empire was well organized, and the thirteen colonies had helped to win the Seven Years' War at great sacrifice in men and money, the British were jealous of their growth and prosperity, and proposed to tax the colonists heavily in order to relieve the English taxpayer."

2. "That the slogan of the American people was 'no taxation with or without representation' was amply demonstrated duing the years from 1763 to 1787." Do you agree? Discuss fully.

3. "While no historian of today would agree with Lecky that the Navigation acts were the principal cause of the American Revolution, it is nevertheless true that economic policies and forces were largely responsible for precipitating the conflict." Do you agree? Discuss fully.

4. "Despite the economic, political, and social forces leading the American people toward independence, the Revolution would never have taken place had not Sam Adams and other rabble rousers organized a lower-class minority into an effective pressure group." Do you agree? Discuss fully.

5. "The American Revolution seems to have been the outcome of a collision between two mutually incompatible interpretations of the English constitution." Do you agree? Discuss fully.

6. Discuss the diplomacy of the American Revolution, and indicate the influence of the wartime alliances on the peace settlement.

V. Confederation and Constitution, 1783-1789

1. "The era of the Articles of Confederation was a 'critical period' not because of any lack of legislative or diplomatic power on the part of the national government, but because of an abuse of power by the states." Discuss fully.

2. Describe the disputes resulting from the Treaty of 1783, and indicate the steps taken to resolve them.

3. Discuss the evolution and significance of the Ordinance of 1787.

4. It has been said that the federal Constitution was at once a "bundle of compromises" on purely political questions and a record of practical unanimity among the framers on economic issues. Do you agree? Discuss fully.

5. Describe and explain the principal devices used in the Constitution to make that document binding on the people of the several states.

6. "Weighed in the scale of democratic liberalism, the Constitution as it stood in 1787 was a monstrous fraud." Do you agree? Discuss fully.

VI. The Federalist Period, 1789-1800

1. Was the Whisky Excise Tax of 1790 a wise measure?

2. Discuss the origins, development, and subsequent history of any two of Hamilton's financial measures.

3. How did the diplomatic shifts in Europe affect the solution of major problems of foreign policy in the United States, 1789-1800?

4. Discuss the origin and settlement of the diplomatic problems of the Washington and Adams administrations.

5. Discuss the Virginia and Kentucky Resolutions as to origin, content, and significance.

6. Describe the conflicts within the Federalist party, and appraise their influence on the elections of 1796 and 1800.

VII. Jeffersonian Democracy, 1800-1816

1. Do you agree that Jefferson's political philosophy "might well be described as one of 'agrarian Federalism'"?

2. "Jefferson's attack on the judiciary was entirely unfounded and served to undo much of the good accomplished under Washington and Adams." Do you agree? Discuss fully.

3. "The election of 1800 did not bring democracy to the United States. Instead it substituted the rule of an agrarian upper class for that of a merchant upper class." Do you agree? Discuss fully.

4. Compare and contrast the financial programs of Alexander Hamilton and Albert Gallatin.

5. Describe and appraise Jefferson's foreign policy.

6. "The United States declared war in 1812 when it was no longer necessary, won the war after it had been concluded, and failed to win any of the things it had fought for." Discuss fully.

VIII. Life and Thought in Revolutionary America

1. The Revolutionary era has been described as marked by an awakening of the national consciousness. How did this influence cultural developments?

2. How did the literary strivings of the Revolutionary period reflect the intense nationalism of that day?

3. "A changed environment and the impact of new scientific ideas had by 1815 created in America a religious structure differing materially from its Old World counterpart." Discuss fully.

4. Would you agree that "the cult of deism and the revivalistic reaction both stemmed more from local American conditions than from foreign influences"?

5. Describe the changing role played by the aristocracy in American life between the beginning of the Revolution and the close of the War of 1812.

6. Describe the contributions of Thomas Jefferson to American social and intellectual life during the Revolutionary period.

IX. The Era of Nationalism, 1816-1828

1. Discuss and appraise the factors which contributed to the growth of a spirit of nationalism in the United States after the War of 1812.

2. Account as fully as you can for the fact that "after 1816 the Jeffersonians adopted the Federalists'. philosophy of government."

3. "After the death of Hamilton, the real leadership of the Federalists passed to John Marshall." Explain and justify this statement.

4. Describe the origins of the Missouri Compromise, stating briefly the arguments used in Congress for and against the measure.

5. Discuss the origins and terms of the Monroe Doctrine.

6. Why was John Quincy Adams unable to carry out the nationalistic program to which he was committed and to which he dedicated his administration?

X. Jacksonian Democracy, 1828-1840

1. "Jackson was not a nationalist; he was a unionist." Discuss in terms of Jackson's presidential policies.

2. Describe the quarrel between Jackson and Calhoun and evaluate its importance in the political history of the United States.

3. Compare Jackson's handling of Georgia during the Indian controversy with his treatment of South Carolina during the tariff controversy, accounting as fully as you can for any differences.

4. Can Jackson's handling of diplomatic problems be characterized as "moderate and correct"?

5. Comment fully on the meaning of the statement: "Jackson sowed the winds; Van Buren reaped the whirlwind."

6. Account for the Panic of 1837, and describe the changes in American political and economic life that resulted.

XI. The Age of the Common Man

1. Account as fully as you can for the fact that the Jacksonian period was an "age of reform," and describe some of the more important crusades.

2. How did American religion during the period reflect both the influence of the frontier and the impact of newer rationalistic concepts?

3. Account as fully as you can for the literary phenomenon known as "the flowering of New England."

4. Explain the widespread interest in communal experiments and other panaceas for the working man, and describe the salient developments.

5. Account for the widespread interest in education, and explain the more important developments in that field.

6. Describe the relationships of the leading literary men to movements for political and social reform.

XII. Slavery and Expansion, 1840-1850

1. Did the annexation of Texas and the Mexican War constitute a "dark lanterned conspiracy of the slavocracy"?

2. Do you think that Polk's program toward Texas was "moderate and just"?

3. "The outcome of the election of 1844 was a foregone conclusion." Discuss in terms of the background, issues, and campaign.

4. Is the Oregon Treaty of 1846 accounted for by the explanation that "possession is nine-tenths of the law"?

5. What methods were open to Congress in settling the slavery question in the territories taken from Mexico? Give

the arguments for and against each. Which was adopted, and did the North or South gain most?

6. Explain the background and significance of each of the provisions of the Compromise of 1850.

XIII. The Decade of Controversy, 1850-1860

1. Explain the failure of the sectional truce embodied in the Compromise of 1850 to prevent a recurrence of the slavery controversy.

2. Which of the two men, Lincoln or Douglas, better represented the views of the West on the important political issues of the 1850's?

3. Describe the political consequences of the Kansas-Nebraska Act.

4. Sketch the evolution of the Republican party, 1854-1860, and explain the sources of its steadily increasing strength.

5. "No reform party can succeed when it depends on ideals alone. Material factors are necessary to attract a sufficient number of voters to win a national victory." Illustrate the truth or falsity of this statement in the history of the Republican party before 1861.

6. Would the election of Douglas rather than Lincoln in 1860 have postponed or made unnecessary the Civil War?

XIV. The Civil War, 1860-1865

1. To what extent can the Civil War be accounted for as a struggle between two antagonistic economic systems?

2. Describe in detail Lincoln's changing attitude toward slavery from the time of his first inaugural address to the issuance of the Emancipation Proclamation, accounting as fully as you can for all differences.

3. Was Lincoln's issuance of the Emancipation Proclamation a contradiction of his earlier profession that the Civil War was being waged not for the destruction of slavery but for the preservation of the Union?

4. "The greatest task of the Civil War was the keeping of the North united. Abraham Lincoln did this; no one else could have done it." Do you agree? Discuss fully.

5. "Short as was the existence of the Confederacy, it lived long enough to justify the dictum that states' rights was an im-

possible creed on which to build a nation." Explain the meaning of this statement and justify fully.

6. Why did England not recognize the independence of the Confederate government?

XV. Reconstruction, 1865-1877

1. "The period of Reconstruction was not a 'tragic era' but a blessing in disguise for the South." Do you agree? Justify your answer.

2. "No president has been so thoroughly misunderstood by his contemporaries as Andrew Johnson." Do you agree? Explain fully.

3. Distinguish between the Lincoln Reconstruction Plan, the Johnson Reconstruction Plan, and the Congressional Reconstruction Plan. Which do you think should have been applied?

4. "The story of the Negro in Reconstruction is not so much the story of the Negro himself as it is the record of the competition of the Southern and Northern whites for the control of a docile race." Discuss fully.

5. Why should the radical Republicans have objected as violently as they did to Johnson's Reconstruction Policy?

6. "The Congressional Policy of Reconstruction was tantamount to a declaration that a successful war, waged for the preservation of the Union, had the legal effect of dissolving it." Explain and discuss.

Index